DICE-K

DICE
K

*The First Season of
the Red Sox $100 Million Man*

Ian Browne

With a Foreword by Terry Francona

THE LYONS PRESS
Guilford, Connecticut
An imprint of The Globe Pequot Press

The Lyons Press is an imprint of The Globe Pequot Press.

Designed by Kim Burdick

Library of Congress Cataloging-in-Publication Data.

Browne, Ian, 1971–
  Dice-K : the first season of the Red Sox $100 million man / Ian Browne; with a foreword by Terry Francona.
      p. cm.
  Includes index.
  ISBN 978-1-59921-347-7
  1. Matsuzaka, Daisuke, 1980- 2. Baseball players—United States. 3. Rookie baseball players—United States. 4. Boston Red Sox (Baseball team) I. Title.
  GV865.M28B76 2008
  796.357092—dc22
  [B]
                                                      2007049966

Printed in the United States of America

10 9 8 7 6 5 4 3 2 1

This book is dedicated to the memory of Richard B. Dunne Jr., who left us way too soon but filled our lives with support and happiness while he was here.

Photo by Brita Meng Outzen

Contents

Foreword

I WAS FORTUNATE TO have the opportunity to manage Daisuke Matsuzaka in his first Major League season, and it was amazing to watch all the cultural adjustments he had to make over the course of the year. He went through a full year of nothing but making adjustments and having a lot of firsts. And all of this was in a strange country and a strange league. I just think that it takes a pretty extraordinary person to do what he did, and thankfully he is extraordinary. Saying that, I think his best days are ahead.

It was neat watching the way Daisuke and our pitching coach John Farrell did such a great job together to make those adjustments easier. Daisuke is a great kid and he has that disarming smile. He has expressed an interest in improving his English, and that will only help the communication going forward. You have to remember that when someone comes from such a different background, many things you might take for granted are quite different. For example, things like weight training and the amount of throwing you do can be very different in Japan from the way they are in the Major Leagues.

In 2007, we knew there were going to need to be some adjustments made by everybody. So rather than force the issue, we just tried to do the right thing every day and be flexible, and at the same time, learn. If there was something we didn't understand, we'd try to learn why. We wanted to learn about him, and we also wanted him to learn about us. It's an ongoing process and that's okay.

What was the toughest adjustment he had to make? I'm not sure you can look at one thing. I think you take the whole pile and put it together. When you think about things like different baseballs, different strike zones, different competition, not speaking the language, the amount of travel, I think there were a lot of things that got thrown at him, and all in a different culture. That's a lot for one person to digest and I think he did it about as well as anyone could expect. There was no time-out where he could go home for a week. Once he got here, he got thrown into it and that was pretty much it.

Even with all the frustrations he had late in the regular season, he was still a 15-game winner. There's a lot there to really like. Early in the playoffs, he had a couple of starts that he probably thought could have been better. But we weren't about to shy away from giving him the ball in Game 7 of the American League Championship Series and he sure was eager to take it. I don't think anybody ever doubted his willingness or his ability to pitch. We always had huge confidence that he wouldn't back down and he wouldn't shrink in big moments. I think we all had pretty good confidence in his ability to rise to that occasion against a real tough Cleveland Indians team and he did.

Then he got to the World Series and won Game 3 of our four-game sweep over the Rockies by pitching a really strong game. It was something to build on, and he was able to go home feeling good about himself. By the time we start Spring Training in February of 2008, things will be totally different. He'll be coming here as a member of our team. He won't be a new guy. His English will undoubtedly be improved. He will not have to be shown what field to go to. There will be no introductions. He'll be coming back. And even with the language barrier, it will be better and it won't be new. I think because all those firsts are out of the way, you're going to see an improved pitcher and that is going to be fun to watch.

Terry Francona
Manager, Boston Red Sox

Acknowledgments

WHERE TO START? IN this case, Japan seems like the proper place. That is where my bosses from MLB.com gave me the honor of traveling to in November 2006, so I could cover the All-Star Series between the Major Leaguers and Nippon Professional Baseball. It was there that I first ran into Daisuke Matsuzaka, who held a press conference to officially inform the Japanese media that he was going to pursue a career in the Major Leagues. And it was in that room that I first became aware of just how iconic a figure Matsuzaka was in his native land. So the first official thanks goes to MLB.com for sending me to Japan for that trip when we had a lot of other worthy writers who could have gone.

Ironically, a few days after I returned to the United States, the news broke that it was the Boston Red Sox—the team I cover on a daily basis—that had won the exclusive bidding rights for Matsuzaka. As the drama built and the Red Sox at last secured the right-hander following an investment of $103.1 million, the wheels started spinning in my head. For years, I had thought about writing a book. But I was waiting for a subject that gripped me. This one definitely did. There were so many elements to it, from Matsuzaka's status in Japan to Boston's willingness to make such an aggressive move on a pitcher with no Major League experience to all the adjustments Matsuzaka would have to make in his first year on United States soil.

A couple of months later my good friend Mark Feinsand, who covers the Yankees for the *New York Daily News,* asked me if I had considered writing a book on Matsuzaka. What a coincidence, I thought. As it turns out, Mark's literary agent, a man named Bob Diforio, was also thinking about it. Mark referred Bob to me, and soon after that, Bob became my literary agent. So thanks Mark, for hooking me up with Bob. Believe me when I tell you that Bob was tireless in finding a market for this book, even though some publishers were skeptical about committing to a subject who could well be a flop in his first Major League season, not to mention a writer who had never written a book. So thanks to Bob, for believing in the project and in me. And thanks to Random House Kodansha in Japan, Lyons Press in the United States and *China Times* of Taiwan for having similar optimism.

The Matsuzaka story had its share of ups and downs in Year One, but it ended in World Series glory for both the pitcher and his team. I thank Daisuke Matsuzaka for being a fascinating subject.

Writing a book is a challenging endeavor that required the assistance of so many along the way. First of all, a big thank you to Dinn Mann, the editor in chief at MLB.com, who gave me the approval to write this book. I promised Dinn that undertaking this project would not interfere with my daily work for MLB.com, and I'd like to think I kept that promise.

Another special thanks goes to Rob Bradford from the *Boston Herald,* who is a tremendous journalist and an even better friend. Rob was my sounding board throughout this process. As someone who had already written a book, Rob always related to the roller coaster of emotions I went through during the process. He also was never shy about making suggestions, all of which I valued.

Thanks to the following members of the Boston media for their guidance and/or camaraderie over the years: from the *Boston Globe,* Bob Hohler, Gordon Edes, Nick Cafardo, Dan Shaughnessy, Bob Ryan, Jackie MacMullan and Amalie Benjamin; from the *Boston Herald*, Jeff Horrigan, Michael Silverman, Tony Massarotti, Karen Guregian, Steve Buckley and John Tomase; from the *Providence Journal*, Steven Krasner, Sean McAdam and Joe McDonald; from the *Hartford Courant*, David Heuschkel and Jeff Goldberg; Jimmy Golen and Howard Ulman from the Associated Press; the inimitable Bill Ballou from the *Worcester Telegram and Gazette*, who can find the silver lining in any cloud; Alex Speier, the highly underrated and talented reporter for multiple publications; Alan Greenwood from the *Nashua Telegraph*, my roommate in the Fenway Park press box; Mike Petraglia, a great teammate and friend who always has my back on off-days; Louise Cornetta from ESPN Radio, who is a supportive friend and savvy director of postgame social outings; Brita Meng Outzen, photographer extraordinaire and a dear friend; Joe Haggerty from the *Woburn Times*.

Thanks also to Paul Bodi, my boss at MLB.com, who has treated me exceptionally well over the years, and to other friends at MLB.com who make it a better place to work including Mark Bowman, Jesse Sanchez, Chris Begley, T. R. Sullivan, Alyson Footer, John Ralph, Jim Banks, John Schlegel, Arturo Pardavila, Jen Royle, Katy Lathan, Thomas Harding, Bryan Hoch, Jordan Bastian, Spencer Fordin, Steve Gilbert, Matthew Leach, Jason Beck, Carrie Muskat, Jim Street, Adam McCalvy, Mark Sheldon, and Mike Bauman.

There were many people who took the time to answer numerous questions for this book. The following individuals were of particular help: John W. Henry, Tom Werner, Larry Lucchino, Terry Francona, John Farrell, Dan Okimoto, Jim Colborn, Reggie Jefferson, Scott McClain, Kazuhiro Takeda, Peter Grilli, Wayne Graczyk, Jim Allen, Osamu Higashio, Sachiyo Sekiguchi, John Blake, Ken Eng, Alex Shear, Hideki Okuda, Mike Piazza and Mike Plugh. While many members of the Japanese media were an enormous help, I want to thank the following three individuals in particular for their assistance in translating some of Matsuzaka's more interesting group interviews with the Japanese media: Takashi Settai, Hiroki Tohda and Sohta Kimura.

I save the best for last, and that would be my family of course. My mom always pushed me to go after my goals while being a doting mother along the way. My stepdad inspired me with his work ethic. My father took me to my first baseball game and has been a huge source of support throughout the years. My stepmom is a gift to our family. My sister brags about her "little" brother to anyone who will listen. My mother-in-law is an incredible person who has been through a lot over the last few months but is as strong as they come. My three sisters-in-law are very cool and made me feel part of the family from the day I met them. My three brothers-in-law are good guys, and more importantly, they all love sports. Nice going, guys. It's good to have someone to watch the game with. I don't have a brother, but my cousin Scott—who had a book published before I did—basically is one. He also knows more about sports than I do, which is impressive.

And my wife—the great Amy Browne—deserves her own paragraph. She is the Most Valuable Player of my household, a true rock. I'm not sure what she's better at—being a wife, a mother, or a best friend. It's probably a tie. She's also a great proofreader with a journalism degree to boot, which came in handy during this project.

To my three sons, Tyler, Ryan and Casey. I love you guys—especially when you let me sleep in.

Introduction

IF DAISUKE MATSUZAKA'S FIRST Major League season had
been scripted into a movie, the alternate ending—one with no
Hollywood fluff or fairytale finish—was there for full public
viewing. The vivid scene took place in the late-night hours of
October 15, 2007 within the walls of the visitors' clubhouse
of Jacobs Field in Cleveland. It was there that this disgruntled,
27-year-old man stared into his locker for close to an hour,
taking only a short break to eat. For several months, this right-
handed pitcher from Japan had been carrying around the burden of massive expectations from his homeland, where he was
nothing short of a living legend and a national treasure. And in
his new country—which included the ravenous fan-base known
as Red Sox Nation—he carried the weight of a price tag of
$103.1 million, though half of that money actually went to his
former team in Japan and not the pitcher himself. And through
all of this, Matsuzaka was learning to live in an entirely different culture, one that spoke a different language than he did.
He was getting used to a new baseball, one that was slicker
and slightly different in size than the one he had thrown for
his entire baseball life. There was a new pitcher's mound to
get used to, this one made of clay instead of the sandy stuff
he had landed on his whole life. The strike zone, less liberal
in the Major Leagues, was another source of education and
aggravation. The travel was far more demanding, with red-eye,

cross-country flights replacing short bullet train rides. For the first time in Matsuzaka's life, he was confined by pitch counts, which was nauseating to a man who had once thrown 250 pitches in a high school game. The season was longer and his rest time between starts was shorter. Oh, and the opposing line-ups were far more powerful and polished from top to bottom than any he had ever encountered in Japan.

Sometimes Matsuzaka looked like he was conquering all of these things. On other nights, it seemed as if he was the one being conquered. The script was unpredictable and nobody could tell whether the ending in the first year would be happy, sad, or somewhere in the middle. But there came that Monday night in Cleveland in the minutes that followed Game 3 of the American League Championship Series. Matsuzaka had just lost a baseball game, 4-2. For the second postseason start in a row, he hadn't made it through the fifth inning. Worse yet, Matsuzaka wondered if his performance was going to be the ultimate undoing for his team, which now trailed 2-1 in the best-of-seven series with two more games to play in the enemy territory of Cleveland.

When the media entered the clubhouse in droves following that game, they wanted answers from Matsuzaka. But Matsuzaka had nothing but anger. He had been out of the game for hours by the time reporters from Boston, Japan and several ports in between roamed the clubhouse. However, Matsuzaka had not taken his uniform off yet. He was sitting in front of his locker, staring straight ahead. His hands were clasped around the back of his head, as to illustrate just how disturbed he was by what had gone on. Matsuzaka hates losing and that, probably as much as his talent, has driven him to win so much over the years. The assumption made by many was that Matsuzaka would unwind for a little longer and eventually stand up and maybe shower, and then discuss his performance with the press. It was a surreal scene in the packed clubhouse. Different players wound up discussing the loss to inquiring reporters while others just kind of lingered. Gregarious slugger David Ortiz was on the couch next to ace Josh Beckett, gleefully talking about how a line drive had narrowly missed hitting him square in the part of his anatomy where a man most doesn't want to be hit. Beckett, meanwhile, was glued to the National League Championship Series on the television, where the Colorado Rockies were on the verge of sweeping the Arizona Diamondbacks and earning a trip to the World Series. But would it be the Indians who would play the Rockies and not the Red Sox? As Beckett did his own salty commentary on the NL game, Ortiz continued to sip on his beer and entertain reporters.

To the left, beyond the couch, Matsuzaka had barely moved a muscle. He was still sitting and staring, his hands still gripping his head. After about a half hour, notebooks and tape recorders moved as they saw Matsuzaka get up. As it turns out, the pitcher was just taking a few steps to a table in the middle of the room, where he dined on the post-game spread. After eating, Matsuzaka resumed his position at his locker, almost as if he never left. All those staredowns Matsuzaka had with American League batters in 2007, and it looked like the final staring contest might just be with a locker. The pitcher sat there for a solid thirty minutes before finally issuing a very brief statement to his translator that was relayed to the media as his quote for the evening. The media left and Matsuzaka sat back down. For how long? Nobody knows. But by the time the clubhouse opened again the next day, Matsuzaka was no longer sitting there, which means the locker eventually won the staring contest.

It might have seemed that Matsuzaka was a beaten man at that time. But what he was really doing was giving his system a full and complete cleansing. "Immediately following the game is a very important time period for me," Matsuzaka would say a few days later. If the Red Sox could get up off the mat and get this series to Game 7, Matsuzaka would be the man on the mound, and he didn't want negativity lingering anywhere close to him. So he sat there and sat there and sat there until finally letting it all go. Of course, getting to a seventh game was entirely out of his control. Only his teammates could control that fate for him. It didn't happen in Game 4, as the Red Sox sunk into a 3-1 hole, meaning all the Indians had to do was win just one of the next three games to go to the World Series. Could the Matsuzaka Year One odyssey with the Red Sox really end this abruptly? It seemed too soon and too empty, considering all the drama that had come with his first year in the States.

Lo and behold, there was more drama still. The Red Sox didn't go quietly into the night. They kept winning. Matsuzaka was salivating at his chance for redemption, one that just about all of his teammates assured him he would get. It was all so befitting the year Matsuzaka had, as so many downs seemed to be followed by an up and vice versa. If there was a key word for Matsuzaka's first Major League season, it was survival. There were some bends for sure. But never any kind of permanent break. Despite all the adversity, he had on numerous occasions showed the will to come back. So he came out blazing in Game 7 against the Indians for the first few innings, faltered a bit in the fifth inning and hung on for the win. Then there was the World Series. All he did on that stage was use his bat—after having four at-bats the entire season—to belt a two-out, two-run single that put a serious dent into any hope of a Colorado comeback. And in that same Game 3, Matsuzaka had a three-hit shutout after five innings before exiting with a couple of runners on base in the sixth. He was the winning pitcher in the game that put the Red Sox on the precipice of their second championship in four years, which they would win the very next night.

The alternate ending in Cleveland was officially scrapped for the happy one in Denver as if a movie director himself had orchestrated the whole thing. And if you hadn't tuned into Matsuzaka all year, you might have thought the ending was indicative of the journey. For wasn't this the way it was supposed to be when the Red Sox outfoxed the rest of the baseball world and secured negotiating rights to this man with the highest posting fee—$51.1 million—in the history of baseball?

In an ideal world, yes. But in the real world, Matsuzaka often felt the strain of learning his new environment in 2007. At times, his greatness back in Japan was lost in translation on United States soil. There were other stretches when he dominated his opponent and you could feel what Japanese baseball watchers must have felt so often over the years. Over the following pages, you will read in rich detail about the entirety of Matsuzaka's initial season in Boston, from the opening press conference at Fenway to the end of the World Series in Colorado.

But to fully grasp the meaning of that, it is important to understand Matsuzaka's background in Japan, and that is also examined. It started with a three-day test of will and endurance at the famed Koshien tournament in 1998, where the 17-year-old Matsuzaka instantly transformed himself into an icon in Japan. Then, there was Matsuzaka's eight-year career with the Seibu Lions, at which time he often had a strong desire to pitch in the United States but still stayed focused enough to be the pitching equivalent of Ichiro Suzuki in Nippon Professional Baseball. Another story that needed to be told was Matsuzaka's international coming out party at the 2006 World Baseball Classic, which put him in the minds of Major League Baseball fans for the first time and helped to set the stage for his move to the Red Sox. And the inner workings of the Red Sox first wooing Matsuzaka and then closing the deal is also explored in this book, with telling insight from the high-powered executives who green-lighted the $103.1 million acquisition price. The context of all the drama that led up to late October adds more emphasis to Matsuzaka's strong finish. There's always something more enriching about a happy ending that comes after conquered struggles along the way.

It was a life-altering year for Matsuzaka, with the media—both American and Japanese—scrutinizing every bit of it. Behind closed doors, Matsuzaka earned respect among his co-workers and bosses for the way he handled it. "I think that when he shows up next year, we're all going to have a little bit of a better understanding of what he went through this year," said Red Sox manager Terry Francona.

1

Koshien—A Star Is Born
(August 1998)

IT WAS ABOUT BASEBALL from the day Daisuke Matsuzaka was born. You see, while Matsuzaka was in the womb, his mother, Yumiko, became riveted by a high school baseball pitching star named Daisuke Araki, who was dazzling in the summer Koshien Tournament of 1980. About a month later—on September 13, 1980—Daisuke Matsuzaka officially came into the world. The first name was no coincidence. Yumiko Matsuzaka named her baby boy after a high school baseball star, albeit one who would go on to have a mediocre professional career in Japan, going 39-49 in his ten years as a pro. In the irony of all ironies, Araki would later go on to become Matsuzaka's pitching coach with the Seibu Lions. Not that he was anything close in stature by then to the man who was named after him. In fact, if you check out the baseball reference.com bio on Araki, a passage reads, "He will be noted more in history for Daisuke Matsuzaka being named after him." You see, Daisuke Matsuzaka was going to wind up being a legend of Japanese baseball, one who would be stacked up with any of the greats past or present. To get to that revered status, it all started, naturally, at Koshien.

Koshien is something that most people outside of Japan can't truly understand. It is the national high school championships, but that doesn't even begin to tell the story. To the Japanese, it might as well be the World Series. There is a spring invitational that serves almost as a warm-up act, but that tourney is not single elimination.

But when it comes to a Japanese sporting event, there is nothing like summer in Koshien, where you win every day or you go home immediately. It started way back in 1915 and every nuance of it is gobbled up by the baseball-crazed country of Japan. Some 4,000 teams enter regional tournaments, and 49 champions go on to Koshien, where every game is single-elimination. The stands of Koshien Stadium are packed with 50,000 people in the searing August heat, with marching bands playing and cheerleaders dancing in the background. "Fans eat it up," said Jim Allen, the veteran baseball writer for the *Daily Yomiuri*. "There's so much emotion. That's the real drawing power. You see crying if you win and crying if you lose." It isn't uncommon for a player to bring a plastic bag with him to Koshien and fill it with dirt from the infield. That is how hallowed the ground is. And that is why Matsuzaka—who grew up in a section of Tokyo called Koto and was a baseball star for Yokohama High School—became a legend from the moment he did what he did there.

As a senior for Yokohama in 1998, Matsuzaka, all 17 years of him, stood up on that mound at Koshien and over a span of three days—August 20–22—went from a high school prospect to a gallant pitcher on the fast track to greatness. That is the power of Koshien. And at that time, that was the power and stamina of one Daisuke Matsuzaka, who had no fear even some nine years before he would pitch in the World Series for the Boston Red Sox. Before getting to the quarterfinal—where the fast track to his storybook run officially got underway—Matsuzaka had already gone twenty-seven innings in his three starts at Koshien, giving up a mere one run and twelve hits while striking out thirty-one. And that was in addition to the spring invitational at Koshien, when Matsuzaka had already lifted Yokohama on his back to the championship, going 5-0 with an 0.80 ERA and lasting nine innings in all five outings. But Matsuzaka nearly didn't prevail in the summer portion.

For in the quarterfinals, he went up against PK Gakuen, a perennial powerhouse, and faced an epic struggle in which his body and mind were tested to their absolute maximum capacity.

If you're lucky enough to obtain video highlights from that tournament, you can see the thin Matsuzaka with the bony jaw and the grey Yokohama jersey with black lettering, the black hat with red lettering, and the No. 1 on his back. You can see that early in the game, Matsuzaka is getting hit a little. In the third inning, he even balked a runner to third, smiling nervously after he did it, and then he gave up an RBI single. He was down 3-0. After ten innings, the score was 5-5. But there was Dice-K—long before he was known as Dice-K—cracking a single that ate up the third baseman to start a rally in the top of the eleventh. And there was Dice-K again, sliding home, and getting a break when the catcher dropped the ball, and reaching his hand back to touch home plate for the go-ahead run, pumping his fist to boot. But a spent Matsuzaka gave the lead back in the bottom of the eleventh. And again in the bottom of the sixteenth, he gave up the lead, this time looking around in disbelief after his wild pitch helped set up the tying run. But he was still out there pitching. And in the seventeenth inning, Matsuzaka would not be denied. He recorded a strikeout to end the game and his manager Motonori Watanabe suddenly had moist eyes. Matsuzaka threw an astounding 250 pitches. No, that is not a misprint. To put it in perspective, Matsuzaka topped out at 130 pitches in his first season with the Red Sox. In Major League Baseball—particularly in the 21st century—a manager wouldn't even contemplate letting a pitcher get anywhere near the 200-mark.

But to Matsuzaka, that was his job. "We practice and practice for those kinds of things," Matsuzaka told Red Sox beatwriter Steven Krasner for an article that was published in Major League Baseball's official 2007 World Series Program. "Of course, having to throw 17 innings is a possibility because of the rules of the game, but not something you'd expect. But at that point, it becomes more of a mental game and I think the preparation I had done, pitching in those situations up to that point, really gave me a good base for being able to pitch in that situation."

If Matsuzaka had stopped there, the story still would have been legendary. But he didn't. The next day in the semis against Meitoku Gijuku, Matsuzaka played left field and watched his team fall into a 6-0 hole entering the bottom of the eighth. But there would be a big Yokohama rally in that eighth, helped in part by Matsuzaka's seeing-eye single up the middle that brought home a run. With the score 6-4, Matsuzaka literally took bandages off his throwing arm and pitched the top of the ninth just twenty-four hours after unleashing 250 pitches. This was just the type of thing that happened at Koshien. He was unscored on and Yokohama scored three to win it in the bottom of the ninth. Courage was taking on new meaning. So was stamina. Jim Colborn, a Major League pitcher from 1969 to 1978, was a Pacific Rim scout for the Seattle Mariners at that time. He was watching something that was changing his entire thinking about what the human arm was capable of. "Those stories are part of his glamour," Colborn said some nine years later. "Matsuzaka really sculpted my thinking about what a pitcher is capable of doing."

But even Matsuzaka's biggest supporters couldn't have imagined what he was capable of doing in the Final against Kyoto Seisho. You'd think he would have been on fumes, but how do you throw a no-hitter on fumes? Yes, he did throw a no-hitter and struck out eleven. From the instant the performance ended, his legendary status was ensured. The no-hitter nearly ended a couple of times. First, there was a hard grounder in the eighth off the first baseman, but the relay to Matsuzaka was just in time. And in the ninth, there was a wobbly bunt that started fair down the first base line but narrowly rolled foul. It would have been a hit. The masterpiece ended with a half-swing on a slider that was maybe a foot outside the strike zone. Matsuzaka was mobbed by his teammates, and for the next several years, he'd be equally mobbed by reporters. In three days, the boy had thrown seventeen innings one day, a flawless inning out of the bullpen the next, and then a no-hit masterpiece the day after that. All he had done during Yokohama's run at Koshien was go 5-0 with a 1.17 ERA. He did it amid the backdrop of the biggest crowds he had ever pitched in front of, not to mention the millions of Japanese fans who were taking in the event from the national television feed.

In an on-field television interview after the game, Matsuzaka's face poured with sweat. His eyes looked almost too weary for emotion, though he did manage a couple of smiles and short, polite answers. Sachiyo Sekiguchi, who served as the Japanese media relations coordinator for the Red Sox in 2007, was kind enough to watch the short video clip on youtube.com and translate Matsuzaka's answers from Japanese to English. How did he feel after such a masterpiece? "It is the greatest thing to ever happen in my life so far," said Matsuzaka. Did he know he had a no-hitter? "I kept checking the scoreboard while I pitched, but I tried not to be overly conscious about it." But it was at the end of the interview that the young Matsuzaka produced his best stuff. The broadcaster told Matsuzaka that throughout the tournament, all of Yokohama's opponents focused on beating him. His answer was succinct and indicative of the type of determination he had. "I became a pitcher that everyone wanted to beat and everyone looked forward to facing. So I tried to be the pitcher that wouldn't be beat."

In 2007, the performance was still being talked about. In fact, his move to the Red Sox seemed to give it more life, as many people in America learned about it for the first time. How did Matsuzaka handle such an intense atmosphere at such a young age? "I'm not the type of person who gets really nervous about pitching in front of a crowd," Matsuzaka told Krasner, who has covered the Red Sox for the *Providence Journal* (Rhode Island) for two decades. "Rather, I think I'm the kind of guy who enjoys it, so ever since performing in such a big crowd [at Koshien], I've always been able to enjoy those moments. If you were a starting pitcher, you'd be expected to throw 200 pitches three days in a row. I actually threw four days in a row."

Matsuzaka sounds almost unimpressed by what he did even nine years later, and, to a degree, he wasn't all that enamored with himself back in 1998 either. But the fans of Japan? "The fans were going crazy, everyone was talking about this amazing pitcher who could just blow everybody away," said Allen. "He was a kid. He threw very hard. He didn't really worry much about anything he threw. He thought everything he threw was going to get everybody out. He was always surprised when anyone got a hit off him, but also very nonchalant about it. 'Oh yeah, well, that's going to happen. We'll see what the next guy does.' He had that dumb look on his face sometimes, like, 'How did that happen?' That sort of look of surprise you see on his face when somebody hits him, like, 'Aha, that wasn't supposed to happen.' He was so confident. That was very clear. And he had so much speed."

The only thing faster than Matsuzaka's fastball was probably how quickly he rose to prominence. For Matsuzaka instantly put himself in the spotlight. And by 2007, it still showed no signs of diminishing. It's just that by then it was in two countries instead of one. But back then, Matsuzaka was still a novelty. He was the next great star to burst on to the Japanese baseball scene. Hiroki Tohda wasn't yet a journalist during Matsuzaka's initiation into superstardom. He was just a high school student who happened to be the same age as Matsuzaka. Tohda had just returned from living in the United States. Matsuzaka's performance at Koshien was Tohda's welcome back present to his native land. "What I thought was, 'Wow, Japanese baseball has a star.' I hadn't seen a high school student pitch like this," recalled Tohda. "It was great fun to watch. I was living in New York for about eight years—elementary school to high school. Then I came back and saw that. He was lights out. He was super." Years later, Tohda would cover parts of Matsuzaka's first season with the Red Sox for Sports Nippon Newspapers. But back then, he was just a fan looking for an athlete to identify with. He found just the man in Daisuke Matsuzaka.

But it didn't all come easily for Matsuzaka. Flash back to one summer earlier when Matsuzaka was trying to will Yokohama's 1997 entry to Koshien. In Japan, students are in high school for three years and this was Matsuzaka's second-to-last chance to pitch on the stage every Japanese youth craved. He was in the semifinal of the qualifying round, which meant he was two wins away from the glory of Koshien. Entering the bottom of the ninth inning, Matsuzaka held a 2-1 lead and proceeded to blow it, losing the game on, of all things, a walk-off wild pitch. The game was played in Yokohama and the result was nothing less than devastating for Matsuzaka. "I think the Dice-K story began that game, the lost game, the walk-off wild pitch," said Masashi Yamazaki, one of the many Japanese reporters who chronicled Matsuzaka's rookie season with the Boston Red Sox. Yamazaki was in the stands for that 1997 meltdown. In fact, it was the first time he became aware of who Matsuzaka was. "After the game, he could not stop crying," remembers Yamazaki.

That's what amateur baseball does to people in Japan. And that's why the significance of a breakthrough performance at Koshien cannot be overstated. For the high schoolers are far more revered in Japan than the pros. "Essentially in Japan, if you are a star, I would say 75 percent of your star power is from Koshien," said Allen. "To really, really be a Japanese baseball icon like Matsuzaka, like [Hideki] Matsui, like Sadaharu Oh, you had to play in Koshien and be a Koshien hero. There are exceptions. [Shigeo] Nagashima was an exception. He never played at Koshien. When Nagashima was in college ball, college ball was very big." Matsui became legendary at Koshien in a highly unique manner, being walked intentionally five times in one game in the summer of 1992. The intentional walk is not utilized nearly as much in Japan as it is in the Major Leagues, so the free passes spoke volumes about the sheer respect teams had for Matsui, even as a high school star. In the opener of that spring's Koshien Tournament, Matsui merely had seven RBIs. Even if Matsui hadn't gone on to become a megastar for the Yomiuri Giants and then become a key member of the New York Yankees, he would have been held in high esteem by the Japanese faithful simply for his exploits in high school.

Why is Koshien so revered by the Japanese? Even an American who is there for a short time can get a sense of that. "When a team loses in the summer tournament, it's the end—the seniors immediately retire and a new team is born," said Alex Shear, an independent producer who collaborated on a documentary film dissecting the meaning of Koshien. "Young men who have spent nearly every single day together with ridiculous dedication to practice, for three straight years, are suddenly split up. The next day, the seniors begin preparing for high-pressure college entrance exams and the next phase of their lives. So when they lose, it's really the end of their youth."

But Matsuzaka rose to the occasion in such a way at Koshien that his future was destined to be in baseball. Later in that same summer, he was at it again in the Asian High School Championship Tournament, which was also played at Koshien. Colborn was again there and again became stunned, though by this time, perhaps he shouldn't have been. "I didn't think he'd last, to tell you the truth," said Colborn. "In one of those games, they interviewed me in about the third inning and I said, 'He just pitched two days ago so I expect him to start losing his stuff in a couple of innings.' Well, he ended up pitching nine or ten innings. I was dead wrong." What Colborn learned about Matsuzaka is that he could just pitch all day and all night and somehow recover. How did he do it?

"I've got no idea," Colborn said. "Well, mechanics are better for one thing. The other thing is, I suspect that the Japanese, it was my impression watching that they don't grow a lot after they're 18 years old. That's not true with people in other parts of the world. When you're growing, the growth plates are at the end of the bones (and) are susceptible to injury. I think the studies I've seen say that if there's excessive amount of growing at the time that the bones are growing, there's a higher risk of injury. I think that's probably why the Japanese can have these reputations of throwing so much because possibly their growing is over when they do the majority of their real professional throwing."

Matsuzaka was far from the only Japanese pitcher or player who seemingly went through hell and back just to win a high school baseball game. It was just something that happened in Japan, where sheer will was as appreciated as graceful skill. "I remember one story, when I was at Koshien in 2004, one pitcher—I believe he was Saibi—pitched his heart out in the usual insane heat and humidity and actually collapsed on the mound," said Shear. "I read in the English language newspaper that he received intravenous fluids and was back at it the next day in the next game. The kid was a hero. That's the kind of attitude Japanese have about high school baseball. It's almost a football mentality. These kids are leaving it all on the field and they will absolutely not give up until they pass out." Play to win to the point of suffering. That is the riveting aspect of Koshien. "Many Japanese baseball fans like the high school tournament better than the professional league," Tohda said. "What they like is that everybody hustles. They run their hearts out. They do everything they can."

That type of mentality was still evident in Matsuzaka by the time he started doing his pitching for the Boston Red Sox. He never wanted to come out of a game. And if Matsuzaka was ever tired, he never wanted to admit it. It was ingrained in him that his job was to pitch, and keep pitching, until the game had been decided. "It was pretty obvious then he was something special, kind of the pitcher's equivalent of Hideki Matsui as a slugger or Ichiro as a pure hitter," said Wayne Graczyk, who has written a weekly baseball column for the *Japan Times* since 1976. It was at Koshien that the origin of the Matsuzaka generation came about. Japanese baseball players who were born between April 2, 1980 and April 1, 1981—the Japanese fiscal year—are referred to as being from the Matsuzaka generation. As great as Matsuzaka was in his pro career for the Seibu Lions, the bulk of his revered status comes from Koshien. Matsuzaka lent credence to how big the high school stage was for him when, after his Major League debut, he said he didn't have the same nerves as he did before his first performance at Koshien. One will never know what would have become of Matsuzaka if he didn't get that springboard of Koshien. But it will always be part of who he is and what he became. "Because he's in the Major Leagues now, we can say that the Koshien tournament was part of his first step," said Tohda. "There were a lot of fans from that point from when he was an amateur. He became bigger and bigger."

And a seed was planted in the minds of certain baseball executives, Theo Epstein among them. Epstein in 1998 was an assistant in the baseball operations department of the San Diego Padres. "I know that he was first on the radar screen for certain clubs in 1998, after Koshien," Epstein, the general manager of the Boston Red Sox, would say in December 2006. "Just from that performance at Koshien, I remember talking about him with baseball people back then. From that point on he was a national hero, a national treasure." Some Major League teams—including the Colorado Rockies and Arizona Diamondbacks—did look into making a run at Matsuzaka before he entered the draft of Nippon Professional Baseball. But it wasn't realistic at that time. Matsuzaka was going to get a far more lucrative deal to play in Japan and wouldn't have to start in the unglamorous world of minor league baseball in America. He was already a legend in his native land, and there was no way he could leave that soon. First, Matsuzaka had to show that his high school prowess was no fluke and that he'd be just as strong at the next level. That validation would not take long. Unlike the man he was named after, this Daisuke would be a star in the pros. But first, he had to find out what uniform he'd be wearing.

2

Seibu Sensation
(1999–2006)

THE 18-YEAR-OLD prodigy—with all that confidence and the stuff to go with it—felt like he was ready to be a professional superstar. He just needed a team to perform his magic for. Literally, the Seibu Lions had to win the lottery before making Matsuzaka their property as the No. 1 overall pick in the draft. It was a strange system. "You could pick a player but if somebody else picked him, the order of the draft didn't matter," said Jim Allen, baseball writer for the *Daily Yomiuri*. "There were lottery picks. If two teams pick the same player in the first round, you can pick him before somebody. You have a lottery. Then the teams draw. This happened with [Hideki] Matsui, it happened with [Hideo] Nomo, I would think it happens with a lot of guys." Three teams had selected Matsuzaka. One was his hometown team, the Yokohama Bay Stars. The others were the Seibu Lions and the Orix Blue Wave, Ichiro's team. "They put three cards in a box or a hat and one of them has his name on it and the other two are blank," said Wayne Graczyk. "And the Seibu manager picked the one with [Matsuzaka's] name. The Seibu manager was named Osamu Higashio."

That name carried some weight in Japan, and that was one reason Matsuzaka would wind up signing with Seibu, despite the fact that Yokohama would have been a better fit for him at the time. Higashio, you see, was a 251-game winner in Japan. And if Matsuzaka would sign with Seibu, Higashio would give him the baseball from his 200th career victory. In Japan, the 200th win is equivalent to 300 in Major League Baseball. It puts you on a pedestal among the greats. Higashio also offered Matsuzaka his uniform number, 21. Matsuzaka took Higashio up on the 200 game ball, but passed on No. 21, saying that 18—which had become trendy for the aces of Japan—was his number of choice. Not long after, the deal was done and Matsuzaka had found his new home. He would not just pitch for the Seibu Lions, but in short order he would become the face of their franchise. He would be their drawing card. It was a franchise—though well-stacked financially at that time and with a fairly recent track record of championship success on the baseball field—that somewhat needed a face. The Lions were not the Yomiuri Giants or the Hanshin Tigers, two storied and tradition-laden franchises in which the team made the player as much as vice versa. "I think he was really very popular even though he played for Seibu," said Graczyk. "But he would have been much more popular if he had played for the Giants or say the Hanshin Tigers. Now that he's gone to the Red Sox, it's like the whole country has taken to him like they did with [Hideo] Nomo."

Still, Matsuzaka's impact for Seibu was immediate and resounding. "The first start he made, it was at Tokyo Dome against the Fighters who were based in Tokyo Dome then," said Graczyk. "The Fighters would draw, for a weekday night game, they would announce like 15,000 but it was more like 6,000 or 7,000 out there. But they had 44,000 that night because Matsuzaka was the pitcher." That night—April 7, 1999—was what Higashio needed as proof that he indeed had himself an ace. To be truthful, he was a tad skeptical after watching Matsuzaka during their first Spring Training together.

"I knew Daisuke had great ability at the time but he was only 18 years old," Higashio said eight years later, from the press box at Fenway Park. "I was not certain Daisuke could make the adjustment to Japanese professional baseball during Spring Training. When Daisuke pitched the first game of the regular season, I knew he could do it. During his first Spring Training, he wasn't so good." And in that Nippon Professional Baseball debut, Matsuzaka reached back and fired a 155 kilometer per hour offering to a talented left-handed batter named Atsushi Kataoka. That is roughly 97 miles per hour. It was a statement pitch. It was a statement performance by a teenage kid who sure looked like a man. Matsuzaka opened his pro career by firing five perfect innings of baseball. He finished with a shutout.

"When Daisuke came to the big leagues and when he was 18 years old, I saw him on the mound that first time," said Kazuo Matsui, a teammate of Matsuzaka's at Seibu for five years, not to mention an opponent of Matsuzaka's in the 2007 World Series for the Colorado Rockies. "He was really confident at 18 years old, and I was like, 'wow.'" There would be other wows to come. Shortly thereafter came the first showdown with Ichiro, and all Matsuzaka did was strike out the great bat-handler in their first three at-bats. It was almost as if things came too easy to Matsuzaka in that rookie year. He recorded five strikeouts at the All-Star Game. And on the season, he was 16-5 with a 2.60 ERA. It might have been a boy against men, but Matsuzaka was getting the best of everyone. That year, Matsuzaka basically wound up and dared hitters to get his fastball. At that time, very few could. His manager enjoyed watching the show, but Higashio knew Matsuzaka's approach wasn't going to get him sustained success. He was going to have to grow as a pitcher. Years later, Higashio would note how Matsuzaka—in the early stages of his pro career—was trying too hard to light up the radar gun.

Very few people knew it at the time, but one of the reasons Matsuzaka was pushing the envelope so much was that he already had dreams of going to Major League Baseball. Interestingly, Matsuzaka confirmed that very thing to Higashio during his visit to Boston in June of 2007, and the manager seemed a little surprised by it. In a way, that demonstrated Matsuzaka's professionalism to the Lions. For even if he already had pangs to pitch in the Major Leagues, he still gave Seibu everything he had. By 2000, Matsuzaka had teammates who had played in the Major Leagues. Men like Tony Fernandez and Reggie Jefferson. Just baby steps into his pro career in Japan, Matsuzaka confided in those men that he wanted to be where they had been before. Jefferson, in fact, had played for the Boston Red Sox for five years, leading up to his arrival with Seibu. "The year I played with Matsuzaka was Ichiro's last year over there and you knew he was coming the next year and it was just going to start a wave. And Dice-K had kind of let it be known that one day he'd want to go over. Sometimes, through the interpreter, he'd ask me and Tony Fernandez some questions. You kind of knew that when his time came, he'd be over here." But the time wouldn't come for a while. Matsuzaka didn't have any options. He was contractually bound to the Lions. And the way he packed the seats, the Lions weren't about to entertain thoughts of letting him go.

But Matsuzaka's desire to pitch in the Majors did not detract from his performances for Seibu. Just like at Koshien, he was a lion on the mound. What struck Jefferson most was just how big Matsuzaka was. Not physically big, but big in the minds of the people of Japan. "It was like nothing else I had ever seen. I played with Pedro [Martinez], Roger Clemens, Randy Johnson, but this guy was just more famous than any of those guys," said Jefferson. "When we traveled, we came out of the hotel, there would be 200 screaming fans just waiting to see him, everywhere he went. I tell people he was like a rock star, like Elvis. It was so unique."

In this case, the sweetest tunes Elvis had came purring out of his right hand. "At that time, I had the same feeling playing behind him as I did a Roger or a Pedro," Jefferson said. "You always felt like you were going to win when he took the mound. I think the biggest comparison for me between him and Pedro was just the competitiveness. Those are two guys who would just do anything to win. Whatever they had that night, they could find a way to go to their strength and get the job done." Jefferson noted that Matsuzaka was 19 years old at that time, and hardly a finished product. But, still, he had the aura. Interestingly, Jefferson noticed some of the very same things from Matsuzaka that teammates in Boston would see some eight years later. "He always had a smile on his face," said Jefferson. "You could tell he loved the game. Even though he had so much attention, you could tell he never let that go to his head. He still worked hard. The majority of the guys over there worked so hard. It was baseball. But he just always had a smile on his face."

Perhaps because of the over-reliance on his fastball, Matsuzaka's ERA swelled from 2.60 in his rookie year to 3.97 in 2000. Still, he was 14-7 and led the Pacific League in wins and strikeouts. Then came 2001, a thoroughly uneven year for Matsuzaka in which he posted a 15-15 record, threw a career-high of 240⅓ innings and walked 117 batters, though he did strike out 214. "He was throwing as hard as he could and people were hitting it," said Allen. "He got hit hard a lot. One guy who caught him very regularly [Kazuhiro Wada], said that basically that was his issue. He had tremendous other stuff, he had to get rid of that feeling that his fastball was good enough." The eerie thing about that is that Matsuzaka went through that precise issue during the worst slump of his inaugural season in Boston. In a way, it makes sense. If you are a power pitcher by nature, you're going to turn to your heater for comfort. But Matsuzaka learned both with Seibu and with Boston it wasn't a sustained recipe for success.

As early as 2001, Matsuzaka started working in his cutter and changeup more often so he wouldn't be so reliant on the fastball and the forkball. In 2002, playing for a new manager named Haruki Ihara, Matsuzaka didn't have a whole lot of time to implement his new and broader approach. For the first time in his career, he was injured. Thanks to a nagging right elbow, Matsuzaka threw just 73⅓ innings, going 6-2 with a 3.68 ERA. But there would be a postseason. In fact, Seibu would make it all the way to the Japan Series for the first time in Matsuzaka's career.

Matsuzaka had done some rehab work late in the season and pitched Game 1 against the Yomiuri Giants. He took a 4-1 loss. Even though the Lions wound up getting swept in four straight, Matsuzaka was strangely brought in out of the bullpen in Game 4. He was hit hard and lost. It was suspected that Lions owner Yoshiaki Tsutsumi—who was on the Forbes list of billionaires before his worth began taking a hit in 2005—had put pressure on manager Haruki Ihara to pitch Matsuzaka. "The owner just wanted Matsuzaka to have the limelight," suspected Allen, who said players had said similar things to him off the record.

You need do nothing more than look at the graphic of Matsuzaka's year-by-year pitching line with Seibu to notice that in 2003 the man matured into a more consistent pitcher. Matsuzaka's dominance, which had always been part of the equation, was becoming routine. Consider that from 2000–02, Matsuzaka's ERA was never below 3.60. For his remaining four years in Japan, it was never higher than 2.90. Matsuzaka no longer was just a man with electric stuff, but now had the knowledge and purpose to know exactly what to do with it. And that will and stamina at Koshien made Matsuzaka a household name in Japan forever. He still had all that. In 2003, the same year the Red Sox would wind up having a heartbreaking collapse to the Yankees in Game 7 of the American League Championship Series, Matsuzaka was shaping himself into the type of pitcher Major League teams desired. This was easily Matsuzaka's best season since his rookie year of 1999, as he went 16-7 with a 2.83 ERA and recorded 215 strikeouts over 194 innings.

Scott McClain, an infielder who had cups of coffee in the Major Leagues both before (1998) and after (2005, 2007) his years with the Seibu Lions, simply loved watching Matsuzaka go to work. The two were teammates from 2001 to 2004. McClain basically saw the unfinished and finished versions of Matsuzaka. "Obviously, going over there, I started playing with him when he was 21, 22. It was real fun seeing him mature into the pitcher that he is," said McClain, who was a September call-up with the San

Francisco Giants during Matsuzaka's rookie year with the Red Sox. "He always had good stuff but he always fine-tuned over the four years I was there." When McClain turns on the rewind button to the years he teamed with Dice-K, the guts and pitching heart seem to resonate more than what actually came out of the pitcher's hand. Memories? "Probably just the fact that he was the ultimate competitor. He always wanted the ball," said McClain. "Shoot, he'd throw 150 pitches in a game like it was nothing. If we were going extra innings, he wanted to go out there again and again and get that win. It was really something to see. I don't think I've ever seen that from a pitcher who is willing to go out and throw in the twelfth inning or whatever. He's at a 160-pitch count and he's wanting to get the win so bad. I think that's what I remember most from over there." For in those years, Matsuzaka's pitch count was all but nonexistent. He pitched until he either won or lost. "We'd be tied 2-2 or 1-1 and he's pitching his ass off the whole game and we're thinking we'll get somebody warmed up in the `pen but there was just no thought of that with him," McClain said. "He'd either finish a game until he won it or he lost." And in case you think Matsuzaka was prodded to be out there so long, McClain remembers it differently. "It wasn't so much the coaches wanting him to go out there," McClain said. "He wanted to be out there."

There were a number of times during the year 2007 that Matsuzaka's teammates in Boston got asked about how the right-hander could handle such a constant dose of media attention. What many of those questioners didn't understand was that Matsuzaka had been dealing with all of this back home since Koshien. McClain would often survey the mob of reporters that circled around Matsuzaka and wonder how he dealt with it so well.

"He was the biggest thing since Sadaharu Oh or whatever," said McClain. "But don't think he really bought into that. He was Mr. Japan as far as I'm concerned as far as the pitching goes. He had someone following him around twenty-four hours a day it seemed like watching his every move. If anyone could come over [to the Major Leagues] and deal with it—he's been dealing with it since he's 18 so I knew it wouldn't be a problem. I think it's a testament to how mentally tough he is and just how well he handles it. As big as he was over there, it just never got to his head. He knew he was a pitcher and that's what he does and that's all he wanted to do and he didn't really get caught up in anything else."

If there was a year to circle in Matsuzaka's Japanese professional career, 2004 would probably be the one. The same year the Boston Red Sox at last became champions of Major League Baseball—snapping an 86-year drought in the process—Matsuzaka would also be the king of his mountain for the first time since Koshien in 1998. Because of the 2004 Summer Olympics, in which Matsuzaka would star while leading Japan to the bronze medal, his overall numbers for Seibu (10-6, 2.90 ERA, 146 innings, 10 complete games, 5 shutouts) don't completely represent how well he pitched that year. Perhaps more telling is the fact that Matsuzaka was the MVP of the All-Star Game for the first time in his career. "He started winning early in the season," said Allen. "I think he won three straight 1-0 shutouts. He never had won big games in the pros. He had lost them. He had that in high school but he had never done that as a pro. He won a bunch of them in 2004. And, then, in the Japan Series."

But before the Japan Series, there was additional drama for Matsuzaka and the Lions. Just like the 2004 Red Sox, which entered the postseason as a second-place team, so, too, did the Seibu Lions. "At the end of that season, he won a game in Fukuoka [against the Soft Bank Hawks]. That was an important game because they had an obscure rule that gave the first place team a one-game advantage in the playoffs if you finished farther than five games out," said Allen. "The Lions were 5½ behind the Hawks and they had to beat them. Matsuzaka won at Fukuoka Dome. Down the stretch, he was just dynamite."

This isn't to say Matsuzaka's '04 postseason run didn't come without some bumps. For in Game 1 of the first stage of the playoffs—there were three stages in all—Matsuzaka struck out ten over seven-plus innings but also allowed seven runs. Still, he got the win over the Nippon Ham Fighters, as Seibu emerged victorious in a 10-7 slugfest. In the second stage, playing the Hawks again, Matsuzaka stepped his game up about two notches, allowing just a run over his two starts—and twelve innings—in the series. It was Matsuzaka who pitched the winner-take-all Game 5 on three days of rest, pitching 6^1/$_3$ innings and allowing a run in a no decision. Seibu went on to win in ten innings, and it was on to the Japan Series for the Lions. Unlike 2002, when it was debatable that Matsuzaka was even 100 percent, he was at full throttle two years later and ready to carry the Lions to championship glory much like he did for Yokohama at Koshien some six years earlier. As it turns out, perhaps Matsuzaka was too pumped up for his Game 2 start against the Chunichi Dragons. He was belted around for nine hits and eight runs over 6^1/$_3$ innings. Most uncharacteristic is that Matsuzaka blew a 6-3 lead in the bottom of the seventh.

But sweet redemption—the kind Matsuzaka would later taste while pitching October games for the Boston Red Sox—wasn't far off. Exactly one week after his poor performance in Game 2, Matsuzaka stared down the Dragons again in Game 6. This time, he was on the road. And this time, he staved off elimination for the Lions by striking out six and allowing two runs over eight innings and 134 pitches. But a strange thing happened in Game 7, which was played the very next day. Matsuzaka had to break out his Koshien recuperative powers again and throw an inning out of the bullpen. The move would have made sense if the game had been hanging in the balance. But Seibu held a 7-2 lead. Matsuzaka gave up a pair of baserunners before Alex Ochoa dented one that was thankfully caught at the warning track to end the inning. Matsuzaka did not come back out for the ninth. The Lions hung on and Matsuzaka was part of a championship team for the first time since Koshien. Built on the financial enormity of their owner, the Lions had been Japan Series champs eight

times between 1982 and 1992. But Matsuzaka had helped them
to their first trophy in twelve years. And that wasn't the end of
his season either.

Matsuzaka still had a few pitches left in him for 2004. The
Major League All-Stars were coming to his turf for the Japan
All-Star Series and Matsuzaka was antsy to face hitters from
the highest level of baseball in the world. He got his chance on
November 11, facing a lineup that consisted of Carl Crawford,
Jack Wilson, Hank Blalock, Moises Alou, Miguel Cabrera, Victor Martinez, Johnny Estrada, Brad Wilkerson and Alex Cora.
David Ortiz, Manny Ramirez, Vernon Wells and Michael Young
were among the MLB stars who were out of the lineup that day.
Perhaps MLB manager Bruce Bochy didn't want to screw up any
swings. Matsuzaka was marvelous, allowing 5 hits and a run en
route to a complete game, 5-1 victory. He struck out six and
didn't walk anybody.

Because the Japan All-Star Series hardly gets any media coverage in the United States—typically it's a wire service story and
maybe appears in an American newspaper or two—word of Matsuzaka still didn't leak out to Western baseball civilization. But
those MLB-ers who witnessed the performance first-hand still
remembered it three years later. "I remember saying to everybody, we all said it in the dugout, 'It's just a matter of time before
he'll be over here with us.' We all knew it," said Crawford, an
underrated star for the Tampa Bay Devil Rays who exchanged
autographed jerseys at the time with Matsuzaka. And Bochy also
knew it. "He went through us pretty easily," said Bochy, now
the manager of the San Francisco Giants. "You just saw not only
great stuff but how competitive he is. We had heard that he really
wanted to come over here and pitch and there was no question in
my mind that this guy could have a lot of success [in the Major
Leagues] with the stuff he has."

For Matsuzaka, pitching in such fashion against MLB had
to feel like a bit of a tease. Yes, his desire to pitch in the United
States still burned inside of him, but he was not yet a free agent.

In fact, if Seibu wanted to push the issue, they could have kept Matsuzaka under their control until after the 2008 season. As it turned out, Matsuzaka would pitch two more years for Seibu before finally being put up for auction to the Major Leagues. Though the Lions would slip to third place in 2005, Matsuzaka was no less stellar, despite a record (14-13) that might have made it seem otherwise. He unleashed 15 complete games and notched 226 strikeouts, both career highs. His 2.30 ERA was the best of his career up to that point.

Something else happened for Matsuzaka in 2005. He married Tomoyo Shibata, an attractive and well-known Japanese TV personality he had been dating for several years. Their relationship had become public in rather quick fashion, thanks to a September 2000 incident in which the 19-year-old Matsuzaka had driven to Shibata's home with a suspended driver's license (he had been hit with a hefty speeding ticket a couple of weeks earlier) and left the car parked illegally overnight. According to published accounts of the incident, Matsuzaka told police that a public relations official for the Lions had actually driven the car. But the cover was blown, thanks to a Japanese tabloid that had photos in hand to chronicle the sequence of events that night. It led to some embarrassment for Matsuzaka, who, according to Wikipedia.com, paid a fine of 195,000 yen, which equates to roughly $1,700. The incident was not symbolic of the way things would go for Matsuzaka before or after. He was never one to get in any kind of trouble away from the baseball field, and that's because it didn't seem he did all that much away from the baseball field. He loved to golf, sure. And he was good at it. But that seemed to be about as adventurous as Matsuzaka got. There were many times that he proudly called himself a "homebody," and was rarely spotted in public during his first year with the Red Sox. What Matsuzaka enjoyed most was spending time at home with his wife, and later their daughter, who would be born within the first year of the marriage. His only other passion, it seemed, was baseball. Matsuzaka absorbed the game, labored over it and obsessed over it.

He wanted to be the best, and he wanted to play against the best, which meant getting to the Major Leagues.

Finally, there was light at the end of the tunnel in that regard. By the time 2006 rolled around, Matsuzaka had just pitched Japan to the championship of the inaugural World Baseball Classic and the possibility seemed very real this would be his last season in his native land. Even if Matsuzaka did have one eye on his future, it didn't diminish his pitching in the least. If anything, Matsuzaka seemed to be making a season-long statement to any Major League teams that might be considering making a run at him. He established career bests in wins (17) and ERA (2.13) while striking out 200 batters over 186 1/3 innings. He had just 34 walks. Matsuzaka was at his pitching peak. He did have a rare bad outing in his final regular season start for the Lions, getting shelled by the Chiba Lotte Marines for seven hits and six runs over five innings in a game that could have landed Seibu the Pacific Division crown. Instead, Seibu again went into the playoffs as a second-place team. Pitching Game 1 against the Soft Bank Hawks, Matsuzaka couldn't have known this would be his last start in a Seibu uniform. He hoped to have another Japan Series title in his back pocket. He was unable to reach that goal. But still, he couldn't have gone out with a better game. Matsuzaka fired a complete-game, 1-0 shutout at the Hawks, striking out thirteen and walking nobody in an epic duel against tough-luck loser Kazumi Saito. The 137-pitch gem was completed when Matsuzaka elicited a weak wave for strike three at his 94-mph fastball. Seibu went on to lose the next two games of the best-of-three series, so that was the end chapter of Matsuzaka's marvelous pro run in Japan. It ended with a record of 108-60 and a 2.95 ERA. But it seemed like Matsuzaka's true career—the one he had dreamed of for so long—was finally going to get started. And just like at the end of his Yokohama years, Matsuzaka again had to wonder where he would wind up pitching next. This time, there would be no lottery system. This time, there would be a high-stakes, blind auction in which only the boldest team would prevail.

3

World Baseball Classic MVP
(March 2006)

To GLOBALIZE THE GAME, as was a strong wish of Major League Baseball commissioner Bud Selig, you create the chance to put individuals on the map who otherwise might not have gotten there so soon. This idea of a World Baseball Classic was all about expanding the miles and the drawing power of baseball. And it came to fruition in March 2006, this tournament featuring sixteen countries with professional players eligible to compete. Selig had long been an advocate of further internationalizing his game and the WBC would be the perfect way to do it. There were four pools of entries in the tournament. The first consisted of China, Chinese Taipei, Japan, and Korea. The second pool was Canada, Mexico, South Africa, and the United States. A third was made up of Cuba, the Netherlands, Panama, and Puerto Rico. And the final quartet was Australia, the Dominican Republic, Italy, and Venezuela.

Such a setting seemed ripe to create an international star. Though it wasn't exactly planned out this way, in hindsight you could say this was Daisuke Matsuzaka's best opportunity yet to work his way into the conscience of baseball America after being a legend in his own country for so long already. One team that wasn't all that keen on such a showcase event for Matsuzaka? Try the Boston Red Sox. Yes, the Red Sox had been focused on

Matsuzaka for years and their interest was intensifying by the week. They had visions of him being an anchor for their 2007 rotation and the last thing they needed was for another big-market team like the Yankees or Mets to have their appetite whetted by Matsuzaka becoming an international hero. But what were the odds of that happening anyway? There were a lot of talented countries and players in this tourney, so there was every chance that Matsuzaka would remain under the radar, which is where the Red Sox loved him to be, at least until he finally became theirs.

Team Japan not only had the most revered Japanese baseball player of all managing them in home run king Sadaharu Oh—he of the 868 lifetime homers in pro ball—but it also had the magnificent Ichiro Suzuki on board as leadoff man extraordinaire. The presence of both of those men took the initial spotlight away from Matsuzaka, though that would change by the time the event was over. Most baseball fans loved the idea of such a tournament, particularly when you consider how long and drawn-out Spring Training can be. But to those in the game, the timing was tough. Juices couldn't help but flow when the top players in the world were representing different countries. But players weren't conditioned to be in peak form from March 3 to March 20, which was the schedule of the tourney. This was when they were supposed to be getting ready for the marathon of a season. So when Team Japan first began working out, Matsuzaka didn't look ready to put together one of those command performances he had so often produced on big stages. In fact it was Koji Uehara who started Game 1 of the first round for Japan at Tokyo Dome and not Matsuzaka. But Matsuzaka would get his turn in Game 2 and despite not having anything close to his best stuff, he went four serviceable innings (three hits, one run, three strikeouts) en route to a 14-3 win over Chinese Taipei that vaulted Japan into the second round of play, at which time the venue would switch to Anaheim, California. Looking a tad out of sorts, Matsuzaka even issued a balk. Under rules of the tournament, he was only permitted to throw 65 pitches in Round One. Matsuzaka ended up throwing 68, because he was in the middle of an at-bat when he reached his limit. Pitching with a baseball that was slicker than the one used in Japan, Matsuzaka had trouble with some of the grips, particularly his slider. And quite frankly, this wasn't his time of year, as much as he tried to make it his time of year. "Looking at Mr. Matsuzaka's pitching lately, looking at the exhibition games and everything, I knew that he was not at his very best," conceded Oh after the game.

But that was all about to change. America—Southern California actually—was going to be the venue for Matsuzaka's big coming out party. After Japan lost a heartbreaking 4-3 game to a United States team loaded with Major League stars, Matsuzaka's start against Mexico was crucial. A loss likely would have spelled the end for Japan's dream of advancing to San Diego for the semifinals and finals. So Matsuzaka, as he so often seemed to do when pressure was staring him in the face, was brilliant. Standing on the mound at Angels Stadium—which stands right down the street from Disneyland—Matsuzaka put together somewhat of a magical performance. This time confined to a pitch count of 85, Matsuzaka held Mexico to one hit over five innings, walking two and striking out two in a 6-1 victory. Keep in mind that this was the same Mexico team that would later knock the United States right out of the tournament. Team Mexico had a collection of current and former Major League hitters, including Adrian Gonzalez, Jorge Cantu, Vinny Castilla, Erubiel Durazo, Miguel Ojeda, and Geronimo Gil. Matsuzaka carved up all comers. Some sixteen months later, Cantu—representing the Tampa Bay Devil Rays at the time—stood in the visitors' clubhouse at Fenway Park and remembered vividly what Matsuzaka had done to his team. "He was fearless. He was tough. He was pounding that zone," Cantu said. "He was pounding that inside corner. Cutters, sinkers, all kinds of two seamers, four seamers. He was hiding his pitches so well and we couldn't figure him out."

Jim Allen, who had been dispatched from Japan to cover the event back in his original home of California, noticed a more mature Matsuzaka than the guy he had come across off and on through the years with Seibu. "He's so confident, so utterly confident in what he's doing," Allen said. "He tries so hard, he's become so professional over the years." It was a command performance Matsuzaka put together against Mexico, one that led a reporter after the game to ask Matsuzaka about his feelings on someday pitching in the Major Leagues. "About moving on to Major Leagues, of course that is the target that I've had, and that's the best stage for any ball player to be at," Matsuzaka said. "But I have no intention of appealing or promoting myself this time throughout the games. And what we would love all of you to see is how great Japan is." The baseball world was also getting a chance to see how great Matsuzaka could be, much to the chagrin of baseball executives like Theo Epstein and Craig Shipley. "The Classic probably didn't help us because he got to come over here, on our turf, and it was easier for people to see him, and some teams that were maybe not as interested got to see how good he is," Shipley said nine months later, on the day the Red Sox were actually successful in signing Matsuzaka. "I think that probably added a few more teams to the mix."

A day after Matsuzaka beat Mexico, Japan took a 2-1 loss to Korea to finish at 1-2 in second round action. Amazingly that record was good enough to get Japan to the final round in San Diego. You see, three of the four teams in the pool finished 1-2, so one of them had to advance. Japan did so because it won the three-way tiebreaker by allowing fewer runs per inning than the U.S. allowed in head-to-head competition involving the three teams only. A weird system for sure, but it was enough to get Matsuzaka and his teammates to the ultimate stage, and a rematch with Korea. This time around, Japan rode not Matsuzaka's, but Uehara's gifted arm to a 6-0 win. That put Japan right into the Finals, where Matsuzaka was going to get the nod in the winner-take-all match with Cuba. It was somewhat ironic that these were the two teams that would square off in the championship game. After all, the U.S., the Dominican Republic, Venezuela, and Puerto

Rico all had a much higher volume of Major League impact players. But the timing of the tournament seemed to throw everyone off. And Cuba was accustomed to international competition. It was their major outlet to showcase talent, because Cubans could only play in the Major Leagues if they defected.

Japan, meanwhile, was trying to enforce the notion that their talent was largely untapped and should be more prevalent in Major League circles. Red Sox chairman Tom Werner, who has a home in Southern California and was at PETCO Park for the championship round, wasn't thinking about those subplots. He was just thinking about Matsuzaka perhaps not pitching a gem at this particular time and possibly putting a dent in Boston's chances of acquiring him once he officially was put up for grabs. "I think the interesting story there is that our organization was sort of hoping that Dice-K would not pitch well," Werner said. "We were going to be aggressive either way but we were hoping he wouldn't have a great experience there and of course he did. I don't know if he opened up other team's eyes, but we were tracking him all along." The only tracking necessary the night of March 20, 2006 was either a seat at PETCO or a look at the nationally televised broadcast.

Then again, the man with the best view of all—and the man who probably knew that Matsuzaka was going to fire a trophy-clinching performance before anyone—was Kazuhiro Takeda, the pitching coach for Team Japan. "In the morning, he was all focused," Takeda remembered as he stood in front of a camera truck at Yankee Stadium in late August 2007. "He didn't talk to anyone. He was just focused on pitching that night." Takeda himself had been a pro pitcher in Japan, but he knew he was watching something special as he eyed Matsuzaka's pre-game warm-up in the bullpen. "When I saw the bullpen session before the championship game, I've never seen a pitcher throw like that before," said Takeda. The stiff neck that Matsuzaka had complained of earlier in the day loosened as his electric warm-up continued.

With a giant globe hoisted on the pitcher's mound during the pre-game ceremony, Matsuzaka was about to go global himself once he got up on that mound. His fastball had some extra kick to it as the adrenaline of trying to win for his country kicked in. "He was throwing his pitches harder than ever in the first four innings," Oh said after the game. "That was something I haven't really seen in the past." Matsuzaka had always enjoyed pitching for his country. In Athens during the 2004 Olympics, Matsuzaka downed Cuba with 8 1/3 brilliant innings in pool play then lost a 1-0 duel to Australia in the semis. He had also pitched in the 2000 Summer Games in Sydney, going 0-1 with a 2.33 ERA. But there was something different about all of this. This was an event run by Major League Baseball and fans were paying close attention. Despite the pitch count limit being raised all the way to 95 for the Final, Matsuzaka was left out there for just 62 pitches over four innings. Japan gave Matsuzaka a four-run cushion before he threw his first pitch in the bottom of the first, and he gave one of the runs back in the bottom of the inning. But after that he was untouched. He scattered four hits and walked none while striking out five. Why such a quick hook? For one, Matsuzaka wasn't fully stretched out by this point in March. And another was that he had pretty much emptied his tank by throwing so hard while he was out there. By the time the night had ended, Team Japan was parading around the field with the national flag. This, after a 10-6 victory that made them champs in the first World Baseball Classic.

Matsuzaka? He was the MVP of the international showcase event, going 3-0 with a 1.38 ERA. The trademark glare he had in his eyes during showdowns with the Cuban batters was replaced by a joyful smile after the game. There was a humorous moment too, as Matsuzaka held up his MVP trophy, only to notice it was already starting to chip. Mike Plugh, who would soon start a "Matsuzaka Watch" blog on the Internet and had been living in Japan at the time, laughed as he watched Matsuzaka take in the moment during the bonus coverage offered to viewers in Japan.

"Matsuzaka was like, 'Yep, it's American style', or something like that, and that was kind of his little joke for the Japanese," said Plugh. "I think everybody kind of knew at that point that the chances of him coming to the States were getting better."

Better than ever, it seemed. Whichever Major League teams would make a run at Matsuzaka would no longer need to sell his worth to fans. And the ones that might not have known much about Matsuzaka had some tangible evidence. World Baseball Classic MVP was now in cement. And Matsuzaka's Team Japan jersey was headed to the Hall of Fame, along with other showcase items from the championship team. Plugh, meanwhile, was a die-hard Yankees fan who already had a blog dedicated to his favorite team. He was also extremely knowledgeable about Japanese pro baseball and salivated over the prospect of Matsuzaka in pinstripes. So that was why he started Matsuzaka Watch, which has every possible nugget of information—statistics especially —you could ever need in educating yourself about this international sensation. Plugh, who also freelances for a detailed baseball statistics analysis Web site called Baseball Prospectus, cringed when he heard pundits spout off about how Matsuzaka might be the next Hideki Irabu.

"There were still people that said Irabu. Any time they heard a Japanese name come up, it was always Irabu, Irabu, oh, this guy is going to come and he's going to be the next Irabu," said Plugh. "I saw Irabu. I knew what kind of pitcher he was. He was a converted reliever that could throw hard and strike guys out but he had very poor control and very poor concentration on the mound and his conditioning and the whole thing. So I was like, I have to show these people in some qualitative way that Matsuzaka's going to come over and he's going to translate. So I started to kind of dive into that." And it wasn't just Plugh. Suddenly, baseball "experts" were starting to talk about Daisuke Matsuzaka as a man who could have a significant impact on the Major League Baseball landscape for 2007. The Seibu Lions weren't in their best financial shape, so there was a fair chance they'd be open to posting Matsuzaka, who had already told them of his wishes to leave. And available starting pitching was thinning out across baseball as, more and more, teams would retain the quality pitchers they had. The time seemed just right for Matsuzaka and it was just a matter of which team was willing to put the most on the line for this untapped international resource of pitching prowess. All the Red Sox knew—from the international scouting department all the way to the highest reaches of the executive offices—was that they wanted Matsuzaka very badly. What they couldn't be certain of was how much competition there would be. They'd have to wait eight more months to find out.

4

Monster Post
(August 20 to November 14, 2006)

LOOKING BACK, PERHAPS RED SOX general manager Theo Epstein was subconsciously orchestrating a game of setup on the late afternoon of August 20, 2006, when he stood in foul territory along the first base line of Fenway Park and fielded a barrage of questions from the blood-thirsty media of both Boston and New York. The Red Sox, as they entered play that night, had already lost the first three games of a critical five-game series with their constant nemesis, the Yankees. They'd go on to get swept in five straight, putting to an end, for all practical purposes, their 2006 season. Not only were the Sox about to fall from 1½ games back to 6½ back in one nightmarish weekend on their home lawn, but they were in the process of getting decimated by so many injuries that it would leave them almost beyond recognition. For the first time since John W. Henry, Tom Werner and Larry Lucchino took over ownership of the team in 2002, the Red Sox were about to have a meaningless September in which virtually all of New England would turn its attention to the Patriots. It was a depressing feeling for a franchise that had generally had such an uplifting vibe to it during Henry's time as principal owner.

A stand-up Epstein had no problem answering the questions. If there was one constant to his dealings with the media, it was that he frequently made himself available when things were at their worst. At this point of 2006, Epstein was ripe for the picking and he knew it. Despite the fact that the Red Sox held a half-game lead in the American League East on the day of the July 31 trade deadline, Epstein chose to stand pat. Part of the reason he did so was that he could see how flawed his team was and he didn't think it was prudent to trade blue chip prospects for return value that might give the club an incremental improvement, but by no means a guarantee to play deep into October. In Epstein's view, when a team is to have sustained success for a decade-plus—which has always been his goal with the Red Sox—there are isolated years in which you have to take a step back. Reading between the lines— not to mention a book called *Feeding the Monster* by author Seth Mnookin which provided a behind-the-scenes look at the inner workings of the organization—it was obvious that Epstein felt 2006 was that year. The team was imperfect, thanks to a pitching staff that lacked depth both in the rotation and in the bullpen. This wasn't the year to deal a top prospect. It wasn't going to make enough of a difference. That strategy would be greatly jus-tified a year later when Epstein watched several of his prospects make big contributions in Boston.

But back to 2006. The Yankees had gone out and gotten a big bat to bolster their postseason run in right fielder Bobby Abreu. The Red Sox were in the running for the patient left-handed hitter, but Epstein pulled back and decided Abreu wasn't worth either the prospects or the financial undertaking. Making Epstein a big target under the late afternoon sunlight at Fenway on August 20 was the fact that Abreu and Johnny Damon—the enormously popular center fielder that the Sox let flee to New York the previous December—had absolutely crushed Boston during the course of that division-altering weekend. So as he spoke to the media, Epstein pointed out that there was no use trying to keep up with the Yankees in the game known through-out baseball as bidding wars.

"We are not the Yankees. We admire the Yankees. I admire the Yankees," Epstein said. "Our approach is a little bit different.

Given our resources relative to the Yankees, we feel our best way to compete with them year in and year out is to keep one eye on now and one eye on the future and to build something that can sustain success. We're not going to change our approach and try to all of a sudden build an uber-team or try to all of a sudden win now at the expense of the future. That's not an excuse."

Epstein continued to elaborate, saying that the Yankees were superior from a financial standpoint and the Red Sox would have to upend them in other ways. "Our goals are now and our goals are to put ourselves in a position to win every year. That's the reality. It's going to occasionally leave us short. It's going to leave us short every time there's a player who's available in a bidding war, taking on a contract, getting the best free agent. We're never going to sell ourselves out just to get that one guy because we have to take a long-term view. Given our resources relative to the Yankees, it's the only way to do it. I think we're good at it. And I think it's going to prove successful in the long run."

So when you fast forwarded the clock a couple of months later, Epstein's words still rang in the ears of media members and fans when it came time to size up what would be, in the truest sense of the word, a bidding war for the international icon named Daisuke Matsuzaka. It was a hot stove season in which available starting pitching was going to be weak. Overrated left-hander Barry Zito was going to be the big prize among the pool of Major League free agent talent and the Red Sox were less than lukewarm with their interest in Zito. Could it be that Matsuzaka—despite having never thrown a pitch in the Majors but seven months removed from his Most Valuable Player performance in the World Baseball Classic—was the most attractive pitcher available on the open market? Epstein certainly felt so. He wasn't alone. But didn't he say the Red Sox weren't going to get in all-out bidding wars? You have to take a man at his word, right? Sure, the pundits all named the Red Sox as a team that would make a play for Matsuzaka. But nobody could have ever guessed the financial commitment they were going to put forth to make it happen.

Well, part of the reason the organizational stance changed is that the poor finish to the season had left such a sour taste in the mouths of the highly competitive ownership group that Henry decided it was time to make a bigger financial commitment and do anything possible to close the gap with the Yankees. Still, the early logic was that Matsuzaka would become yet another feather in the cap of the financial powerhouse that is the Yankees. The Matsuzaka sweepstakes hadn't officially gotten underway yet, but the buzz was starting to surface in October when the pitcher announced he would not be pitching in the Japan All-Star Series in which Major League All-Stars, led by Phillies slugger Ryan Howard, would play a five-game tour in Japan. Matsuzaka had been advised not to participate and it was clear why. His agent Scott Boras did not want him to risk injury when he would be trying to get a multi-million-dollar contract to play Major League Baseball in a matter of weeks. Still, Matsuzaka was a big topic of conversation during the tour of Japan, as everyone speculated on where he would wind up. Mets third baseman David Wright playfully lobbied for Matsuzaka during an office visit with then-Japanese prime minister Shinzo Abe. "The Mets need help with starting pitching. Any chance you could make a call to [Daisuke] Matsuzaka?" Wright said to Abe.

As everyone knew, however, this one was going to come down to baseball politics. What first had to happen was for the Seibu Lions—Matsuzaka's pro team in Japan for eight years—to post him. The pitcher had told the Seibu Lions back in 2005 that he wanted to go to the Major Leagues. Those who knew Matsuzaka the best were aware that he actually had been experiencing a craving to pitch in MLB many years before that. Nevertheless, the sides agreed to revisit it again after 2006, at which time the club would let their drawing card go pursue his dreams. If Matsuzaka had simply pitched two more years in Japan, he would have been a free agent following the 2008 season. But then Seibu wouldn't have gotten any compensation from the Major League team that signed him. This way, both sides could win. The Lions could get many millions that they needed and Matsuzaka could go to the Major Leagues at the age of 26, while he was still very much in his prime.

The posting process—in which MLB teams have a short window to submit a blind bid to a Japanese player's current team—was how the Mariners landed the great Ichiro Suzuki in 2001. Ichiro was the first star everyday player to make the jump from Japan to the Majors, and the Mariners won exclusive bidding rights with a post of roughly $13 million. Hideki Matsui had been a full-fledged free agent when he went to the Yankees for three years at $21 million prior to the 2003 season. So the Ichiro bid was the most relevant point of comparison in a system that was largely untapped. Pundits had speculated widely that the Matsuzaka bid could go to the range of $20–$30 million.

On November 1, Matsuzaka held a press conference in the ballroom of the posh Takanawa Prince Hotel in Tokyo to inform the media that the Lions were on the verge of posting him, though it hadn't officially occurred as of yet. Peter Miller, the son of former Players Association legend Marvin Miller, had been living in Japan for years and felt Matsuzaka's media gathering was "the announcement before the announcement." Miller, who was doing some consulting work for MLB during the All-Star tour of Japan, explained that Matsuzaka needed to brace his fans for his pending exit and this was his way of doing that. Matsuzaka had been a pitcher Japanese fans had treasured ever since his magical performance at Koshien as a high schooler in 1998.

Their love for Matsuzaka aside, the process was getting easier for the Japanese to take after seeing Hideo Nomo, Ichiro and Matsui all go on to the Major Leagues to have great success. There were just four American media members present at Matsuzaka's packed conference, including yours truly, Eric Neel of *ESPN the Magazine*, Adam Rubin of the *New York Daily News* and David Lennon of *New York Newsday*. Miller, through some Japanese officials, tried to get the American writers a private session with Matsuzaka in which a translator would be used, but the pitcher declined. Miller did his best to translate what was said to the plethora of Japanese writers and cameras for the benefit of the English speakers in the crowd. "I'm not nervous about anything," Matsuzaka said. "I think I have to raise my level a bit but I think I have it within me to succeed. So I'm full of confidence. Even last year, I thought about being eligible for posting. But this year seems to be the time."

It was indeed the time. The Lions were once stacked financially under the leadership of Yoshiaki Tsutsumi, who was for a time one of the wealthiest men in the world, thanks to his genius in real estate. But by 2005, Tsutsumi had been arrested in a financial scandal and the wealth of the Lions was in the process of taking a severe drop. They were now at a point where they could use a sizable posting fee from a big market Major League team. So they posted Matsuzaka, their prized pitcher for so long, on Thursday, November 2. Any Major League team was now free to submit its best bid for Matsuzaka by November 8 at 5 p.m. EST.

The Red Sox stayed publicly mum on the matter but were furiously scurrying to finalize their bid. "We were all pretty enthusiastic about it," Lucchino said. "John Henry in particular thought that it was the type of thing that we should be bold about." Perhaps the biggest impetus behind the big push was Craig Shipley, Boston's vice president of international scouting, who had quietly fallen in love with Matsuzaka's arm and mound presence while scouting and analyzing every aspect of him in Japan for several years. Shipley constantly lobbied Epstein to make the strongest bid possible for Matsuzaka. But Shipley made his infatuation known to nobody but his bosses in Boston. Shipley, an Australian who played in the Majors from 1986 to 1998, was not one of those scouts who would roam the field during batting practice and talk up the players he was interested in. If anything, he was likely to throw a smoke screen or two. Jim Allen, a baseball writer for the *Daily Yomiuri*, had plenty of conversations with both Shipley and Jon Deeble, Boston's other Far East scouting guru during their scouting trips through Japan.

"They were like, 'Oh no, nobody pitches that many innings,'"
Allen said. "They said they were more interested in [Hiroki]
Kuroda with the Carp. Nobody knew if Kuroda was going to be
a free agent because Kuroda never said anything basically." For-
get about Kuroda, who wound up re-upping with the Carp for
another season before making himself available to Major League
teams in 2008. The Red Sox were completely fixated on Matsuzaka. The first time Epstein was asked about the pitcher in a
public setting was in October at an informal roundtable session
with the media at Fenway Park, and the GM didn't blink. "It's
our policy not to comment on players under contract with other
organizations, and he qualifies, even though it's not a Major
League organization," Epstein said. "We've scouted Japan and
the Japanese leagues, we're pretty active scouting internationally.
We won't have any comment on any individual player."

Consider how that stance differed from Epstein's glowing words back in December 2002 on Jose Contreras when the
Cuban defector was set to become available to the highest MLB
bidder. The Yankees wound up signing Contreras, seemingly as
much to irk the Red Sox as to add the talented pitcher to their
team, where he would struggle mightily before being traded to
the White Sox halfway through the 2004 season. Though Boston kept their interest level in Matsuzaka a complete mystery,
they didn't do a good job staying secretive about how much they
liked Contreras. When the Yankees did bring Contreras home
on Christmas Eve 2002, Lucchino famously referred to Boston's
rivals as the "Evil Empire," which sent George Steinbrenner—
perhaps not a *Star Wars* fan—into a tizzy.

What was clear was that Epstein's strategy changed after
Contreras. In the ensuing years, he was silent on what players
he had interest in. He felt stung by his openness on the potential
prowess of Contreras. From then on, Epstein's typical stance was
to issue a "no comment" on any prospective signee, be it domes-
tic or international. Despite what they were saying—or better
yet weren't saying—in public, the Red Sox desperately wanted

Matsuzaka. They looked at it as a unique opportunity to land an elite pitcher at a time when there were hardly any available. The sour taste of 2006 had left the franchise hungry again, from ownership on down to baseball operations. "I think adversity among this group leads to resolve," said Henry. "We were very focused in September as to what we wanted to accomplish."

It's just that the info was kept remarkably in-house. "There's an old saying from the neighborhood I grew up in Pittsburgh that three people can keep a secret as long as two of them are dead," Lucchino said. "In this case, we had four or five people, six people if you count Shipley and Theo and John [Henry], Tom [Werner], me, and another scout or two along the way. So you're talking about six or seven people who knew of the keen interest. It was an affirmative strategy. Theo was advocating that we just hide in the tall grass, hide in the tall grass as long as possible."

In that tall grass, a shockingly bold battle plan was scripted. The bid that Henry and Epstein—with significant input from Shipley—formulated was designed with a clear goal in mind: Outbid everyone, even the deep-pocketed Yankees. The way they looked at it, this was as close to a sure-fire way of landing Matsuzaka as there was. If they could win the bid, they would be the only team able to negotiate with him. The Red Sox were going to exploit the system, fully exposing its vulnerabilities.

"We thought the Yankees might bid $50 million and we were determined to top that," Henry said. "The rationale was that the post was providing a free option. Free options don't occur very often and he was a number one pitcher in our view." So Henry came up with an interesting bidding number: $51,111,111.11. The 11 was lucky superstition for Henry. When he initially threw his hat in the ring to buy the Red Sox in 2001, Henry made himself known to potential investors and bankers only as "Investor 11." Henry also would later note the good karma of the fact that he and Matsuzaka shared the same birthday—September 13. But the all-out process to land Matsuzaka had little to do with superstition, good luck or shared birthdays. It was about making a dramatic push to land a world-class pitcher.

How much convincing did Henry need from Epstein and Shipley that this was a wise baseball move? "A lot," said Henry. "You have questions about any pitcher that has not pitched in the majors. But we had a lot of faith in Craig Shipley, Theo and baseball ops."

Similarly, did Henry have to persuade the minority owners of the club that investing $51.1 million to speak with one man was a wise business move? "Technically we don't have to go to the partners on payroll, but Tom [Werner] and I have fiduciary roles and we discuss everything in detail with our partners. The NASCAR decision was much more controversial than Matsuzaka." Yes, the Red Sox had also become players in auto racing, when Henry bought 50 percent of Roush Racing and turned it into Roush Fenway racing on February 14, 2007. But the race for Matsuzaka would soon involve just one horse after the Red Sox submitted their record-setting posting bid.

The Red Sox, nervously excited about the process, waited until just minutes before that 5 p.m. deadline on November 8 to submit their sealed bid. Epstein, with the aid of Henry's personal assistant Sylvia Moon, faxed the bid to the Major League Baseball offices in New York. The Red Sox were determined to keep their enormous bid a secret until the last possible moment. Lucchino and Henry, who were conducting some other business at MLB headquarters on 245 Park Avenue in New York earlier that day, walked upstairs to confirm the bid was received, and also, to see if they could pick up any inside information. No luck there, as the process was kept tightly under wraps by MLB's international department.

During their visit, Henry and Lucchino saw a couple of other equally diligent baseball executives—general manager Omar Minaya and international guru Tony Bernazard of the New York Mets. "They were the only other club that was there," said Lucchino. "Everyone else was doing it by phone or proxy or something.

There was just so much gaming going on." It opened Minaya's eyes at that moment that the Red Sox were as thoroughly interested in seeing the process through as he was. "I think both of us wanted to be there," Minaya said. "We wanted to make sure the process . . . I just wanted to hand-deliver it. We could have done it by e-mail, but we just felt we wanted to hand-deliver the envelope. When we saw them there, we definitely knew they were strong bidders and contenders. It was kind of different, you know what I'm saying?"

At that hour, Boston's major move had still been kept under wraps from even the ravenous media that covers Red Sox Nation. "We were particularly proud of that, because that's not always the case, particularly in Boston where there is such penetration in the media," said Lucchino. In fact, word of the bidding was quiet on all fronts, with the only real news coming from Seattle, where the Mariners, who already had a Japanese superstar in Ichiro not to mention a sizable Japanese population, surprisingly announced that they would not be making a bid. With the presence of Boras looming, some teams knew the process wouldn't be for them.

As mammoth as their bid was, the Red Sox were by no means optimistic that it was going to blow everyone out of the water. If Theo and the Trio—as Epstein, Henry, Lucchino and Werner had sometimes been dubbed in the media—had learned anything during their years in command of the ballclub, it was that you could never rule out the Yankees. It seemed that Steinbrenner would go to any measure to flex his financial power, even if it was out of pure spite.

It was not surprising that Lucchino had confided in long-time friend Dan Okimoto, whom he had gone to Princeton with more than forty years earlier, that the Red Sox had entered the sweepstakes for Matsuzaka. Lucchino had always gone to Okimoto for advice any time he was dealing with a matter of Japanese relations. Okimoto had Japanese parents and in his more than three decades as a professor at Stanford, he had often gone to Japan on business. His understanding of the culture was thorough.

Lucchino had informed Okimoto that the Red Sox were going to get in on the Matsuzaka auction and asked him if he'd come on as a consultant if the club was able to outbid everyone else in the bidding process. Okimoto dutifully agreed to help his friend. But Lucchino told Okimoto several times he wasn't optimistic the Red Sox would win it.

Already knowing the monster bid the Red Sox had submitted, Lucchino asked Okimoto how much he would have posted. "I said, 'I don't know, the Mariners bid $13 million for Ichiro, so maybe $18 to 20 million,'" said Okimoto. Lucchino chuckled and basically told Okimoto the Red Sox had made a far more substantial offer than that. Not that he was sure it would do any good. "Larry was convinced the Yankees were locked in on him and would outbid the Red Sox for Matsuzaka," said Okimoto.

This time, however, in this particular negotiation, the Yankees would be badly outspent. Not that anyone knew this just yet. The Seibu Lions had until Tuesday, November 14 to officially announce who the winning bid was from and whether they would accept it. But a buzz began to circulate on November 10 that it was the Red Sox who had made the best offer. ESPN's baseball insider Buster Olney feverishly reported, citing sources, that Boston's winning bid was in the $38–$45 million range. Other media outlets followed the news from there, and had sources saying similar things. That number in itself was a shocker. When the true bid of $51.1 million (give or take a few ones after the decimal point) was leaked, jaws dropped throughout baseball. For a player who had been dubbed the Monster by his followers back in Japan, the Red Sox, who had been flanked by the Green Monster at Fenway Park for nearly a century, put forth a monstrous bid. Consider that it was nearly four times the amount of what the Mariners submitted to the Orix Blue Wave to land Ichiro some six years earlier.

"We didn't know we were going to stun the world," Lucchino would say months later. "We just knew we wanted to win the auction." With the general manager's meetings taking place in Naples, Florida, that was the natural venue for MLB to announce the Red Sox as winners of the Matsuzaka bidding sweepstakes. The announcement was jointly televised in the United States and Japan, with Epstein reading a prepared statement and answering questions for roughly five minutes. Knowing the type of respect that was bestowed on baseball players over in Japan, Epstein referred to Matsuzaka as "Mr. Matsuzaka" several times during the press briefing. The GM stayed tight-lipped through the press conference, informing the assembled media that there wasn't a whole lot he could say until a deal with Matsuzaka was officially reached. Epstein knew better than to get giddy over a successful step one of a multi-faceted process. But the one thing he was thrilled about was that there were no leaks along the way that forced another team to come up with a bigger offer. "For several years now, he's been a real target," Epstein said. "We've been trying to keep a low profile. I don't think we were mentioned very prominently among the most likely suitors for Matsuzaka. That was by design." Stealth, indeed.

By winning the posting war, the Red Sox earned themselves an exclusive negotiating window of thirty days with Matsuzaka and his shark of a lead representative—Boras. The Red Sox needed to get the deal done by midnight at the end of December 14. Otherwise, Matsuzaka would be returned to the Lions for another season and the Red Sox would get their $51.1 million back. One thing Epstein mentioned was that the Red Sox would be inviting Matsuzaka and Boras to Boston during the negotiating period. Little did Epstein know it at the time, but Boras would basically steer Matsuzaka away from Boston during the negotiating window. Perhaps if Matsuzaka got too close to the adoring public of the electric city of Boston, it might soften his negotiating stance. Boras would not let that happen.

But the posturing and the "gaming" (as Lucchino might call it) that would be in store over the next thirty days, were not front and center during that night the Red Sox had won bidding rights. It was a joyous night in Red Sox Nation, as the sting of 2006 finally vanished amid the excitement of Boston's bold push to land Matsuzaka. NESN, the lucrative cable television network that is owned by the Red Sox, preempted regularly scheduled programming to do a live special on the club winning rights for Matsuzaka. Talk radio station WEEI-850 AM broke away from talk of the juggernaut football team, the New England Patriots, and dissected Dice-K. The Red Sox didn't allow euphoria to seep in. They knew that their latest matchup with Boras would be a grind-it-out special.

As for the other players in the posting race, the Mets finished a distant second, with a bid that was, as Minaya would confirm months later, nearly $40 million. "I had seen him for a long time, I saw him when he was about 19 years old," Minaya said. "He was always a pitcher that was a very good competitor, had a lot of pitches, great location, great pitchability. We thought he was definitely one of those front of the rotation guys. We liked him."

Minaya, who had been one of the foremost executives in finding top prospects from Latin America, was hoping to find a game-ready ace from Japan this time around. "We identified him as the No. 1 free agent in the market this year as far as pitchers," Minaya said. "We made what we thought was a very good bid, it was $39 million-plus. Of course, we were second to the Red Sox. We never thought of the number $50 million for him. But we should give credit to the Red Sox. They probably wanted him more than us."

The Yankees, for once, were badly outbid, putting together a blind post of somewhere around $30 million. "You put your best foot forward and you make your evaluations," Cashman said later that night to reporters at the GM meetings. "He's a tremendous pitcher and I congratulate the Red Sox." Ever-aggressive Rangers owners Tom Hicks also threw his team into the ring with a bid in the range of $25 million. Other teams who were said to have made bids were the Angels, Cubs, Diamondbacks, and perhaps the Dodgers.

Though it will take years to know whether Boston's lavish bid for Matsuzaka was a good business move, the Mets and Yankees—the silver and bronze medal finishers in the race—both were hurt in the short-term otherwise known as the 2007 season. There was no other place in the market to get a pitcher who could pitch 200 innings and strike out 200 batters. Zito—another Boras client—wound up going to the Giants for the enormous cost of $126 million over seven years. The Mets had a late-season collapse and missed the postseason. In a year in which Tom Glavine began to show his age and Pedro Martinez missed much of the season because of injury, Matsuzaka undoubtedly could have made a significant difference for the Mets, particularly in the National League, a less imposing place for pitchers.

After losing Matsuzaka to the Red Sox, the Yankees would later react with two questionable business moves. They essentially used the posting money they set aside for Matsuzaka and put it out there in a $26 million bid for another Japanese lefty named Kei Igawa. After winning the rights to Igawa, the Yankees handed him $20 million over five years. Mind you, Igawa wasn't even close to Matsuzaka's level as a pitcher during their years in Nippon Professional Baseball. And Igawa, to be kind, was a complete flop during 2007 for New York. Pitching in just 14 games—12 of them starts—Igawa was 2-3 with a 6.25 ERA.

Then, there was the matter of Roger Clemens. Sure, the Rocket was a legend and he had already helped the Yankees win a pair of World Series titles in his first go-around with the team. But by 2007 Clemens was an arm for hire, challenging teams each year to woo him out of retirement by paying him a ridiculous amount of money. By May of 2007, the Yankees were reeling because they didn't have enough pitching. While they wouldn't reach back into owner George Steinbrenner's deep pockets to bring home Matsuzaka, they had no trouble outbidding themselves for Clemens. They gave the 44-year-old pitcher a pro-rated salary of $28 million for the final four months of the season. If Clemens had even come close to duplicating what he did for the Astros from 2004–06, it wouldn't have been that bad a move. But the Rocket—whose reputation took a huge hit when he was named as an alleged steroid user after the 2007 season—was a shell of himself in his return to the Yankees. Clemens went 6-6 with a 4.18 ERA in 17 starts and was bothered by various injuries.

Matsuzaka undoubtedly would have served the Yankees better than Igawa or Clemens in 2007 and beyond. If the Yankees had gone the extra mile for Matsuzaka, could they have been champs in 2007 instead of bowing out in the Division Series for the third year in a row? One will never know, but it is certainly food for thought.

The Red Sox had trumped them all, but still had a lot of work to do with Boras, who is as tough a negotiator as any agent in sports history. One of the most preposterous theories out there in the wake of Boston's big bid was that it was simply a means of keeping the pitcher away from the Yankees. If the Red Sox couldn't strike a deal with Boras, they'd get their $51.1 million back and keep Matsuzaka away from any other Major League team for one year. "That's ludicrous," Werner said. "The truth is, we were focused on his talents and felt that in this market, he would be an outstanding addition to the staff." The other hole in that theory is that MLB had the authority to monitor the negotiations, and if they sensed the Red Sox were anything less than sincere, they could start the posting process all over again.

Those who wondered how the Red Sox could invest $51.1 million just for the rights to talk to a player were missing the bigger point. The posting fee was merely part of the overall investment the Red Sox were willing to make in Matsuzaka. What the Red Sox were doing was front-loading a hefty portion of the freight to guarantee they were still in the game to finish the deal. They knew all the leverage would be on their side, and in hindsight, it was a savvy way to go about it. "The one thing that was working in our favor here is we looked at it like we were willing to spend $100 million for his services for six years," Werner said.

"That was sort of a number that we had sort of felt reasonably comfortable with."

As it turns out, that was the difference. The Mets, as much as they wanted Matsuzaka, weren't willing to go that high in terms of total dollars. "At the end of the day, we didn't see him as a $100 million-plus pitcher," said Minaya. "The bid was $50 and they ended up signing him for $52, we saw that number being, in reality, in real dollars, that was going to be about $125 million when you add [the contract], the amount of the [bid] and the interest. The total cost, that number was going to be $120, $130 million. We liked him, but we didn't like him that much."

With the Mets out of the picture, it would come down to a couple of worthy adversaries—the Red Sox and Scott Boras. And Boras, who had never been a player in the Japanese market, felt that the bid should in no way be counted against what his client would make. In fact, if anything, Boras felt that such a whopping post only enhanced his client's value. "The licensing fee is certainly something that shows that this is a premium guy," Boras told writers who staked out the lobby at the GM meetings in the hours after Boston's winning bid had been accepted by the Lions.

The thirty-day clock was officially running for Boras and the Red Sox, but Epstein, Lucchino and Henry had all had enough experience with the power agent to know that the negotiations would inevitably go almost all the way down to the wire—if not completely to the buzzer—before a deal would be complete. Now that the Sox had blown everyone out of the water in Phase One, the real intrigue was about to begin.

5

The First Supper

(Mid-November–Early December 2006)

How could United States Senator and former New York Knick Bill Bradley have anything to do with the ultimately successful quest of the Red Sox to sign Daisuke Matsuzaka? Better yet, what did ultra Major League bust Hideki Irabu have to do with the Red Sox signing Matsuzaka? You have to go way back to Princeton— and more specifically, the graduating class of 1965—to start solving that riddle. Bradley, the star of the Princeton basketball team, teamed with a point guard named Larry Lucchino. Bradley had a highly intellectual roommate who was not on the basketball team named Daniel Okimoto, who was the son of two Japanese parents and was born in California shortly after the bombing of Pearl Harbor. Bradley introduced Lucchino and Okimoto, and the two became fairly good friends in their years at Princeton.

Lucchino went on to Yale Law School before settling into a highly successful career in professional sports. Okimoto, an academic all the way, built quite a career himself, as a widely respected professor of political science at Stanford. "He started the Asian American research program at Stanford, which is kind of a big deal," noted Lucchino. Oh, by the way, Okimoto also served as a top policy advisor when Bradley ran for president of the United States in 2000. But it was a few years before that when Okimoto was in San Diego with his son for an American

Legion baseball tournament and he happened to come across a newspaper article about Padres president/CEO Larry Lucchino. Could this be the same Larry Lucchino?

"There was a picture of him, and sure enough it was Larry," Okimoto said. "I quickly gave him a call. He said, 'Let's have breakfast together.' The next day, we met and had breakfast and talked about the San Diego Padres and what he was trying to do and so forth. I knew Larry had gone off to Yale Law School but I lost track of him after that. We basically had no contact for many years."

During their reunion breakfast, Lucchino asked Okimoto for suggestions on how to turn the Padres into a more successful franchise, despite their small market status. "I said, 'Well, Larry, you have two choices. You can either raise revenues or you can cut costs,'" recalled Okimoto. "Larry said, 'Well, thank you very much, that's enlightening.' Okimoto laughed and then cut to the chase. "I said, 'Let me be more specific.'" It was then that Okimoto suggested to Lucchino that he go after a Japanese baseball star. That same year, Lucchino's first with the Padres, the Dodgers had a Japanese pitching star named Hideo Nomo who had electrified fans from Los Angeles to Japan. "The Dodgers reaped a bonanza of benefits from having Nomo pitching for them, not the least of which was financial," Okimoto said. "So I said, 'Larry why don't you find a Japanese star who could come and give your franchise a kind of marquee image, not only here in the U.S., but also in Japan.'"

Lucchino not only thought it was a good idea, but asked Okimoto to be part of the process. "I said, 'Larry, I'm an academic, I'm not a baseball man even though I do love baseball.' He said, 'Well, give us some advice on how to go about doing this. Help us out.' So I said, 'OK.'" So Okimoto joined the San Diego Padres board as an unpaid advisor. "It was really out of friendship and loyalty to Larry that I agreed to help him out," Okimoto said.

For Okimoto not only had a ton of contacts in Japan from his business dealings there, but also had a thorough understanding of the culture and psychology. It was his recommendation prior to the 1997 season that the Padres go after a hard-throwing and thickly built right-hander named Hideki Irabu, who was pitching for the Chiba Lotte Marines. Okimoto quickly formed a friendship with Marines head honcho Akio Shigemitsu. What wound up happening was that the Marines signed a strategic alliance with the Padres in which the clubs would share information and San Diego would even provide some minor league players to go play for Chiba Lotte. Because of that agreement, on January 13, 1997, Shigemitsu agreed to give Irabu to the Padres without a posting fee or any other form of compensation. Under the old system, Lucchino noted, wooing a player from Japan was pretty much "about relationships." Okimoto had definitely fostered that friendship with Shigemitsu to seal the deal. The only problem was that Irabu had no interest in playing for the Padres. That steadfast refusal—which included failed contract negotiations that lasted for more than four months—led to a trade to the New York Yankees. But along the way, Okimoto and Lucchino would learn several lessons about the process that would help them years later with a pitcher far superior to Irabu. Without question, Hideki Irabu wound up being a complete flop, and he was out of Major League Baseball by 2002.

In fact, it was just fifteen months after Lucchino and the Padres had traded Irabu that Okimoto saw one of the most amazing pitching performances of his life. Of course, he saw it on television from the United Lounge at the airport in Tokyo. It was Daisuke Matsuzaka pitching a no-hitter for Yokohama High School in the championship game of the famed Koshien Tournament. Okimoto recalls his jaw basically dropping while watching the young Matsuzaka throw comfortably in the 90s while also displaying wicked offspeed stuff. "He was an incredible talent, much more talented than Irabu," said Okimoto. "So I called Larry and said, 'You've got to come to Japan, you've got to come see Matsuzaka and meet him. You have a tiny window of opportunity, maybe ten days to two weeks before the draft. You might

be able to sign Matsuzaka to a Major League contract before the
Japanese draft takes place.'" It's just that it was unheard of for a
Major League team to sign a Japanese player out of high school.
Not only that, but there was an unwritten rule of sorts between
Major League Baseball and Japan that MLB would not raid the
Japanese talent pool from the high school ranks.

Though it occurred nine years earlier, Lucchino still had a
detailed remembrance of that phone conversation with Okimoto.
"I said, 'Dan, there's no way we're going to be able to go over
and draft this kind of high school star and be able to take him
away from Japan right now. It just isn't in the cards.' He said,
'I'm telling you, you should do it.' But we didn't do it," said
Lucchino. Okimoto accepted the answer but gave his long-time
friend a firm reminder. "But I said to Larry, 'Remember the name
Daisuke Matsuzaka because you'll be hearing more about him in
Japanese professional baseball,'" Okimoto said.

In truth though, Lucchino, who has a tireless work ethic and
always has countless irons in the fire, did not think of Matsuzaka
much, if at all, for the next several years. That was until Epstein,
in a meeting of the organizational brass early in 2006, discussed
making a strong run at this international sensation—Daisuke
Matsuzaka. Craig Shipley and Jon Deeble—the international
scouting gurus of the Red Sox—had been covering Matsuzaka's
every step for years and it was a wild twist of irony that Lucchino
and Okimoto wound up being back in pursuit of this man they
first spoke of on that August day in 1998. As soon as the Red Sox
had won the exclusive bidding rights for Matsuzaka, Lucchino
brought Okimoto on board. This time, he offered to make him a
paid advisor for the thirty-day negotiating window the Red Sox
had with Matsuzaka. But Okimoto wouldn't take money from
his long-time friend and confidant. Okimoto told Lucchino he
would help him out of "friendship and goodwill, not only to you
and the Red Sox ownership and management, but goodwill in an
international sense in terms of U.S.-Japan relations." It turns out
Okimoto also has a brother-in-law and a sister-in-law who reside

in Marblehead, Massachusetts, and are huge Sox fans. By the time the courtship was over and Okimoto had helped the Red Sox get Matsuzaka, the only request he made was for his relatives to get tickets to select games at Fenway. That would not be a problem.

But before that, there was a lot of work to be done. The first concrete suggestion that Okimoto would make to the Boston brass was to arrange an informal dinner with Matsuzaka and Scott Boras, a meet and greet session of sorts. Okimoto knew this couldn't happen at some ritzy restaurant. Knowing that Matsuzaka had been in Southern California, where Boras is located, and that Red Sox chairman Tom Werner has a home in Southern California, it was clear to Okimoto what should be done. So he advised Werner to host a dinner for Matsuzaka and Boras that would end up including Henry, Lucchino, Epstein, and manager Terry Francona. Werner's beautiful home in Pacific Palisades would provide the perfect setting.

It wasn't as if the Red Sox could simply have a dinner, toast a few cocktails with Matsuzaka, and say good night. They had to make a strong, strong impression, and Okimoto outlined this to Lucchino and the others. "It's Matsuzaka's first face-to-face look at you and his first impression of how serious the Red Sox are about signing him," said Okimoto, who urged the men to show Matsuzaka their "human side."

"It was a get-acquainted dinner," Okimoto said. "It was a low key, informal way to introduce ourselves to Matsuzaka. I was convinced that if Matsuzaka saw the commitment, the excellence, the successes, of the Boston Red Sox senior management team—ownership and senior management team—he would be enormously impressed and would leave the house wanting to sign with the Boston Red Sox and thinking that he would be a Boston Red Sox. I said, 'If you show this side to yourself of basic honesty and decency and excellence, no one including Scott Boras will be able to demonize the Red Sox.'"

The feast took place on November 19, a mere five days after the Red Sox had won the bid. Okimoto and Lucchino convened at Los Angeles International Airport that morning and drove together to Werner's house, discussing every avenue of not just the pending dinner, but how to put Matsuzaka in a Red Sox uniform. In the hours leading up to the dinner, Okimoto put minds in motion. "When we assembled first at Pacific Palisades, the first question I asked everyone was, before we started discussing anything was, 'Gentlemen, what is it you want to achieve tonight? What do you want to have happen before Daisuke Matsuzaka and Scott Boras walk out the door?' That forced everyone to see, what is it that we're after here? What are we trying to do with this meeting, this dinner?"

Okimoto had a unique and sensible way of looking at everything, and his objective view as an outsider came in handy considering how deeply involved the others were in the process. "His role in this should not be minimized. He was a very useful advisor, navigator, diplomat in the process," said Lucchino. "We always felt like we had sure footing in this arena because we had Dan Okimoto to help us."

On this night, Okimoto was one of the guests at the Werner household. Werner, who had a Hollywood background and produced the wildly successful "Cosby Show" in the 1980s, was not intimidated by having such a big event at his home. "I thought it was nice that Boras called it quaint," said Werner. "That was a nice word for it. I think we felt it was important that it was not in a restaurant. Obviously I was delighted to have it at my house. We wanted to make it warm and respectful."

And according to everyone who was there, it was just that. "Yes, the introduction," said Henry. "It was a very warm dinner with a lot of laughter. Tom's home was perfect for such an occasion. It was a very relaxed atmosphere. We wanted to let him know we were baseball fans and determined to win championships. We wanted him to know how excited New England would be to have him join us."

Leave it to Gordon Edes, the intrepid veteran baseball writer for the *Boston Globe,* to uncover exactly what the menu items were. Edes noted in his article that both of the cultures were represented in the dining experience: "Organic yellow miso soup with wild mushrooms. Mixed baby green salad with mint, pomegranate, and ginger soy dressing. Pan-seared Chilean sea bass with spicy lemongrass gastrique and jasmine rice. Filet mignon with red onion confit and wok-seared sesame haricot verts. Coconut macaroons with wild berries and satsuma tangerine coulis," wrote Edes, who had to be getting hungry while typing all of that for his readers.

But eating was a mere sideshow on this crucial night for the Boston Red Sox. Okimoto served as a choreographer of sorts during the dinner. As is custom in Japan, the important people— as Okimoto put it—sat at the middle of the table. That was Matsuzaka, who sat directly across from Henry and Werner. Slightly off to the side were Lucchino and Epstein. Boras sat opposite them. There were two interpreters, one of them who sat next to Matsuzaka. Francona was at one of the table's ends. "It was very enjoyable," Francona said. "It was an interesting evening. I thought they handled it with a lot of class. And I was actually kind of proud of the way we did it. I thought we did a good job."

There was a sell to make, but the Red Sox did it in a most genuine way. On that first night, there would be no talk about money. It was about human beings. The men from the Red Sox, at Okimoto's request, all told Matsuzaka stories of themselves and their backgrounds. "We wanted Matsuzaka to know that we were all men of integrity," Werner said. "That we all cared about this being a good experience for him. We had heard that he was, all things being equal, leaning towards going to New York. So we talked a lot about the special qualities of the Red Sox and Boston and the quality of life that his family would have because he's a very devoted father." A replica of the 2004 World Series championship trophy was also brought into the room so that Matsuzaka could get a peek at it. Werner mentioned that a dream would be realized if Matsuzaka could one day pitch in a World Series for the Red Sox.

Okimoto, who was probably the most objective observer in the room, thought the Boston contingent did a phenomenal job. "Each of the people present, they told a compelling story," said Okimoto. "John Henry about his success in financial markets, Tom Werner about his success in entertainment and the passion that both of them brought to ownership of the Red Sox and so forth. It was all very successful I thought in terms of establishing a rapport with Matsuzaka. By the time dessert came, I had asked the gifts to be brought out."

Yes, the gifts. Yet another key suggestion by Okimoto was for the group to provide gifts not only for Matsuzaka and Boras, but for Matsuzaka's wife and child. Gifts are the ultimate sign of respect in Japanese culture.

In light-hearted nature, Boras was given a clock because, after all, time was ticking on the negotiations. As the birthday-like parade of presents was ushered into the room, Matsuzaka stood up and opened them one by one. For his wife, who was still back in Japan, there were tour books about Boston, among other things. There was a children's book written by the Red Sox wives for his daughter. By design, the Red Sox saved the best for last.

Okimoto, in particular, loved the idea of Matsuzaka being presented with a Red Sox jersey with his name and number (18) on the back. "That will have a powerful effect on him psychologically," Okimoto predicted to Lucchino and the others. "But save that gift for last. Let him open everything else up first and then save that uniform for last." So, on cue, with everything but trumpets blaring, the Red Sox uniform was placed in Matsuzaka's hands. Okimoto needed but one look at the pitcher to see that the idea had produced the desired result, and then some. Most of the night, Matsuzaka had been stone-faced, much like he is on the pitcher's mound, and undoubtedly just how Boras wanted him to be on this night. With this brilliant stroke of genius, however, the Red Sox had briefly disarmed the man who was still not quite in their possession.

"There was a beam on his face that was indescribable," Okimoto said. "For me, the Japanese are poker-faced, they don't really show their emotions like that. But oh my God, he beamed. I knew when I saw that beam that he was going to be a Red Sox." According to Okimoto, Matsuzaka then volunteered to the group that it had been his dream since he was a child to pitch in the Major Leagues and that he was very eager to achieve that dream. "This was completely unprompted," Okimoto said. "I'm sure Scott Boras must have been squirming in his seat. He just voluntarily poured out his feelings."

Matsuzaka and Boras left shortly thereafter, with all sides feeling good about the way the night had gone. Naturally, Lucchino wanted Okimoto's assessment of the evening. And his old pal from Princeton was more than happy to provide the following: "I said, 'Hey, if we don't bumble this completely, he's a Red Sox. But there's a long way to go between now and signing him.'"

Collaboration began in earnest. Epstein, Shipley and baseball operations continued crunching numbers in advance of their first official proposal to Boras. Werner put his Hollywood background to use by suggesting that the Red Sox produce a highly persuasive and poignant DVD that would be sent to Matsuzaka's home in Japan and hopefully tug at his heartstrings even more than the dinner had. A year earlier, Werner had directed a similar production in trying to lure the legendary Roger Clemens back to Boston, where he won the first three of his seven Cy Young Awards. The Red Sox lost that battle, though Clemens and wife Debbie admitted to being highly touched by the video. The difference was that Clemens—sappy video or not—had choices as a full-fledged free agent. Matsuzaka's option, at least for 2007, was the Red Sox or nothing, at least if he wanted to realize that dream he confided in Werner, Lucchino, Henry, and the others during that dinner.

The first baseball video Werner ever produced—*Opening Day at Fenway Park*—occurred in 1970 while he was a junior at Harvard University. This hardball film made some thirty-six years later, which Werner definitely suggested but did not actually produce, would be to impress a pitcher, not a professor. The Matsuzaka video ran about nine minutes long and took two days to put together. It had several elements to it, intertwining Dice-K highlights from his years at Seibu with historic Red Sox moments. There were picture-perfect views of Boston's most noted skyscrapers, and Japanese fans extolling the virtues of both Boston and the Red Sox. Then, Boston mayor Tom Menino, with his thick Boston accent, filled up the television screen. "Matsuzaka-san, we welcome you to Boston. We can't wait to see you at Fenway Park. Let me just say, if you come to our city, you'll really enjoy it." And, right after Menino's words were finished, there was a view of the Citgo sign that hovers behind the Green Monster with the familiar theme song of the Boston-based sitcom *Cheers* playing in the background. From there, the video traveled back to Fenway Park, highlighting the unique nuances of the yard that was built in 1912. Cy Young, Roger Clemens, and Matsuzaka's future teammate David "Big Papi" Ortiz were then shown in vintage reels.

And Curt Schilling, who is rarely at a loss for words, was the next celebrity to speak to Matsuzaka electronically. Schilling, who was easily the most accomplished member of Boston's current pitching staff and well-known to Japanese fans for his legendary "bloody sock" performance in the 2004 postseason, was filmed in an office building with Boston skyscrapers in the background. "Daisuke, Curt Schilling here. It's cold in Boston right now but I'm hoping that when you show up here in February to be part of this staff, we can heat things up a little bit. We're excited about the potential of having you here. I'm excited about brushing up on my Japanese, becoming friends, and pitching in the same rotation as you. There's nothing like Boston baseball. I look forward to having you and hopefully I'll see you in Spring Training."

Then there was a sushi chef speaking to Matsuzaka in Japanese. And after that it was Peter Grilli, the president of the Japan Society of Boston, standing in front of a Japanese restaurant called

Ginzi saying, "Matsuzaka-san, konnichiwa!" The swift-moving and fun video then played the Fenway favorite song "Sweet Caroline" by Neil Diamond, which is blasted out of the loudspeakers in the bottom of the eighth inning of every Red Sox home game with 35,000 fans in unison blurting out the lyrics. After two random Red Sox fans called for Matsuzaka to come to Boston, Hideki Okajima, the lefty from Japan who was a far more unheralded acquisition by the Red Sox than Matsuzaka, joined in the video. "I signed a contract today," said a smiling Okajima in Japanese. "I hope to enjoy baseball with you." After that, another standard song on the Fenway playlist—"Dirty Water" by the Standells, which is played after each Red Sox victory—was boomed into the video. The production then headed for its grand finale. There was the footage of the Charles River and Freedom Trail—two favorite summer spots for tourists of Boston—plus a montage of the 2004 World Series run and historic Red Sox moments, with "A Day in the Life" by The Beatles playing in the background. It ended with the indelible highlight of Keith Foulke clinching the World Series against the Cardinals, followed by the World Series victory parade and a close-up of the trophy.

The only question was, did Matsuzaka actually see the video? And did he like it? It wasn't until after the Red Sox had signed the pitcher that Werner got confirmation that his work had been seen by the audience it was intended for. You see, Grilli was there at Fenway on the December day Matsuzaka was unveiled, and introduced to the pitcher. Werner gets a chuckle out of the story. "Larry Lucchino after the press conference went to Daisuke and said, 'I'd like you to meet Peter Grilli.' And Daisuke said, 'Oh, I know you. You're that awkward Japanese-speaking foreigner in Boston in the video.'"

While Werner was the entertainment king, Lucchino was the true business shark of the Red Sox brain trust. He knew how to schmooze just about anyone and very easily could have gone into politics instead of baseball. Once again, Okimoto came up with a suggestion that Lucchino followed. Go to Japan, said Okimoto.

Get public sentiment in your favor out there in the event that negotiations break down. "I said, 'Look, you have to go to Japan and meet the Seibu Lions and express your appreciation to them for posting Matsuzaka. Show your sincerity towards the Seibu Lions and establish a pipeline of communications because you may need it at some point in the negotiations later.'" And, as Okimoto noted, it would also give Lucchino a chance to meet with the Japanese press and spin things further. "Describe Matsuzaka as a living national treasure," suggested Okimoto.

So shortly after Thanksgiving, Lucchino got on a plane and went to Tokyo. "We were aware that with Scott Boras, it generally goes down to the eleventh hour," said Lucchino. "So we calibrated our efforts in recognition of that fact. We knew we'd use all thirty days. We kind of divided and conquered. I went over to Japan to show the flag and to deal with his incumbent team and Japanese baseball. We thought if somehow we made it clear that this was not a defensive bid, that this was a sincere bid from a team that would take good care of him, we could build up some public pressure for him, requiring him we hoped to accept a reasonable proposal."

While Epstein said on the night of winning negotiating rights that there would be no public updates of the negotiations along the way, Lucchino did make it known to reporters in Japan that the Red Sox had made their first offer. "We have sent a formal offer to Matsuzaka and his agent Scott Boras," Lucchino told the Japanese media at that time. "I believe it is fair and comprehensive and offers a great deal of security and a substantial level of compensation." It was later learned that that first offer—to which Boras never even provided a counter—was for six years at $36 million.

Lucchino wasn't doing anything spur of the moment. His whole plan was essentially the execution of a script that he certainly had time to think out during the endless flight to Tokyo. "Create a backdrop that this was a reasonable proposal from a reasonable team that had a lot of respect for Japan and

Japanese baseball and Dice-K," said Lucchino. "This would make it harder for his representative to portray us in some fashion that might make it easier for Dice-K to reject our proposal and go back to Japan." Okimoto couldn't help but look back at the Irabu situation when advising the Red Sox in how to handle the early stages of the negotiations. Looking back on it, Okimoto feels that the original Irabu offer—which Lucchino presented in Tokyo to Irabu and agent Don Nomura—was too low and that they basically lost Irabu at that moment.

It was on the day of the Dice-K dinner at the Werner household that Okimoto and the Red Sox executives first discussed strategy for the negotiations. "I said, 'Face is important in Japan.' If you insult somebody by lowballing them, even though you have an intention to come back in negotiations to give them a substantially higher salary, that initial impression will stick," Okimoto said. "It could alienate them and harden their determination not to give in. We talked about what would be a fair price. I stayed out of all that. But I said, basically look, what you ought to do is instead of offering 50 percent of what you're eventually going to pay him, offer him 75 percent, 70 or 75 percent, and then negotiate the final 25 percent. You want to establish your integrity and the strength of your desire to sign Matsuzaka."

As it turns out, that initial offer ended up being 69 percent of the final $52 million Matsuzaka would eventually sign for. Still, at least one executive was skeptical of the plan knowing the cutthroat adversary Boras had always been. "Someone said, 'Geez, if we're at 75 percent, we may wind up paying 150 percent,'" recalled Okimoto.

In hindsight, there was just no going back to Japan. Though the monetary game was just getting started, Lucchino saw some things that he loved during that brief stay in Japan—namely Matsuzaka saying good-bye to his team and a nation of beloved followers. In fact, Lucchino probably felt like doing cartwheels when he saw the way things were unfolding. "What we found out when we were there is how extremely unlikely it would be that he would return to Japan from the good-byes he said to his team," Lucchino said. "We were over there when his team was flipping him up on the blanket at the team party and they were saying good-bye to him and all that. It was just music to our ears to see and hear all of that from up close." So Lucchino flew back to Boston with every reason to feel good about the situation. The optimism didn't last all that long though. Even if he didn't have the leverage he was accustomed to, Scott Boras was going to make everyone sweat.

6

Jetting to the Finish
(December 11–15, 2006 and beyond)

AROUND THE SAME TIME Major League Baseball's Winter Meetings were being conducted amid the backdrop of Florida's Disney World in early December 2006, the Red Sox were getting increasingly agitated at the pace of their negotiations with Matsuzaka. Things had slowed to a crawl as Boras had yet to counter the original offer. Still, Epstein had other things on his plate, so he passed the time by making two other key acquisitions off the free agent market in right fielder J. D. Drew and shortstop Julio Lugo. Drew, incidentally, was also represented by Boras. But in the course of those negotiations with Drew, which resulted in a stunning five-year, $70 million contract for a player who had never so much as made the All-Star team, it didn't appear as if two birds were being killed with one stone. Though the Drew deal wouldn't officially be signed until January because of some quirky medical issues, Boras and Epstein came to the genesis of that pact far easier than the Matsuzaka signing.

Quite frankly, the issue of the $51.1 million bid that Seibu received was slowing everything down. The Red Sox viewed that as part of their total acquisition cost for the pitcher. Boras felt it was entirely independent and, in fact, just further proof of how much his client should command on the open market. Maybe Boras was just posturing and knew in his heart that a deal would ultimately get done by that well-documented deadline of midnight when December 14 turned into December 15. One thing was clear, however. The Red Sox were no longer sure.

"It was frustrating for us," said Henry. "Scott often passes on deals for clients he doesn't think are appropriate. So we knew there was a real possibility we would not be able to make a deal." As real as that possibility was, the Red Sox were not going to go down without every stone unturned. Boras still hadn't made a counter offer? Fine, said Henry. He decided to do something about it. On Monday, December 11, Henry offered up his Learjet so that his lead negotiators in this deal could literally bring Matsuzaka home. So that morning, Shipley—the executive who had put more man hours into the Matsuzaka project than anyone else—was the first to board the plane in South Florida, where Henry's home and other business ventures are based.

The plane flew north to Boston to pick up Lucchino and Epstein and swiftly headed to Southern California, where the offices of Boras are located and where Matsuzaka had been stationed for the last couple of weeks. Shipley—once a Boras client during his days as an active Major Leaguer—stayed in the background while Epstein, Lucchino, and Werner served as front men. "We wanted to make the trip to Southern California, unsolicited, to provide every opportunity for this negotiation to have a successful conclusion," said Epstein. And shortly after landing, the Red Sox told Boras they were in town and wanted to meet, in order to provide as Epstein called it, "A second, improved contract offer of considerable magnitude, despite the fact that we haven't received a counteroffer. We sincerely hope that this will lead to a deal," said Epstein in a session with the media later that night.

Lucchino is an in-your-face kind of guy to begin with. He had made his mark in business long before the advent of cellphones, e-mail, and text messaging. "My view is that too much in baseball is done by telephone," Lucchino said. "More face-to-face conversations would lead to better agreements. So we went out there uninvited as you may know, saying that we know when the deadline is and we're going to get a lot more done if we're there than if we try to do this all by phone. We're a lot harder to demonize if we're there. So we just went out there uninvited and it proved to be a very important decision in the whole process."

To Epstein, the situation was cut and dry. This was the final push. Henry's jet would be flying back to Boston on Wednesday morning, December 13, at which time Boras and Matsuzaka would hopefully be in tow so that the pitcher could get his physical completed in advance of the deadline. No deal would be done without a thorough physical, which made it imperative for the sides to agree to a contract in principle. That same night, Boras invited the media to his office for a press conference. "The progress is something I'm not going to comment on," Boras told the assemblage of reporters. "I'm not going to characterize the negotiations. This is not a customary negotiation. The question is, with a posting fee, how do you handle that?" The Red Sox, who had barely said a public word about the negotiations, felt they had no choice in this matter but to counter whatever Boras was going to say to the masses. At 11:27 p.m. ET on the night of December 11, an e-mail from Red Sox PR man John Blake went flying into the inbox of every member of the Red Sox media. "The Boston Red Sox will hold a conference call, at 12:45 a.m. EST early Tuesday morning, December 12. On that conference call, Red Sox President/CEO Larry Lucchino and Executive Vice President/General Manager Theo Epstein will be available to discuss the on-going negotiations with pitcher Daisuke Matsuzaka."

So in the wee hours of that morning, Lucchino, Epstein, Werner, and Henry took twenty minutes of questions from the deadline-tested media. And it was on that call that the public first became aware of the fact that Lucchino and Epstein had gone to California on Henry's jet. Henry participated in the call from his home in Florida. It was clear that the blood was boiling for this typically mild-mannered owner. "I think it's also fair to say that we're on Scott Boras' doorstep because he hasn't negotiated with us directly thus far," Henry said. "We're taking the fight directly to him, the fight to try to have a negotiation here." During that first night in town, the Red Sox did turn their cheek at the fact Boras had never countered their original offer and came in with a more lucrative deal. Making a second offer before you get a counter isn't the way teams like to do their business. But Epstein felt Boras had left the club with little choice. "It's highly unusual, but again, signing Matsuzaka is extremely important to the Boston Red Sox," said Epstein. "We're very committed to making sure that happens. Although it's normally not good policy to make a second offer without receiving a counteroffer, we want to demonstrate to Matsuzaka and to fans of Japanese baseball around the world just how important this is to us."

Epstein, who is polished in just about everything he says to the media, once again had put together a good strategy that had the Red Sox looking like the good guys. "We'll present the second offer, an improved offer, one that we hope will get this deal done," Epstein said. "We're not frustrated. We're just doing everything possible under the sun to get a deal done. That's all we can do. We can control the Boston Red Sox actions, and we plan to leave no stone unturned." Epstein also noted that for the second time, it was the Red Sox who had flown cross-country to try to make in-roads. And he mentioned Lucchino's trip to Japan. Clearly, the Red Sox had maxed out their efforts and they were looking for some reciprocation from Boras.

That second offer? Six years at $48 million, a jump of $2 million per season. It was still not good enough. There would be more talks on Tuesday, which would be the pivotal day in that it was the last day before the plane would be flying back to Boston.

December 12 was an all-day, all-night event. Epstein, Lucchino, and Shipley would use every ounce of what was left on the clock to get Matsuzaka and Boras on that plane the next day. There would be multiple meetings with Boras that day, one of which even included Matsuzaka. "He was reserved," remembered

Werner. "But I didn't take that as anything else than letting his agent make the recommendation." Stressful? Perhaps. But also par for the course known as poker with Scott Boras. "They were pretty stressful but Theo, Shipley and I were all aware that it was going to come down to an all-night session the last night because that's part of the melodrama you associate with Scott Boras negotiations," Lucchino said. "It was a tag team effort. We were all fully expecting that it would go the distance."

Finally, with time ticking away, the Red Sox produced what they felt was their last, best offer to Matsuzaka. Six years at $52 million. Boras said thanks, but no thanks. Is this how it was really going to end? An odyssey that began so long ago for so many members of the Red Sox organization was just going to die a slow death because of a staredown with Scott Boras? According to the *Boston Globe*'s Gordon Edes, Boras would later request a last-ditch, one-on-one session with only Epstein in the early morning hours of Wednesday. Epstein advised Boras that if the topic was more money, forget it. The Red Sox had maxed out their package, which, including the posting fee, was at $103.1 million. Still, Epstein and Boras had one last session that went until roughly 4 a.m. on Wednesday, or better yet, about five hours before Henry's plane was set for takeoff. Boras did ask for more money. A lot more. He wanted six years at $66 million. Epstein made it clear that would not happen. However, some ground was made at that time with a whole batch of creative perks that Boras wanted with the sole purpose of making his client and family as comfortable in his new country as humanly possible. Fine, Epstein said. They could do the perks. But the money was staying at $52 million.

Without a deal in place and the sun threatening to come up soon, Boras exited the meeting and a weary Epstein still didn't know what the next few hours would bring. The way Lucchino remembers it, Boras phoned the Red Sox at about 7:30 a.m.— roughly ninety minutes before the departure of Henry's plane— and said that he wouldn't be accompanying the contingent back to Boston, and neither would Matsuzaka. Perhaps by this point, Epstein, Lucchino, Shipley, and Werner were all too sleep-deprived to read too much into it. Forty-five minutes later, Boras called again. He and Matsuzaka would be flying to Boston after all.

So what happened in those forty-five minutes? "You're going to have to find that out from the other side," Lucchino said six months later. "We can all speculate what happened, but I can't tell you that with any certainty." Boras chose not to give his side of the story, declining a chance to be interviewed for this book. As Lucchino said, "We can all speculate" as to the reasons Boras first said Matsuzaka wasn't boarding Henry's flight and then abruptly changed his mind less than an hour later. Here would be a logical game of speculation. Boras didn't have leverage because Matsuzaka truly and deeply wanted to pitch for the Boston Red Sox, and would be able to do so at an annual salary that nearly tripled what he had been making for the Seibu Lions. And by agreeing to so many perks, Matsuzaka accurately sensed that the Red Sox would not only care for him, but for his family as well.

With Red Sox executives Epstein, Lucchino, Werner and Shipley already on board, there was a sense of elation from all sides when Matsuzaka and Boras stepped on to the plane. Mind you, there was still not a signed deal. There were technicalities to overcome and a physical to pass later that day. But getting Matsuzaka on the plane was the biggest hurdle and everyone knew it. As tired as Lucchino was at the time the negotiations swung in his team's favor, he has an indelible image of Matsuzaka's entry on Air Henry.

"One of the more vivid memories I have of the process is that Dice-K, even when we saw him and talked to him, he did not smile at any point," Lucchino said. "I attribute that to the sort of legendary mien that he had, that he was just a poker-faced guy and all that. But when he sat down in John's plane, he just looked at us and he just smiled from ear to ear. He seemed so happy to be on the plane and to be going. There was sort of this recognition that it was symbolically over, if not literally over. This smile that lit the plane cabin."

Once the Red Sox saw the smile, they could finally sleep. "I think that everyone was exhausted," said Werner. "It was exhausting. On the way back, everyone slept. And [the deal] wasn't closed. But it was encouraging." As Matsuzaka smiled and the Red Sox exhaled, the ravenous fan base of Red Sox Nation did what it does best—it started obsessing. Some web-savvy fans, knowing that flight patterns were public record, began charting the status of Henry's plane so that it could be gauged exactly when Matsuzaka would be arriving. Nobody quite knew the status of the negotiations at this point, but the fact Matsuzaka was coming to Boston with the Red Sox could only be viewed as good news.

One of the more bizarre timing aspects of the day was that Lugo—the shortstop the Red Sox had agreed to terms with a week earlier—was actually introduced late in the afternoon in one of the most distracted press conferences in the history of Fenway Park. Red Sox PR man John Blake announced to the small media gathering that there would be no information about the status of Matsuzaka and said there would be no questions on the matter. This was a press conference for Lugo, who had been in town to take his physical. With Epstein understandably out of pocket, assistant general manager Jed Hoyer and Francona represented the team at the Lugo announcement. Shortly after the formal part of the session ended, people wanted answers on Matsuzaka. Was the deal done? "Well I know that the whole group is at 35,000 feet right now, other than that, I have no comment," said Hoyer.

At around 5:20 p.m. on the afternoon of December 13, Henry's plane at last landed at the Hanscom Air Force Base in Bedford, a nearby suburb of Boston. With about fifty fans and seventy-five photographers on hand to survey the unique scene, Matsuzaka disembarked and went straight for the back seat of an SUV, which was escorted by a state police car. What will be best remembered about that scene was the way Matsuzaka's smile seemed to beam right through the window of the car he was sitting in. He waved to the fans as the car headed straight for Massachusetts General Hospital for the all-important physical. Under the microscope of the team's medical staff was a completely healthy pitcher with a very strong right arm. "He didn't just pass the physical," said Lucchino, "but he passed with flying colors." Not long after that, the deal was done. Four weeks of angst had instantly been lifted. "There was complete euphoria among all of us when the deal was made," Henry said.

And an interesting deal it was. When details of the contract leaked out, it was clear that the Red Sox had done everything in their power to make sure Matsuzaka and his family would be as comfortable as possible in their new environment. The pact included a physical therapist, a massage therapist, an interpreter, eight first class, round trip tickets between Boston and Japan, a sizable Spring Training housing allowance, use of a town car for his family to get to and from games, and the number 18 that he wore in Seibu and traditionally went to ace pitchers in Japan. The deal itself was structured with a $2 million signing bonus and base salaries of $6 million in 2007, $8 million in each of the next three seasons, and $10 million annually in the final two years.

"Because we always anticipated that there may be problems in the first year, we were eager to walk the extra mile on some of these conditions, terms, amenities to make sure he had the best chance to be successful," Lucchino said. "We were always planning on that. We thought it would be crazy to be penny-wise and pound-foolish. If we're going to do this, we should give him the best possible opportunity to succeed."

One of the more underrated aspects of this story is how the power brokers of the Red Sox had come together in such a unified front to make this deal happen. For in the previous winter, Epstein temporarily left his post as general manager when contract negotiations fell apart at the last minute. But the real root of his departure was not the dollars, but his relationship with Lucchino, which had deteriorated greatly over the years. Epstein only returned to his job after heart-to-heart meetings with Lucchino, Henry, and

Werner in which the sides agreed things would have to be different and that the money-makers in the organization would have to find common ground with the baseball operations staff. For so long, Lucchino was about making the splash and getting the big headline, while Epstein was a long-term thinker, just as interested in the state of his farm system as the current Major League team. But they tried to meet somewhere in the middle. Just the fact that they were able to go to Southern California to bring Matsuzaka home and work in such a collaborative way was an enormous improvement over the way things had fallen apart late in the calendar year of 2005. Epstein and Lucchino were both extremely smart business men with rational and creative minds, willing to work late into the night and think outside the box. When they were both going in the same direction, it was clear good things could happen, and Matsuzaka was a case in point.

In fact, if Okimoto hadn't read about some of the history, he would have never known about the strife that once existed in the executive offices of Yawkey Way. "I had heard that there were maybe rifts among the senior management of the Red Sox. I saw none of that," Okimoto said. "I saw only a fierce focus on getting this done and a collective pulling of thinking and efforts to make sure that it would happen. There was kind of a spirit of camaraderie there that was gratifying to see."

All that was left now was the press conference, which would be one of the most unique in the long history of the ballclub. With all of Red Sox Nation buzzing about the successful acquisition of an international icon, the actual unveiling took place on December 14, which would have been the deadline day for negotiations if no pact had been reached the day before. With the sun shining on a mild New England winter day, the highly formal press conference took place in a ritzy function room behind home plate. Typically, the media strolls into a press conference about fifteen or twenty minutes before it starts. But this occasion was different as over an hour before the actual announcement, there were twenty television camera trucks lined up and down

Yawkey Way. Inside, some three hundred media members—many of whom were from Japan—packed the room, making it perhaps the most well-attended player acquisition announcement in the long history of the franchise. After the announcement, there would be a sushi feast—which the Red Sox paid several thousand dollars for—to fuel writers between stories.

What will best be remembered about the day is a highly humorous moment that took place before the actual announcement, when the Red Sox—led by Henry, Lucchino, Epstein and others—gave Matsuzaka an on-field tour of Fenway Park. With a baseball in hand, Matsuzaka, decked out in a dark suit jacket and tie, stood on that Fenway mound that he was still four months away from standing on for real. Henry, of all people, crouched behind home plate and prepared to catch the first pitch Matsuzaka ever threw at Fenway Park. But with a soggy green tarp covering home plate, Henry lost his footing and fell right on his back as he tried to make the catch. Matsuzaka couldn't help but chuckle, and neither could Henry. The owner got up off his back. Sylvia Moon, Henry's assistant, later made one of those small movie picture books to commemorate the hilarious moment. In fact, by May 2007, Werner still had the little book in his desk drawer at Fenway. It was titled "The Pitch and the Catch, Dec. 14, 2006," and as you flip through the pages with your thumb, you can see the progression of Henry trying to catch the ball and then falling right over. "You know, we didn't go over signals," laughed Henry. "I put down four fingers expecting a changeup. He crossed me up." With all the pitches Matsuzaka possessed in his arsenal, how could you blame Henry for that mix-up?

Once it was time for the formal part of the afternoon to begin—which was, of course, televised live in both Boston and Japan—a procession of key figures came into the room and walked toward the dais. It was Henry, followed by Werner, Lucchino, Epstein, and Matsuzaka. Once they sat down, Shipley, the scout who had devoured all things Matsuzaka for the last several years, joined the group. So did Boras and a translator named Tak

Sato, who would gain infamy by the end of the afternoon. In an effort for Matsuzaka to be comfortable on the big stage, it was agreed on that Sato—an employee of Boras—would interpret the conference, rather than someone who actually had experience translating at such a big event.

The result was that Matsuzaka's personality didn't come out during his first meet and greet in Boston, but his smile sure did. Here was an example of the way things were lost in translation by Sato: Matsuzaka was asked if it was a dream of his to play in the Major Leagues. Sato translated his answer as, "I don't like to use that word *dream*. Playing in the Major Leagues is a goal." A day after the announcement, the *Boston Globe,* on its Web site, hired someone a little more fluent in translation to decipher what Matsuzaka had actually said and here is what Columbia University grad student Taka Tanaka came up with: "I don't really like the word 'dream' to begin with. I think a dream is something you can have without realizing," Matsuzaka said. "I've always believed that I could pitch here and have held it as a goal, and acted on it. I think that because I've believed in and acted on it all along . . . that's why I'm here today." That answer was far more expansive than what writers had at their disposal in their live copy from the press conference. Fortunately for the media members—not to mention the fans who get to know the emotions of the players through print—the Red Sox wound up hiring a translator for Matsuzaka named Masa Hoshino, who did an excellent job translating Matsuzaka's answers into English throughout the season.

In truth, the event was more symbolic than substantive. As Epstein put it in his opening remarks, "Today is a very important day, a very significant day for the Red Sox. We are welcoming Daisuke Matsuzaka to the Red Sox family. Today, what we're really doing is announcing the signing of a national treasure." But how would that translate into the highest form of competitive baseball in the United States? Despite all the hype, the Red Sox were prepared for Matsuzaka to feel his way through 2007.

Aside from going to a whole new world, there would be very real baseball adjustments, including a slicker ball, a different pitching schedule, far more travel, and fiercer competition. But the way the media had come out in droves to chronicle every aspect of the acquisition, there didn't figure to be much leeway for Matsuzaka in Year One.

And speaking of the media, the Red Sox started preparing for the added onslaught they would have in Year One. In fact, before the Red Sox had actually completed the contract with Matsuzaka, Blake went to the team's Spring Training base in Fort Myers, Florida to try to get an idea of how things would work logistically. During the first two weeks of camp, the Red Sox work at the minor league complex because there are far more practice fields. The media doesn't have a press box at that complex, but instead works out of trailers. Blake immediately decided that the Red Sox would now need four media trailers instead of two. Also, the press box at Fenway Park would need to be redesigned before Opening Day to make room for all the Japanese reporters. Architect Janet-Marie Smith hit the ground running on that project, improving the sightlines in the third and fourth rows and building a state-of-the-art work room behind the press box that made a world of difference. The project got done in time. "Janet-Marie Smith and those guys did a great job finding the space and redoing the press box to make the third and fourth rows usable," said Blake. "I don't know what we would have done without that work room. We would have been really up the creek. There would have been no space to put everybody. That was a huge advantage and we laid out some additional photo positions up top so we were covered on that."

While Blake handled the media side of things, Red Sox pitching coach John Farrell was going to be the man with the most responsibility in getting Matsuzaka set up from a pure pitching standpoint. Farrell was entering his first year as a Major League pitching coach but was well-suited for the role, given his five years as the director of player development for the Cleveland Indians. Farrell's top skill is probably his organization. So he wanted to smooth out some adjustments with Matsuzaka before Spring Training started. To make that happen, he had to go meet Matsuzaka. That took place in January, as Farrell hopped on a plane and went to the headquarters of Boras, where Matsuzaka was doing his workouts in the ultra-modern facility. "Really, it was just a chance to observe his workouts," Farrell said. "It was a day that he did throw long-toss. The whole goal was that it was a first opportunity to meet in person, rather than it being in Spring Training when so many other things would be taking place. I just wanted to devote some time to our initial conversation and initial meeting. And really to get some ideas and thoughts on Spring Trainings that he had been involved in and begin to outline what our Spring Training would entail."

Farrell learned quickly that Matsuzaka would need to be eased off some of the throwing he had done in the past. In Japan, Spring Training is two months long compared to the six weeks it is in the Major Leagues. "Their goal is that, and this is what I came to learn, is to get 2,000 pitches thrown in the month of February off the bullpen mound," Farrell said. "Well, that's a huge number. If you're throwing every other day, let's say that gives you 14 times, you're looking at 100 to 150-pitch bullpens." That wasn't going to happen in Fort Myers. "We kind of blended the two worlds together," said Farrell. "We gave the ability to have some lengthier bullpens. I think our goal was to remain open-minded and for this to be an education process as we went through it. Granted, there were parameters around it, but there was some flexibility within those parameters. I think the biggest objective that I wanted to accomplish was that with him coming in here, we wanted to make sure he got enough work to prepare because that's where I think any athlete is going to generate and gain some confidence from."

Matsuzaka also had one more media session before Spring Training, inviting reporters to come out to the Boras headquarters and observe part of his workout on January 31. The *Boston Globe* and *Boston Herald* dispatched reporters some three thousand miles out west just to cover a few hours of Matsuzaka. That was how big a story he was going into the year. The Associated Press and MLB.com also covered the event, as did the typical mob of Japanese media members. He spoke in general terms of his workouts and of adapting to a five-man rotation. And he was eating well. "The vegetables and the fish taste great," said Matsuzaka. In a couple of more weeks, he'd be out of the warm-weather climate of California and into the warm-weather climate of Florida, where his Major League career would at last get underway.

7

Spring Fling
(February—March 2007)

IN CASE ANYONE WONDERED how long it would be before Dice-K's arrival took over Spring Training, consider that he was surrounded by reporters nearly the minute he disembarked his plane at Tampa International Airport the night of February 12. It is generally a custom for the American media—even in aggressive markets like Boston or New York—to allow a player to reach his destination, get settled, and then surround him once he gets to the ballpark. But because of the great interest in the story, Matsuzaka's marketing firm discreetly released the info of his flight itinerary to the thirsty Japanese media, and also to a lesser degree, some members of the American media. For example, the biggest wire service around—the Associated Press—was on hand to watch Matsuzaka, at least symbolically, step into his new world. It was clear the Japanese media, fueled by demanding bosses who wanted around-the-clock coverage of their national icon, were going to leave no stone unturned, even if it was chronicling the smallest details of Matsuzaka's integration into his new world. During the early weeks of Spring Training, you could always tell what part of the field Matsuzaka was on just by watching the Japanese media. If they moved, chances are, Matsuzaka was moving in front of them. Part of the in-your-face aggressiveness of the Japanese media was tied to the way things happened back home, where reporters were denied access to the clubhouse and often had to stake out players, or even dine with them, in hopes of a candid quote or two. Just as Matsuzaka and the Red Sox would be getting an education in the other's life, the Japanese media would also see over time how differently things are run in America. And as the season wore on, there would also be instances in which Matsuzaka couldn't understand the protocol of certain factions of the American media, not to mention the ravenous fan base of the Red Sox.

Matsuzaka had flown in from Los Angeles, where he had been doing his last-minute workouts at the state-of-the-art facilities provided by Boras. Looking a bit weary as he got off the flight, Matsuzaka entertained some brief questions at the baggage claim area before making the two-hour drive to Fort Myers. "I have a few days left before camp officially starts," Matsuzaka told the assembled media. "My excitement has not reached its peak, but I would love to meet my teammates."

That happened over the course of the next few days, as Matsuzaka participated in some early-bird workouts and started getting a feel for the life he had signed on for. On the eve of the official reporting date for pitchers and catchers, there would be yet another massive press conference of 150 strong—this one with the pitcher literally seated in a chair on top of the Red Sox dugout at City of Palms Park and the questioners sitting in the box seats. Matsuzaka said all the right things while keeping the legend of the gyroball alive.

He also playfully said that his first Major League pitch would be a fastball, and he requested that the batter not make contact. It was clear from the start that Matsuzaka's dynamic personality— which came out much more in smiles and laughs than words— wouldn't hurt his initiation into America. After all, charismatic stars are always easier to like, right?

The gyroball—real or imagined—would create some comedy all spring. The pitch was supposedly the brain-child of a Japanese physicist named Ryutaro Himeno, who had demonstrated the sharp breaking action of the pitch on a computer. Nobody could say for sure they had ever seen it for real. The way Matsu-zaka's pitches dipped and darted, it was easy to see why he was the pitcher being most linked with the gyro. John Farrell denied its existence, saying that the pitch in question was basically just Matsuzaka's changeup, which was delivered with a circle grip that gave the ball the break normally associated with a screwball.

Matsuzaka was getting a kick out of the whole thing. "How should I answer?" Matsuzaka said through Sachiyo Sekiguchi, a woman who had been hired by the Red Sox as media relations coordinator for the Japanese media. "I knew this question was coming today. And I was preparing some optional answers for this particular question. Should I say, 'I have that [pitch].' Or I could say, 'Which particular [pitch] are you referring to?' Overall, if I have the chance, I will pitch that ball." Long before Matsuzaka's first official pitch, it was clear he was already toying with the minds of the batters he would face. And in the power-packed American League, Matsuzaka was clever to be seeking every advantage he could get, even one gained by purely psychological means.

That night might have been the last publicly calm one he'd have for some time. Though his face was already imbedded in the minds of Red Sox fans, Fort Myers hadn't quite caught on yet. Just hours after the press conference, Matsuzaka dined at a Japanese/Chinese establishment called Tim's Magic Wok. He sat at a table with a circle of associates—including Sekiguchi—and nobody in the restaurant bothered him. That's because nobody in the restaurant knew who he was, at least until a sportswriter told the female sushi chef that the man seated toward the back of the restaurant was perhaps on the cusp of becoming a Major League All-Star. Considering the legend Matsuzaka was at home, it was unfathomable to imagine he could ever dine in such peace back in Japan. Matsuzaka would never be granted the privilege of blend-ing into a crowd once he arrived in Boston. Red Sox Nation is famous for fawning over even the 25th man on the team during public outings. Some players, such as erstwhile Sox center fielder Johnny Damon, loved the attention. Others, such as hefty lefty

David Wells, who never became comfortable with the Boston fishbowl during his two years with the team, couldn't stand it.

But if anyone had been groomed for it, it was this 26-year-old man from Japan who had been stalked from the moment he became a legend all those years ago at Koshien. "In Japan, he's like all four Beatles rolled into one," former Major Leaguer and Japanese pro player Orestes Destrade said in the presence of several reporters before Matsuzaka's exhibition start at Jupiter, Florida against the Marlins. Destrade, who serves as a studio analyst for ESPN, played for the Seibu Lions (1989–1992, 1995) and had clear perspective on how the stars are treated in Japan. So, too, did Joe Torre, who managed the Yankees from 1996 to 2007. The Yankees had opened their 2004 season in Tokyo against the Tampa Bay Devil Rays and Torre couldn't help but be amazed at the way his own Japanese star Hideki Matsui was adored there. Sitting in the visitor's dugout in Fort Myers roughly three years later, Torre still remembered the scene vividly.

"We were going back to the hotel from the ballpark after one of the exhibition games, and [Matsui's] car was in front of us," said Torre. "It took about thirty seconds to draw a crowd when he stopped at the light. It was the most incredible thing I'd ever seen. People getting out of cars in front of him, flashing their phones and taking pictures through the window of the car, it was incredible stuff. After seeing that, as I say, he's oblivious to it. He's used to it. I don't think anybody could handle it better than him, let's put it that way."

That would be Matsuzaka's challenge. The $103.1 million price tag would force him to gain as much, if not more, attention than the sweet-swinging Matsui, who is known as Godzilla to Japanese baseball followers. Matsuzaka was known as the Monster to his fans back home. But over in the United States, he simply had a monster following. On the morning of the Red Sox's reporting date, the players' parking lot entrance was surrounded by cameras, all there for the sole purpose of seeing precisely what time Matsuzaka got to the park. It would be like that every day for the rest of camp. Clearly, Matsuzaka was an obsession to Japanese fans, and the imbedded reporters were charged with feeding it with their reports and snapshots. The fiercely competitive American media, watching their Japanese counterparts go to work, seemed compelled to bring a similar depth to the coverage. *Boston Globe* columnist Dan Shaughnessy had the most sarcastic take on Dice-K fever.

"It's a little embarrassing the way we're reacting to the introduction of this Japanese hurler," Shaughnessy wrote in a February 15 column. "Are we not staid old Boston? Have we not been the professional sports home of Bill Russell, Ted Williams, Larry Bird, Bobby Orr, and Tom Brady? Didn't we already go through the process of acquiring the best pitcher in the world—a guy from a foreign land—named Pedro Martínez? Didn't we watch the Red Sox trade for Curt Schilling, who had already been a World Series MVP? Didn't Roger Clemens win 192 games here? Same as Cy Young? So why is Dice-K, who arrived in Florida the week of the 43rd anniversary of the Beatles' first appearance on *The Ed Sullivan Show* touted as the soon-to-be Fenway Elvis?"

The answers to Shaughnessy's questions, which by the way were valid, would have to come through time. In the meantime, the hype continued at a dizzying rate and the Red Sox tried to deal with it as best they could. John Blake might have had the toughest job of anyone in Spring Training, just trying to manage all of the media. "The Spring Training part of it, especially the first few days, was certainly more than we expected," Blake said. "I felt a little over-run there the first day or so before we really got a handle on it." Blake did his due diligence, trying to find out what it was like when Ichiro Suzuki and Hideki Matsui made their introduction to America. "I had talked to the Yankees and Mariners and tried to get a feel for the kind of numbers that they had the first springs for Ichiro and Matsui," said Blake. "At the beginning, I felt like we nearly doubled those numbers. We had well over 120 Japanese media there at the beginning. With the six networks, everything else, and trying to do all of that at that minor league facility, it was a little hard those first couple of days. He was on so many fields and we had to kind of work through all that. I think eventually we got a system down to some extent."

It was Sekiguchi who kept the Japanese media informed of Dice-K's daily schedule. And there would be a lot of media—not just in Spring Training but throughout the year. On a daily basis throughout 2007, fourteen Japanese newspapers—half of which were exclusively sports publications— covered Matsuzaka. There were also two wire services, not to mention six television stations and eight photographers. Much like Japanese baseball players, the Japanese media seemed to take pride in their work ethic. They seldom took a day off. In fact, one in particular went the whole season without missing a game. That was Takako Nakamichi, freelance TV director for FUJI-TV, who attended all 162 games and the fourteen postseason contests. And she did it all with a smile on her face. One American writer started calling Nakamichi iron woman as a spinoff of Cal Ripken's Iron Man moniker bestowed on him for playing in more consecutive games than any player in history. "For her, the most important thing was never to miss a game," said Sekiguchi. "I gave her a little gift for having never missed a game."

There was a Spring Training photo opportunity for the ages— at least for those who were wielding cameras from Japan—when the Red Sox and Yankees met up for their lone exhibition season matchup on March 12. Because the Red Sox had a union meeting during the pre-game hours and did not take batting practice, there was no way for a chance meeting between the two Japanese icons, Matsui and Matsuzaka. So the younger Matsuzaka made it a priority to set up a meeting behind home plate. It is very much a Japanese custom for the younger player to show proper respect to his elder. To anyone with a background in Japanese culture, the exchange made perfect sense. The American audience at City of Palms Park that night got an education.

"In Japan, there's the *sempai/kohai*," said Wayne Graczyk, a baseball columnist for the *Japan Times,* in explaining the dynamic. "You went to the same school I did, but I was there five years before you so I'm your *sempai,* you're my *kohai.* You have to respect me. If we were on different teams and we were playing each other, before the game you would have to run out on the field and find me and come over and tip your cap and show some respect. If you're a pitcher and I'm a hitter, and you struck me out, you'd probably have to apologize for striking me out even though it's your job."

And, like clockwork, both Matsuzaka and lefty reliever Hideki Okajima—another Red Sox rookie from Japan—came out to greet Matsui shortly before game-time, and an avalanche of photographers lined up for the "money shot," in which there were several bows and a couple of handshakes between the Japanese players.

It was easy for all regular observers of the team to see the way Matsuzaka eased his way into camp and instantly became likable to his teammates. Despite all the hype he came in with, Matsuzaka worked hard to be one of the guys, something not all that easy to do given the language barrier and the price tag he came in with. But he pulled it off, and there didn't seem to be any resentment in the clubhouse.

"He's very respectful to his teammates, he works his tail off, he's part of the team," said Tim Wakefield, the elder statesman of the Red Sox. "It's tough, coming from Japan to the United States, the culture is different. But the game is still the same and I think that's helped his adaptation over here. He's been wonderful so far, I have the utmost respect for him." Sure, players would get tired of answering the same questions about Matsuzaka to the media. But nobody ever seemed to hold it against the pitcher himself.

The first "big" event of camp came on February 24 when Matsuzaka faced batters for the first time. Not batters in an opposing uniform, but Red Sox minor leaguers in a live batting practice session. Johnny Pesky Field, named in honor of the franchise's most enthusiastic ambassador, was the site of Matsuzaka's first live pitches. It was a surreal scene, as the foul lines were surrounded by club executives such as Lucchino, Epstein, and

Shipley, the latter of whom played such a big role in the scouting and subsequent signing of the pitcher. And yes, there were media members, media members and more media members tracking each pitch. The foul territory area beyond the diamond was literally infested with observers on all sides.

To the untrained eye, it's hard to get much of a read on batting practice. Still, Matsuzaka seemed to impress the big crowd, though Shipley privately confided the next day that the pitcher didn't have his usual command of his offspeed stuff. Following the BP session, Blake inadvertently set the tone for the type of circus this had become. "Bobby Scales is now available," boomed Blake, as he motioned toward the veteran minor leaguer, who was holding court with the media in the courtyard area stationed between the clubhouse and the complex of fields. Scales was one of the hitters who dug in against Matsuzaka which, on this day, made one of the most anonymous players on the Spring Training roster a must-get for the media.

Only Francona seemed to have the power to put the event in its proper perspective. "You've got to remember, I had Michael Jordan [in the minor leagues]. And this guy can't dunk," quipped Francona. "So I have seen it." Francona managed the NBA legend during his brief—and ultimately unsuccessful—bid at trying to play Major League Baseball at Double-A Birmingham in 1994, and remembered a similar type of media frenzy. "When Michael would take batting practice, you'd hear the cameras, kind of like you do when Daisuke [pitches]," Francona said. "It's a little similar—that, and, I think, Pete Rose. Those are maybe the three who come to mind."

As the media tripped over each other during the six weeks of spring, the Red Sox matter-of-factly worked with their new pitcher on making the transition. He put in time with Jason Varitek, coming up with signs and words that would make sense to pitcher and catcher. Varitek, on game days, went so far as to tape a list of English baseball phrases translated into Japanese on to his left arm. Red Sox pitching coach John Farrell spent much of his winter learning to speak Japanese. For Matsuzaka and Okajima, there were English lessons three mornings a week. Not only was Matsuzaka trying to get a grasp of the English language, but he was trying to transition his pitching schedule from one system to another. It was as if the Red Sox were weaning him off his old program, week by week.

Even by the time the season ended, this was still something Francona, Farrell, and Matsuzaka were trying to refine. "So much of his program just went on feel," Francona said. "What we're trying to do is go with more of a program where you don't go on how your body feels but you go on a consistent program where hopefully you can get your body to feel the same and be consistent over the course of the year. That was probably our biggest fight, to not go on feel."

Japanese pitchers are legendary for the amount of pitches they throw between starts. Matsuzaka fired a 103-pitch side session one week into camp, which would have been unthinkable for any other pitcher on the team. A proud Epstein labeled it a virtual clinic, noting how Matsuzaka mimicked game situations, checking runners and working repeatedly out of the stretch. "You almost wanted to videotape it and show it to our young guys in minor league camp about how to get the most out of your practice," said Epstein.

The day before his March 6 start at Jupiter against the Marlins, Matsuzaka threw a 60-pitch side session. Again, it's highly unusual for a Major League pitcher to throw a bullpen session the day before his turn in the rotation, even during Spring Training. But these things were getting adjusted through time, as Matsuzaka needed to get prepared for pitching in a five-man rotation instead of the six-day schedule he always worked out of in Japan. Eventually, he would throw two days before his start instead of one day. "He's not throwing nearly as much as he has in the past because of the schedule of the way we do things here," said Francona. "So he's learning also. I just think our philosophy is you don't just cram something down somebody's throat. You try to learn about them as they learn about you."

The difference between Japanese baseball and the Major Leagues is enormous from a preparation standpoint. In Japan, they are almost militant, believing that a player must punish himself with a grueling training regimen to succeed. In America, players work hard, there's no doubt about it. But they do it more on their own terms and believe far more than the Japanese do in saving energy for the rigors of the long season. Without a doubt, Spring Training was far more laid back for Matsuzaka than it ever was in Japan. He tried to be as diplomatic as possible when asked about it.

"Obviously, the biggest difference is the hours spent in formal practice, there are a lot more hours spent in formal, team organized practice in Japan," Matsuzaka told Red Sox beatwriters at a luncheon in late March. "But that's not to say that the practice time here is inadequate. Rather, I prefer the way it's set up here because you have your team activities and then that gives you a lot of time to work on personal things that you might want to work on. I haven't had any problems with the Spring Training format here."

Matsuzaka, who seemed to have no problem being a young ambassador of Japanese baseball, was also trying to make a seamless transition in his new land. By his words, he was clearly trying to please both his countrymen in Japan and his new teammates in Boston. "When I talked to my friends in Japan who have seen video of us practicing during spring camp, to a man, they say, 'Wow, it looks like you guys have a lot of fun over there.' But I don't think that's to say that the environment here is more relaxed. I think it's rather that, when you look around, everybody is laughing, everybody on the field is having a great time. I think in Japan, you know, there's a little bit more tension, first of all. And the guys who are really laughing their heads off, there's usually only four or five guys at any given time. So I think that image that the whole team is having fun together really gives the impression that things are a little more relaxed."

Preparation semantics aside, from a pure pitching standpoint, Matsuzaka clearly belonged. He seemed to make it clear early that this would be no Hideki Irabu bust story. There was some comedy when his very first "game" pitch in a Red Sox uniform was belted into the left field corner for a double by a Boston College batter named Johnny Ayers. "I don't think I would have been as lucky. Definitely was just trying to take in the atmosphere a little bit and stay relaxed. Took a couple of deep breaths and hope for the best. I was looking first pitch fastball and I got it," said Ayers, almost sheepish at putting a dent in Boston's new star.

For the rest of that exhibition, which was seen by some 14 million viewers back in Japan, Matsuzaka was untouched. The rest of the exhibition outings were what they are for all established pitchers—a mixture of sincere competitiveness and constructive experimentation. Some things stood out for those who got to see the man pitch live for the first time. Matsuzaka had a very distinct delivery, in which he'd rock his hips back in forth a few times as he eased into his windup, pausing with his glove over his head before exploding into his delivery. Matsuzaka also possessed gorgeous offspeed offerings—particularly his changeup and curve. Several awkward swings per game became standard fare for a Matsuzaka outing. The young Marlins had no problem feeding the hype machine after Matsuzaka stifled them for three innings.

"I didn't see any gyroballs, but a couple of my teammates did, and they said they don't want to see it again," Marlins second baseman Dan Uggla said in all sincerity. What was more interesting than whether or not the gyroball existed was how many pitches Matsuzaka actually did possess. He had a truckload. It was such a wide variety that Jason Varitek would sometimes have to use his thumbs for signs because he literally ran out of fingers.

Matsuzaka possesses a four-seam fastball, which ranges from 92 to 95 mph. He works in a two-seamer from time to time, throwing that pitch anywhere from 90 to 92. There was also a cutter, a curve, a slider, a changeup, and a splitter. In the spring, Farrell thought the changeup could be the true difference-maker.

"To me, his changeup is what will really set him apart," Farrell said. "Just the overall arm speed and deception he creates with his changeup is phenomenal."

With all those pitches in his back pocket, not to mention a kind of aura that seemed to hover around him, the story of Daisuke Matsuzaka, steadfastly enormous in Japan, was picking up loads of steam in the United States. During March, Matsuzaka hit the trifecta of sports magazine covers. First out of the gate was the March 5 *Sporting News*, in which you could see a smirking Matsuzaka gripping a baseball, accompanied by the headline, "Secrets of the Gyroball (if it even exists) . . . Baseball's Filthy New Pitch." Up next was a casual Matsuzaka on *ESPN the Magazine*, dressed in a workout shirt, holding the baseball outward with his index finger pointed toward the viewer, as if to say, "Welcome to my World." The tease at the bottom of the page said, "The Care and Feeding of the Dice-K Monster."

Then came the true confirmation that he had arrived as an impact player in all parts of America's baseball universe. Matsuzaka was the cover boy on *Sports Illustrated*'s baseball preview issue, with a headline for Tom Verducci's in-depth feature that read, "Fever Pitch, Why Daisuke Matsuzaka Is Worthy (And What America Will Learn From Him)." As the spring drew to a close, the first signs of minor irritation developed toward the overly-probing media. Matsuzaka chose not to speak after no-hitting the Reds through five innings. You see, he was disappointed that he walked five and threw an uneconomical 104 pitches. In the clubhouse, Matsuzaka sat in front of his locker, wearing a white Nike sweatshirt and an icy look on his face. He was stewing. Anyone who walked by him could see that. Reds PR staff had worked overtime to build a makeshift podium in the outskirts of the stadium to accommodate the Japanese media, and thanks to Matsuzaka's rare silence, it never got used.

With only a brief written explanation from Matsuzaka, the media peppered Francona in a post-game dugout sitdown. The manager, weary as it was from the dog days of spring, wasn't amused. "Again, he doesn't have the right to have Spring Training because of every camera and all you guys. You guys are going to drive me nuts. This is a Spring Training game in Sarasota. You guys are going to make this hard. Let's just ease off. Now I know why he didn't want to talk to you guys, I don't blame him."

Overall, though, Francona was the epitome of a good sport with the never-ending inquiries regarding his new pitcher. There were some playful moments with the Japanese media. One reporter said to Francona, "You said recently that Daisuke is very engaging. When did you first pick up on that?" "When he engaged me," quipped the manager, before going into a more serious answer. Slowly but surely, barriers were breaking. Later that week, on the suggestion of Blake, Matsuzaka and Hideki Okajima had lunch at a Fort Myers country club with ten members of the Boston media. It was a roundtable type session that also included two interpreters and Blake. For the first time, the Red Sox beat writers were able to get to know Matsuzaka a bit in an informal setting, away from all the stress of the workplace. The pitchers shook hands with the writers and exchanged pleasantries in English.

"Hi, nice to meet you," said Matsuzaka, who then asked the waitress for "Iced tea, please." For two men who had just integrated into an entirely new culture, their assimilation appeared to be going rather smoothly. Never did the lightheartedness of Matsuzaka's personality show more than when between bites of his chicken wrap, he did a mock impersonation of former Sox ace Pedro Martinez taking down Don Zimmer in the infamous melee that happened during Game 3 of the 2003 American League Championship Series. Matsuzaka was having so much fun that he forgot the wooden table was below him, and upon his follow-through of the Pedro takedown, Matsuzaka's right arm slammed against the table. Perhaps he hit his funny bone. Without a doubt, the moment created laughter for the lunch party.

The questions from the Boston media ran the gamut. What do you do for fun in Fort Myers? What kind of music and movies do you listen to? Who is your favorite American sex symbol?

That last one, which could have been an embarrassing question, was deftly handled by Matsuzaka. "They're all so pretty, I can't really pick just one. It's hard for me to pick just one. They're all very, very pretty." Then, out of the blue, Matsuzaka picked one of his favorites. "Angelina Jolie, obviously she's very pretty but there's an aura about her. She also has a strength and poise that I find attractive." Who could argue? None of the men seated at the table did, that's for sure.

The lunch seemed to serve its purpose, with the media feeling as if it had caught a candid glimpse of the man they were set to cover like glue for the next six months, or better yet, six years. As long as Spring Training can feel, the interest in Matsuzaka never seemed to hit any kind of lull. It felt like March was one big media event for the Red Sox. On the last day of camp, Epstein was asked how many interview requests he had from Japanese media members. "When we go upstairs I can tell you almost exactly because I get a bottle of sake for every one. Just count the bottles of sake," said the GM, referring to the Japanese custom of providing gifts as a way of showing respect and/or gratitude.

Predictions for Matsuzaka became a rite of passage in Spring Training. "It's going to be a tough season to be frank," said Takashi Settai, a staff writer for *Nikkei*. "He's never done the five-day rotation before. Nobody knows whether he'll get through it or get injured." Japanese TV crews interviewed countless American reporters for their take. The safe number seemed to be 15 wins. Nobody seemed to go too far below or above that number. Perhaps Matsuzaka would make that number seem conservative—or optimistic—by the time his rookie season ended. Everyone sure was fascinated to find out. After six long weeks in Florida, it was time for the Matsuzaka dress rehearsal to give way to the Opening Act, which, of course, would last all year long.

8

Grand Openings 1 and 2
(April 5–17, 2007)

OF ALL PLACES FOR the Red Sox to ring in the Matsuzaka era, they ventured to Kansas City—hardly a hotbed of baseball the last fifteen years. But the media arrived in droves—approximately 220—making up the biggest pack of reporters to show up at Kauffman Stadium since the 1985 World Series. "You guys are going to eat a lot of box lunches this year," Royals PR man Mike Swanson said to a Red Sox beat reporter on the eve of Matsuzaka's debut, which would come in Game 3 of the season. Typically, the cold cut sandwiches packaged in boxes with a bag of chips only become in vogue during October, when the amount of media outweighs the manpower in the press kitchen. But just as Swanson alluded to, box lunches were the meal du jour for the first three games in KC.

"I can't have my people washing dishes all night," said the lighthearted Swanson. Matsuzaka, meanwhile, was simply hoping to feast on the Royals on raw, frigid Thursday, April 5 in Kansas City for the finale of a three-game series. The teams had split the first two games, with Sox ace Curt Schilling getting rocked in the opener and Josh Beckett—who would swiftly supplant Schilling as the team's No. 1 starter—pitching Boston to victory in the second game. Francona tried to quell the media concerns about the way the weather would impact Matsuzaka's first game. "Their mountains have snow, right? He must have pitched in some cold at some point," Francona said.

True enough, but what Francona didn't say was that all of Matsuzaka's home starts for the Seibu Lions took place under the controlled climate of a dome. The worry with pitchers in cold weather is that they'll lose command of their offspeed stuff, since those offerings rely on such touch and feel. Perhaps the adrenaline of the day rendered the weather irrelevant for Matsuzaka. Or maybe he's just that good. Let the record show that the first Major League batter he faced—David DeJesus—poked a single up the middle on the third pitch. It was eerily similar to the way things began against Boston College and Johnny Ayers some five weeks earlier. But even more resounding this time was the way Matsuzaka responded. The Royals were pretty much unheard from the rest of the day. DeJesus did go deep in the sixth, accounting for the only run Matsuzaka allowed in an electric showing which included 10 strikeouts. It was the first time in five years that any Major League pitcher had registered double-digit K's in a debut. The Red Sox won the game by a score of 4-1.

Sox designated hitter David Ortiz, as beloved a figure as any player who has ever worn the Boston uniform, found himself awed by the television as he enjoyed the warmth of the clubhouse between at-bats. "He reminds me of Pedro [Martinez] when he's pitching," said Ortiz. "He has total control of the game when he's out there, you know what I mean? I don't know how he does it. There might be some Japanese drink. I'm going to try to talk to him to see if he can get me some of that. When you watch him on TV, it's like a Nintendo game. He's got pitches that . . . they just disappear when they get to the plate. Nasty." For Ortiz to even mention Matsuzaka in the same sentence as Martinez said volumes. For Martinez, a certain Hall of Famer once he is eligible, is like a big brother to Ortiz. Some three years after Martinez had left the Red Sox to play for the Mets, Ortiz still had a photo taped to his locker at Fenway of the two of them celebrating during a game. So, clearly, Ortiz wouldn't make such a lofty comparison lightly.

Red Sox chairman Tom Werner watched the game from his office in Southern California and did his best to temper his excitement. "Again, you temper all these things. I was saying to people, 'Please don't put the pressure on him.' I was pleased, but it wasn't like, this guy is Tom Seaver." Werner had other things on his mind as the day wore on, as he was involved in a serious car accident that left his vehicle totaled and his nerves still a little shaken even more than a month later. "I'm glad I have side impact airbags," Werner said. There was no opening crash for Matsuzaka. Owner John W. Henry, who has a boyish passion for baseball, was in Kansas City for the spectacle. "Incredibly exciting," Henry reflected six weeks later. "Every time he pitches, it is an event throughout Red Sox Nation and Japan."

For the third member of Boston's ownership trio, energetic and intense club president/CEO Larry Lucchino, the moment reminded him of yet another big moment in his career as a baseball executive. "When we opened Camden Yards in 1992, [architect] Janet-Marie Smith and I embraced each other right after the game and said, 'It plays, it plays, it plays well,' because it was a 2-0 score and it was a two hour and two minute game," said Lucchino. "I sort of had the same reaction with this. It was like, 'He really can pitch.'"

And yes, in case you were wondering, they were watching in Japan. Oh, were they watching in Japan. Peter Grilli, president of the Japan Society of Boston, was in Tokyo on business when that Dice-K debut began at 3 a.m. Japan time. It would have been interesting to count the total amount of sand in the eyes of Japanese businessmen and women later that day. "I got up and watched it and I had a whole bunch of business meetings the next day, the next morning," said Grilli. "Everyone was sort of rubbing their eyes and yawning all day long. It's amazing. I think half the country watched it."

Back in Red Sox Nation, at least a small level of anxiety was lifted for those who went so far—literally in some cases in terms of travel miles—and invested so much to bring Matsuzaka to

Boston. "It was an organization-wide effort to get this guy," noted Epstein. "We put a lot on the line, but this is really just the beginning. It's always great to watch a pitcher who has a lot of different weapons." And then, there are the grinders behind-the-scenes who never get all the credit they deserve for making these types of acquisitions possible. In a classy gesture, Francona after the game credited the two executives—Craig Shipley and Jon Deeble—who had spent more time monitoring Matsuzaka up close than anyone else in the organization. "It's easy for us to take our bows today. But I think Ship and Deebs, I wish I could show you the scouting report, because what they wrote down was pretty true. That's a pretty neat day for them. I hope they share in the fun of this day."

Now that they had really seen it up close, the players seemed more willing to buy into the hype they had been hearing about for so many weeks. "That's why we outbid everybody," said third baseman Mike Lowell, who is generally the most insightful quote in the Boston clubhouse. "That's why we paid a lot of money for him. I don't think this organization bid money on a hope." The Royals didn't much care about hope or hype. They were just glad to get Matsuzaka and the Red Sox out of town so they could go back to being the small-market, under-the-radar team that had marked their recent history.

"I'm just happy it's over and they're out of town," Royals outfielder Mark Teahen told the *Boston Globe*. "I'm just happy we're getting back to two or three reporters and back to the quiet that we have here. It was quite a thing the past few days."

A blogger—who also doubles as one of the most clutch pitchers of his era—was more than happy to give his thoughts just hours after Matsuzaka completed step one of many. "Daisuke. Wow," Curt Schilling wrote on 38pitches.com, a forum that had become the ace's therapeutic platform for his unfiltered thoughts. "I can't say I was surprised, but it was fun as hell to watch. The kid can flat out pitch and the line score he trotted out was even more impressive when you factor in he wasn't as sharp as he can be. The one word that continues to come to mind every time I see him is poise.

"Regardless of the 'pressure' the media thinks he has on him, I don't think anyone will ever exceed the expectations he has for himself. His track record speaks for itself. In the biggest games of his life, he's pitched his best. That takes different makeup, and a confidence level you can't fake." Of course, being one of those people himself, Schilling knew of what he was speaking. He tried his best to convey encouragement to his fellow pitcher, which he later recapped on his well-read blog. "The only two things I could muster up in Japanese today were 'Ten-o-sheen-day' (that's how I pronounce it, not how it's spelled), which means 'have fun' and 'Yokoo Yatta' or 'eeyo' which means 'good job.' Obviously I got to say the second one often, he was lights out today," recapped Schilling, who produced more words on some days than the sportswriters who were paid to produce copy.

There was one person inside the confines of Kauffman Stadium who seemed to have little in the way of adjectives or awe. That, of course, would be one Daisuke Matsuzaka. In fact, from an emotional standpoint, it didn't stand up to his crowning moment in high school. "I'm having a hard time responding to your question because it was really such a normal day for me," Matsuzaka said. "I think when I look back, my first start at Koshien, there was definitely something emotional about that day. As for today, it's a day I've been waiting for for a very long time, but even given that fact, it felt surprisingly normal." The Red Sox certainly weren't going to complain about normalcy if it was going to include 10 K's and one run allowed.

With hyped Opening 1 out of the way, it was now time for hyped Opening 2. First, there was an uneventful series in Texas, in which the Red Sox lost two out of three to come home at .500 over the first six games. For maybe the first time in team history, the second home game of the season was far more anticipated than the first. By the time the Old Towne Team got back to Boston for the Fenway opener, everyone just wanted to get it out of the way so the Matsuzaka-Ichiro showdown could unfold the next day. In fact, the highlight of the day probably came in the introductions, when Matsuzaka trotted out to the baseline during pre-game introductions and was given a rousing ovation. That only whet the appetite even more for the next night, when he would actually take the mound in the city that had been abuzz over his arrival for months.

So after summarily thumping the Mariners behind Beckett on a sunny Tuesday afternoon, the stage was set for Matsuzaka's Fenway first. Often times, the quotes of Japanese players seem to be watered down by translation by the time they get to English newsprint. But every now and then, you get a true gem like the one Ichiro reeled off to a bilingual freelancer for the *Seattle Times*. "I hope he arouses the fire that's dormant in the innermost recesses of my soul," said Ichiro. "I plan to face him with the zeal of a challenger." Talk about a stage-setter. The refrain of Kevin Millar and the Red Sox for one memorable summer of 2003 at Fenway was "Cowboy Up!" Judging by Ichiro's quote, perhaps now it was "Samurai Up!"

Fenway was in a zany, October-like frenzy for this one, with the club doling out 350 media credentials. To accommodate all of their new friends from the Japanese media, the Red Sox worked tirelessly on expanding their press box, knocking down walls to create a state-of-the-art workroom that included plasma televisions and plenty of work space for those who couldn't fit into the main box, which had also been spruced up with better sightlines for those in the back rows. At 7:08 p.m. ET on this Wednesday night in April, Matsuzaka strode to the mound. There was still daylight, but the flashbulbs created a strange symmetry. The Boston skyline stood out amid the blue sky. It was hard not to notice the Dunkin Donuts sign atop the bleachers in right field with Japanese letters that translated to, "Welcome to Fenway Park." As Matsuzaka completed his warm-ups and got ready to face the Mariners—naturally Ichiro would be the first hitter he faced from the Fenway slab—a spontaneous buzz filled the Fenway air, with roars of anticipation. "A magical moment," said Henry.

And then came the blinding lights. Amid the recent advent of camera cell phones and easy to carry digital cameras, Joe Fan could chronicle everything with a mere click. As Matsuzaka's first Fenway offering—a crisp curveball—came bending in at 7:11 p.m., a virtual light storm unfolded. The pitch was a called strike. Somehow, Varitek saw it into his mitt despite the glare. "Of course I noticed [the bulbs] and it wasn't easy to throw with all the flashbulbs going off but I'm glad I got a strike," said Matsuzaka, showing yet another example of his ability to zone in despite the chaos around him.

Mike Lowell and Kevin Youkilis hovered from their corner positions at third and first, respectively, and had a rare request from within that went something like this: Don't hit that baseball at me, particularly with any type of authority. The snapshots were all well and good for the camera-toting fans. But for those who are paid to react instinctually to the sometimes lightning-quick speed of a baseball, this was far from conducive. The flashes never stopped during that first at-bat with Ichiro, which finally concluded with a quick hopper back to the box that Matsuzaka pounced on before throwing out his fellow countryman at first. Deep exhales came from the infielders.

"Oh yeah, I could feel the flashbulbs too," said Lowell. "I didn't want Ichiro to hit me a ball because I wouldn't be able to see the damn ball. I mean, there were so many bulbs going off. I said, hopefully he hits a ground ball because if it's right at me, I'm going to be seeing stars." In fact, that was what all the media and fans had come to see—two of the great stars from Japan.

Some 3,000 miles to the West, Rockies second baseman Kazuo Matsui, who played behind Matsuzaka for five years with the Seibu Lions, literally stood still for a few moments during his preparation for a game at Los Angeles to take in the Ichiro-Matsuzaka showdown from a clubhouse television. "Turn it up," Matsui, who doesn't speak much English, instructed. Wrote Thomas Harding of MLB.com, who surveyed the scene: "Matsui hung on every pitch, talking with teammate Willy Taveras as the count ran full before Suzuki grounded to the pitcher's mound. It was a rare matchup of Japanese sensations."

As with all hyped events, the storylines can change. The story of this memorable night involved a blossoming pitcher from Venezuela named Felix Hernandez. For a couple of years, baseball was abuzz that this man was going to emerge into a franchise pitcher. In fact, Epstein, during his brief sabbatical from the Red Sox, said at a January 2006 charity round-table that if he had to start a team with one player, it would be Hernandez.

The example of why came fast and furious on this night fifteen months later as Hernandez somehow moved the Matsuzaka-Ichiro showdown to sideshow status. Hernandez no-hit the Red Sox for seven innings and only J. D. Drew's single up the middle in the eighth prevented him from entering the history books. His complete-game, 1-hit gem lifted Seattle to a 3-0 victory that hardly dampened the enthusiasm of the night. As much as the Red Sox and their fans wanted a win, it was hard not to marvel at the pure brilliance of Hernandez. Matsuzaka wasn't so bad either, giving up eight hits and three runs over seven innings, striking out four. For April, the drama could not have been any higher. Matsuzaka got the best of his countryman this time, sending him down four times, including a pair of K's.

Matsuzaka had the utmost respect for Ichiro from their many showdowns in Japan—the *Boston Globe* highlighted each one of them in a graphic in the paper that morning—and the two had bonded while playing together and winning the gold medal in the 2006 World Baseball Classic. Ichiro could have become a free agent following the 2007 season, but instead would sign a mammoth extension by July. Early in the 2007 season, there was some buzz about the possibility Ichiro and Matsuzaka could become teammates in Boston a year later. Though Matsuzaka had made Ichiro look bad in a number of at-bats over the years, it was clear the reverence he held for the already entrenched Major League hit machine.

"I had the opportunity to play on the same team with Ichiro for the first time ever during the WBC," Matsuzaka said during Spring Training. "By being on the same team with Ichiro-san, I felt his greatness and his ability and also his reliability. I felt his greatness directly through that experience. If I could be on the same team with him, there would be nobody I could count on more."

It was hard for any Japanese player not to think the world of Ichiro, who was a trailblazer in America for Japanese position players much like Hideo Nomo was for pitchers. In Ichiro's first Major League season of 2001, all he did was win the American League's Rookie of the Year and Most Valuable Player awards, becoming the first player to win both awards in one year since Boston's Fred Lynn back in 1975.

Putting aside the Ichiro angle and the Hernandez gem, this was still a crucial night for Matsuzaka. Finally he had landed in this historic baseball town. And unlike Kansas City, when his emotions were hardly palpable, this was clearly a meaningful night in his life. "With the great welcome I received from the fans here being at home, I got the sense early on that I'd finally arrived here in Boston," said Matsuzaka. "So at the very beginning, my psychological state may have been different, a little bit heightened compared to usual, but I wouldn't say that was a bad thing."

Matsuzaka would have made his next start in the annual Marathon Day game at Fenway five days later, but two rainouts changed that schedule and moved him to Toronto the night of April 17. It was a move that didn't sit well with at least one member of the Japanese media, who had planned his time accordingly to be at Fenway, but could not change things at the last minute to go to Toronto. "Geeeeezzzzzzzz," said the outraged writer in the middle of the press conference at which Francona had announced the switch. In unison, Francona and PR man John Blake admonished the writer, explaining to him that his behavior was inappropriate.

After all the pomp and circumstance of the first two outings, Canada felt a lot more like normalcy. Matsuzaka's fastball exploded over the first three innings, as he struck out four
and allowed just one hit. But then came his first Major League
meltdown. Matsuzaka simply lost it in the fourth, giving up two
hits, three walks and two runs while throwing a 38-pitch inning.
Almost magically, he reverted right back to the dominant form
of the early innings for his final two frames—the fifth and sixth.
"It was like he had temporary amnesia for a couple of minutes,"
said Francona. In a way, what occurred that night in Toronto was
a sign of some of the inconsistency Matsuzaka would have in his
first season with the Red Sox.

One thing that stood out was Matsuzaka rushing his delivery with men on base. He also conceded he was trying to be too
fine against Frank Thomas, the future Hall of Famer who drew
a walk. And when Matsuzaka walked Greg Zaun with the bases
loaded, he showed the first outward display of emotion in his
Major League career, waving his right hand in disgust. Perhaps
finally, some of the adjustments were starting to weigh on a man
who had been so unflappable for most of his baseball life. But he
was now pitching at the highest level of the world, and it wasn't
going to come easy. Next on Matsuzaka's calendar would be Boston's ancient rivals, the Yankees. Fair or unfair, all Red Sox players are measured by their performance against their counterparts
from the Bronx. In other words, the scrutiny would be back at
full throttle by the time Matsuzaka took the ball at Fenway for a
Sunday night game televised nationwide on ESPN no less.

9

Rivalry Initiation, Growing Pains
(April 20–May 9, 2007)

To ANYONE WHO HAS never been to Fenway Park for a Red Sox-Yankees game—be it April or October—the atmosphere is strikingly different than when any other opponent is in town. The fans are revved up, the media is maxed out and the players can't help but feel that extra voltage of electricity. Red Sox-Yankees is deep in the blood of fans on both sides. In Japan, the Yomiuri Giants and Hanshin Tigers also have a boiling rivalry, with the Giants considered to be the Japanese equivalent to the Yankees and the Tigers often compared to the Red Sox. But could that rivalry possibly have all the historic subplots as this one?

Just consider the various angles that make up the rich backdrop. There was the sale of Babe Ruth from the Red Sox to the Yankees following the 1919 season, which then led to one team going 86 years without a championship and the other becoming a dynasty many times over. The 1940s and 50s brought the classic Ted Williams vs. Joe DiMaggio—who was better?—debates. There was the hostility of the 1970s, when the players on both sides hated each other. The Bucky Dent homer in the one-game playoff of 1978 became so painful to Red Sox fans that they actually gave the light-hitting shortstop the letter *F* as a middle initial (use your imagination and you can come up with what it stands for). There was pure rejuvenation that took the rivalry to another level in 2003, with blood boiling so high in Game 3 of that ALCS that bench coach Don Zimmer ran to the Boston side of the field to charge Pedro Martinez, who had no choice but to toss the old man down. And there was the Red Sox collapse in Game 7 of that same ALCS, which would have created a permanent F in Aaron Boone's middle name if not for Boston's epic and historic comeback from 3-0 down against New York in the '04 ALCS.

There's always something with these teams, and this was Matsuzaka's first taste of it. He was able to watch comfortably from the dugout as the Sox produced exciting wins over their archrivals in the first two games of the series. In fact, it was Oka-jima who stole the show in the first two games, twice coming on to get pivotal outs against the teeth of the Yankees' batting order. The Friday night opener was sure to have a special place in the 2007 Red Sox highlight video. After the Sox had rallied all the way back from a 6-2 deficit against the great Mariano Rivera in a furious eighth inning rally, it was Okajima and not closer Jonathan Papelbon who came on for the ninth. Papelbon, who had developed arm problems the previous September, was being protected after pitching the last two days. So on came Okajima, who retired a ridiculously hot Alex Rodriguez (12 homers in the first 15 games of the season), among others for his first Major League save.

There is no quicker way to a Sox fan's heart than having success against the Yankees, and it was then that Okajima made his first mark in Boston during an April in which he, and not Matsuzaka, would be named the American League's Rookie of the Month. An antsy Matsuzaka had to wait around for his turn until finally getting it in that prime time Sunday ESPN show-down against an emergency starter named Chase Wright. At this point of the season, the Yankees' pitching rotation was depleted, almost beyond recognition. The matchup was so heavily in favor of Matsuzaka, who gave Sox fans no reason to doubt him at that point of the season, that fans were tempted to bring broomsticks to Fenway instead of scorebooks. The stage seemed perfectly set for Matsuzaka's first big Yankees moment. And then, like so many other preconceived sporting scripts, the night took an entirely different turn. After retiring the first two batters, Matsuzaka didn't have it in the first. He walked Bobby Abreu and then hit Alex Rodriguez on the shoulder blade. Matsuzaka did a nice job following the advice of teammate Julian Tavarez, who sidled up to his Japanese teammate during the late stages of Friday's win and told him that the way to get A-Rod is to pound the inside part of the plate.

Despite the adverse situation it put his team in, the plunking of A-Rod did nothing to diminish Matsuzaka's popularity rating throughout Red Sox Nation. To be kind, Red Sox fans despise the sight of A-Rod. This, after fawning over the prospect of his arrival in December 2003, only to see the union stand in the way of a mega-swap between Hall of Famers that would have sent Manny Ramirez to the Rangers. The Red Sox wanted to restructure Rodriguez's mammoth contract and the union blocked the move. Naturally A-Rod went to the Yankees instead and was part of the epic collapse against the Red Sox in the 2004 American League Championship Series. Matsuzaka did not share the loathing of A-Rod. In fact, in a somewhat awkward moment, Matsuzaka slightly tipped his cap to A-Rod after hitting him. It was an obvious sign of respect, and highly common in Japan when a pitcher hits a batter. Consider the way Warren Cromartie, who had played in Japan after a successful career in the Major Leagues, excused himself for punching a player after being hit by a pitch. "I had to do it," Cromartie said in Robert Whiting's wonderful book on Japanese baseball titled *You Gotta Have Wa*. "The guy didn't tip his hat, the way Japanese are supposed to."

But in the macho world of the Major Leagues, apologizing for something that occurs in the line of duty is to show a sign of weakness. Matsuzaka later confided to Japanese media members how torn he was about whether to tip the cap. Interestingly, Matsuzaka offered no tip of the cap later in the game when he drilled Derek Jeter. "A-Rod and I have the same agent," joked

Matsuzaka to a couple of Japanese reporters he trusted. But Scott Boras notwithstanding, you could be pretty sure Matsuzaka would not take his cap off the next time Rodriguez was hit. In fact, that moment came in August, and Matsuzaka kept his hat on his head. But this was one of those strange moments when Matsuzaka seemingly forgot about the new world he was in. He made it clear that if he could press the rewind button, he would have handled the move in a more Americanized fashion. A bigger problem than the etiquette issue was that the Yankees had gotten early baserunners and took a 3-0 lead on Matsuzaka and the Sox.

Nobody could have known what was coming in the bottom of that third. Certainly not Matsuzaka, who watched in sheer awe as his teammates put a surge of emotion through Fenway Park by belting a record-tying four home runs in succession off a shellshocked Wright. First came Manny Ramirez, who hit a laser deep into the Fenway night and onto the street beyond the Green Monster. Then it was J. D. Drew striking a liner over the Boston bullpen in right-center. Lowell made it a trifecta by belting one over the wall in left and Varitek completed the madness with a Monster mash of his own. For Matsuzaka, who became so accustomed to the Small Ball style of Japan, this was something to behold. "Of course in Japan I have never seen nor heard of such a thing taking place," Matsuzaka said after the game. It wasn't exactly run of the mill stuff in the Major Leagues either, where the Red Sox became just the fifth team in history to pull off such a quartet. As thrilled as Matsuzaka was to watch it unfold, it didn't help his pitching any. In fact, he looked strikingly ordinary for the first time in his brief time with the Red Sox. The Yankees came back for single runs against Matsuzaka in the fifth and sixth to reclaim the lead, and only a three-run rally by the Red Sox in the bottom of the seventh enabled Matsuzaka to earn a win on a night he gave up five runs.

The consensus in the aftermath was that it was just one of those rare nights that can happen to any elite pitcher over the course of a season when the stuff just isn't there. It happened to the great Curt Schilling on Opening Day. At least at this moment, there was no reason to suspect Matsuzaka was about to slip into a mini-slump. But five days later, Matsuzaka again took the ball against the Yankees, this time in New York at fabled Yankee Stadium, and he was again less than the superstar everyone expected him to be.

Contrary to popular belief, April 27, 2007 was not the first time Matsuzaka had set foot in the legendary baseball yard known as Yankee Stadium. Flash back to eight years earlier when Matsuzaka, fresh off his first professional season in Japan, ventured to America during late October and got a taste of the Major Leagues on its biggest stage. He attended Game 2 of the Yankees-Braves World Series in Atlanta, then set foot in the Bronx for Games 3 and 4. Matsuzaka saw the Yankees sweep that Fall Classic, and perhaps a seed was planted during that October visit. There are plenty of people in Japan who suspected that it was Matsuzaka's goal to wear pinstripes. Matsuzaka wittily diffused that notion when asked about it at his Spring Training luncheon with Red Sox beatwriters. "I think rather than saying that I was a fan of the team, I had something for pinstripes as a uniform. Even teams in Japan, whether it was high schools or whatever, and when I first joined the Japanese National team, at the time, our uniform had vertical pinstripes too. From that moment on, I just had a thing for vertical stripes. That being said, I don't really like the Hanshin Tigers."

Like any player who suits up for the Red Sox, it probably wouldn't be long before he flat-out didn't like the Yankees either. It's just sort of a natural progression. Perhaps Matsuzaka was awed at the majesty of pitching on the mound at Yankee Stadium. Much like his Toronto start ten days earlier, it all fell apart for Matsuzaka in the fourth inning as he gave back a 2-0 lead. Shockingly, he walked the first three batters of the inning—the imposing trio of A-Rod, Jason Giambi and countryman Matsui. It was here, with the bases juiced and nobody out, that Matsuzaka felt

Yankee Stadium rock just like he did during the World Series he attended eight years later. Only this time, he was on the mound, not in the stands. This time, the buzz was deafening instead of intoxicating. The roar of the Yankee faithful is a rhythmic sensation unique unto itself. It has contributed to the demise of many an opposing team or pitcher over the years, and Matsuzaka was feeling it head on.

"In the fourth inning when I found myself in a little bit of trouble, I heard the massive ovation for the Yankees from the stands," said Matsuzaka. "And of all the cheers I've experienced in my career, it was probably one of the loudest I've experienced. That being said, I don't think it had too much of an effect on my pitching or my composure." Matsuzaka didn't become unnerved by any means. He had simply put himself in an impossible situation. That's where a bloop will do you in, and Jorge Posada's fell right in front of a sliding Manny Ramirez to bring a run home. Matsuzaka nearly rescued himself with just the one run, striking out Robinson Cano and getting Doug Mientkiewicz on a popup to third. But Johnny Damon, as he had done so many times for the Red Sox, found a way to put the ball in play. His half swing landed the baseball right into short right field to bring home two more. Derek Jeter applied some more heat by slapping a single to right and it was 4-2.

"If I got into all the things that happened in the fourth inning, that would be a very long story and it would sound like a lot of excuses," Matsuzaka said to a packed room of scribes from Boston, New York and Japan. "To keep a long story short, I'll just say that there's a few things technically that I still need to work on."

Just when it seemed Matsuzaka was falling apart, he got it all back together. He was unscored on the rest of the night and exited following six innings and 117 pitches. How could he be so dominant in some innings and so ordinary in others? The pitcher, the team and the opponents were all trying to figure it out. The Red Sox did what they do, thumping Andy Pettitte around a little bit and eventually winning by a margin of 11-4. Matsuzaka got the win—his second in a row over the Yankees—but it didn't really feel like it. He had come over with such fanfare that he wasn't just expected to win, but also to pitch brilliantly. He wasn't doing that, and the weight was getting to him. A perfectionist to the highest degree, he wasn't giving in. There was growing sentiment that he was trying to be too fine, as if not to disappoint his expectant following.

"When we've given him an early lead, I think there's a tendency for him to be over-cautious and work too hard to protect that lead," said John Farrell. "What I mean by working too hard is that he thinks and delivers every pitch so it has to be perfect, or just to exact locations. When you pitch too fine and work too hard, inevitably you're going to run in deep counts, you're going to fall behind in counts. To me, he just needs to continue to trust his stuff with more general location rather than just trying to be so specific. He's got tremendous stuff and multiple weapons to attack hitters."

The adjustment to this new world wasn't small, be it the size and slickness of the baseball, the feel of the mound, or the prowess of the opposition. In a telling sign of what he was going through, Matsuzaka warned that his struggles might continue. "The sort of pitching you saw today might be what you see for a few more starts as I get used to the opposing lineups," he said. "But that being said, it's the type of pitching I would like to avoid." But there was no avoidance at Fenway six days later. It was that night—May 3 in a make-up game against the Mariners—the man with the $103.1 million price tag hit rock-bottom. To be kind, he had nothing. Fans had barely sat down after the national anthem and Matsuzaka had walked the game's first three batters. After finally getting his first out, he hit Richie Sexson. The Mariners then started treating Matsuzaka like a batting practice pitcher, belting him around for five runs before the Red Sox had taken their first at-bat. In fact, the inning came a few feet from going from sheer disappointment to utter disaster. With two on and two outs, Ichiro, taking his second at-bat of the inning, laced one to deep center that Coco Crisp hauled in right in front of the wall. Mercifully, Matsuzaka's worst inning as a Major Leaguer was over.

Somehow, the Red Sox went on to win the slugfest of a contest by a score of 8-7. Matsuzaka (five innings, five hits, five walks, seven runs) was not involved in the decision, yet he was decidedly angry—with himself. There was a coldness in his eyes during his post-game press conference that hadn't been seen following his other starts. Usually, there was a lightheartedness with Matsuzaka. A smile that sort of gleamed amid the bright camera lights. Not this time. The first inning meltdown? "I wonder," Matsuzaka said glumly. "I don't know what really happened myself."

After the game, the Red Sox were in hurry-up mode, packing their bags and getting ready to take the bus to the airport for a flight to Minneapolis. Rest assured that Matsuzaka, his ERA having ballooned up to 5.45, was not singing in the shower following the abysmal performance. "He was a less than happy human being after his last start which was interesting to see," Curt Schilling told his faithful listeners on WEEI-850 AM a few days later in his weekly spot. "It's always nice to see a new teammate when he snaps for that first time. You get a feel for the competitor that he is and he had a pretty good one." Host John Dennis asked if any food hit the floor. "A lot of things hit the floor," said Schilling. But Matsuzaka knew that anger wasn't going to fix all that ailed him. In Japan, discipline is what athletes go to in good times and in bad, and Matsuzaka knew that he would work his way through it.

It was part of Matsuzaka's deep approach to success that kept the Red Sox confident even during his deepest of struggles. For it was Lucchino who during Matsuzaka's December introduction at Fenway urged fans to view Matsuzaka as a long-term acquisition who shouldn't be judged on his rookie year. Months later, the president/CEO of the Sox explained his thinking.

"I do think that we're all so influenced by the Japanese long term mentality as we spent time in Japan, talked about Japanese culture, talked about the Japanese players' perspective, it brought out this longer term perspective that came to the surface and I wanted to communicate that to people because I thought it was right, I still think it's right," said Lucchino. "I think this is a major transition into a major new league and there are a whole lot of things that could go wrong. Knock on wood, many of them haven't happened yet. It struck me that controlling expectations, given the overwhelming response to the deal, to the signing, to the negotiations, was a prudent thing to do."

Though Matsuzaka never used the new baseball as an excuse in any of his dealings with the American media, there were Japanese reporters who became aware through conversations with the pitcher that he was having a hard time controlling his slider. In Japan, the slider was a money pitch for Matsuzaka, but he was losing confidence in it fast in the United States. But Matsuzaka wasn't one to throw his hands up. He just kept working at it. There was a mammoth, 109-pitch side session over the weekend in Minneapolis in which Matsuzaka and Farrell poured through the checklist with a thirst to fix the glitches. "The one thing that we tried to stress to him is that he doesn't have to be perfect with every pitch, even if he does miss a little bit with his target, he still has a chance to get some people out," said Farrell.

And there was also an alteration to his training program. Matsuzaka would lighten up on the weights and go heavy on cardio. "There was a pretty sizeable adjustment made with all that and I can empathize with a pitcher who hadn't lifted much upper body weight in the past and all of a sudden he's involved in it, it's going to cause some difference to the way he feels to generate rhythm, particularly with his offspeed pitches," Farrell said. "Again, this was all part of the educational process back and forth. This is what we do for these reasons and at the same time, we want to make sure he feels comfortable and confident because his performance and production is what matters most."

Back in Toronto for the second time in less than three weeks, Matsuzaka took the field at Rogers Centre more than four hours before he would actually throw his first pitch. There he was in the middle of a near empty stadium, sprinting. There he was, playing catch for twenty-five minutes. To the members of the Japanese media, this wasn't out of the ordinary. For American reporters, who are used to seeing Major League pitchers stick within the confines of the clubhouse for the most part in the pre-game hours of a start, it was enlightening.

All the time Matsuzaka had spent trying to climb out of his slump paid dividends. Under the roof of Rogers Centre, the aura was back. There were eight strikeouts, just one run allowed and a 9-3 win for Matsuzaka and the Red Sox. Aside from the modification to his training, Matsuzaka noted that he had loosened the grip on his splitter, and it was a pitch that dove against the Jays, causing several swings and misses. But perhaps hardened by the lumps he had taken during his three-start slump, Matsuzaka was guardedly optimistic about where things would go from here. "I made a few technical adjustments heading into the game today and I think it's too early to tell if that made all of the difference," Matsuzaka said. "I do hope that with small, incremental changes, this will lead to gradual improvement over time."

October 27, 2007 — Matsuzaka picks Game 3 of the World Series to produce his best start of the postseason, helping the Red Sox to an eventual sweep of the Colorado Rockies. Photo by Phoebe Sexton/Boston Red Sox

December 14, 2006–Matsuzaka throws his first pitch at Fenway Park at an introductory press conference. Owner John W. Henry fell down trying to catch it. Photo by Brita Meng Outzen

December 14, 2006 — Matsuzaka unveils his new jersey at an introductory press conference at Fenway, flanked by Red Sox owner John W. Henry, general manager Theo Epstein, chairman Tom Werner, and president/CEO Larry Lucchino. Photo by Brita Meng Outzen

February 20, 2007 — Matsuzaka grins as he catches a line drive during pitcher's fielding practice in the early weeks of Spring Training. Photo by Brita Meng Outzen

February 20, 2007 — Matsuzaka takes time to sign some autographs during Spring Training.
Photo by Brita Meng Outzen

March 12, 2007 — Matsuzaka and teammate Hideki Okajima are reunited with Yankees outfielder Hideki Matsui prior to the Red Sox-Yankees exhibition game.
Photo by Brita Meng Outzen

April 10, 2007 —
Matsuzaka gets a big
ovation during pre-game
introductions of the
Fenway Park season
opener against the
Mariners.
Photo by
Brita Meng Outzen

March 27, 2007 — Tim Wakefield passes time in Spring Training by trying to teach
Matsuzaka how to throw a knuckleball.
Photo by Brita Meng Outzen

June 16, 2007 — Matsuzaka beats Barry Bonds and the Giants, 1-0, at Fenway Park.
Photo by Brita Meng Outzen

October 5, 2007 — Matsuzaka comes out flat in his first postseason start against the Angels, and pitching coach John Farrell tries to pep him up. The Red Sox went on to win the game on a walkoff homer by Manny Ramirez. Photo by Brita Meng Outzen

October 21, 2007 — Matsuzaka pumps his fist after striking out Asdrubal Cabrera for a pivotal out in Game 7 of the American League Championship Series against the Indians. Matsuzaka ended up getting the win to vault the Red Sox into the World Series. Photo by Brita Meng Outzen

October 27, 2007 — Matsuzaka uses his bat of all things to key the Red Sox to victory in Game 3 of the World Series at Coors Field in Denver, lacing a two-run single in the eventual 10-5 victory.
Photo by Phoebe Sexton/Boston Red Sox

10

Complete Turnaround
(May 14–June 5, 2007)

TIGERS MANAGER JIM LEYLAND, an authoritative voice who loves and respects being around the game, wasn't quite sure what to make of Matsuzaka when his team arrived at Fenway Park the night of May 14. Leyland pulled aside a couple of Boston writers. "How good is this Matsuzaka guy?" Leyland asked as he stumbled on the pronunciation of the Japanese legend's last name. He would find out in a matter of hours. If Matsuzaka's Fenway coming out party was supposed to be that April night when Ichiro and the Mariners came to town, the reality was that it took place on this Monday night against the defending American League champions from Motown. All of the things which had been troubling Matsuzaka at times—the different feel of the mound, the smaller strike zone, the bigger baseball—suddenly seemed to go away. It was as if Matsuzaka was at Tokyo Dome firing a gem against the Nippon Ham Fighters.

Matsuzaka sliced and diced his way through the strike zone, walking nobody on that night. He struck out five and got sixteen ground ball outs. His pace was smooth and easy. There was a Curtis Granderson homer to right in the third inning, but nothing else of consequence all night. There was a simple fact that made this a night to savor for Matsuzaka: CG. Manager Terry Francona allowed him to go the distance. No Red Sox pitcher had fired a complete game all season, and, as a matter of fact, wire-to-wire jobs in baseball have turned into a lost art. Managers use their bullpens in this day and age, sometimes to a fault. Interestingly, the Red Sox had just won a wild Mother's Day game the day before in which Orioles manager Sam Perlozzo, who would be fired a month later, took out pitcher Jeremy Guthrie with one out in the ninth, even though he had a 92-pitch shutout in progress. The Red Sox celebrated with one of their best comebacks in team history, rallying out of a 5-0 deficit and winning 6-5.

If anything was tough for Matsuzaka to adjust to in his rookie season, it was the importance of pitch counts. This is a man who made his reputation with a 250-pitch, 17-inning victory in high school, which was made all the more impressive by the fact he saved the next day's game and fired a no-hitter the day after that. Pitch count? That wasn't prominent in the vocabulary of a man who fired 72 complete games in his eight-year professional career in Japan. In 2006, Matsuzaka's last in Japan, he had 13 complete games. For context, consider that as a team, the Red Sox had three complete games in 2006, one of which was a five-inning job in a game shortened by rain.

There Matsuzaka was, at 109 pitches through eight innings. That was one more pitch than he had thrown in his entire seven-inning outing against the Blue Jays five days earlier. After mowing the Tigers down in that nine-pitch eighth, Matsuzaka sat right down on the bench, and was stretching out his arms, and loosening his neck, while his team batted. He didn't look like a man who had punched out on the time clock. Jonathan Papelbon loosened up out in the bullpen as the Sox batted in the eighth. Jerry Remy, the wildly popular Red Sox analyst for NESN, certainly sounded logical when he uttered to his large audience, "He's probably not coming back out, as Papelbon is up. When he was walking back to the dugout, it was almost like he expects to be back out for the ninth, that's the way it is in Japan."

The Red Sox had a lengthy bottom of the eighth and toward the end of it, Papelbon was no longer warming up. This time,

Francona would have no hook. For Francona is a sensible sort. He doesn't just look at pitch count, but he looks at how the pitcher got to that number. There was not a lot of stress on Matsuzaka throughout the performance, and Francona didn't find a reason not to let him finish: "He didn't look like he needed to come out. He was better at the end than he was at the beginning. I didn't see a reason to take him out."

When Matsuzaka trotted back out for the ninth, the crowd of 36,935 erupted. The electricity that engulfed the ballpark at that moment, and for that inning, felt eerily similar to what the masterful Pedro Martinez used to elicit in his glory years (1999–2000). It wasn't just that Matsuzaka was going to go the distance. It was as if the Fenway faithful was going to will him there. Henry, Lucchino and Werner—the ownership trio which green-lighted the costly acquisition—were part of the support system. "There was an undeniable buzz about making sure he came out in the ninth and finished the ninth," Lucchino said. "It was like we saw something special." Matsuzaka could feel it. "The fans gave me a huge ovation and that definitely pumped me up," he said.

And after Gary Sheffield led off that ninth with a bloop single to left, Matsuzaka went right back into rocking chair mode. He put a 92-mph fastball right on the outside black that Magglio Ordonez watched for strike three. There was a flyout to center, and then Pudge Rodriguez was all that stood in the way of Matsuzaka's first complete game on United States soil. Throughout the at-bat, there was a "Let's Go Dice-K" chant from the crowd. Then, on a 1-2 pitch, Matsuzaka got a groundout to third baseman Lowell and the 124-pitch masterpiece was over. "Dirty Water," the signature victory song for the Red Sox, boomed from the Fenway sound system. What followed was one of the more eclectic post-game gatherings around home plate. There was a huge smile on the face of Matsuzaka as Varitek congratulated him. Then there were handshakes, pats on the back, hugs and bows, the most pronounced of which was between Matsuzaka and "Big Papi" Ortiz. As Matsuzaka trotted back to the dugout for the ninth and final time on that night, there was a deafening roar that almost felt like a call for an encore at a concert. Matsuzaka had truly arrived at Fenway. "The fact that I was able to pitch my first really good game, first good showing at Fenway, that I'm really excited about." Suddenly, Matsuzaka's slump seemed like it was months earlier instead of a mere couple of weeks.

Meanwhile, Leyland, who would be entrusted with managing the American League All-Stars just two months later, got the answer to his pre-game queries. "He's the real deal, he's good," Leyland said of Matsuzaka. And five days later, Matsuzaka was good again. When the Saturday afternoon game against the Braves began at Fenway, it seemed Matsuzaka had yet to exit the groove he was in against Detroit. He came out of the gate with six shutout innings and then seemingly became a victim of boredom as the Red Sox built a 12-0 lead by the time Matsuzaka came out for the seventh. He gave up three runs in that inning but fired a scoreless eighth inning. With 103 pitches after eight, another complete game could have been in the works. But this time, Francona decided there was no reason to push the envelope with his team up by ten runs. "He wanted to go back out after eight, but I just didn't see the reason today," Francona said.

As far as Matsuzaka was concerned, he didn't see a reason not to go back out. "Given my pitch count at the end of the eighth inning, I was expecting to go back out there for the ninth. I think given my pace up to that point, it would have been normal to go back for the ninth but the manager came in and spoke to me and said that given our big lead, 'Go and get some rest.'" Such words, however supportive they may have been, sat in Matsuzaka's stomach about as well as sushi that had been left in the sun for five hours. "I think it's probably a bit of a culture shock for him," said infielder Scott McClain, who played behind Matsuzaka for four years at Seibu and spent the summer of 2007 playing for a minor league team called the Fresno Grizzlies. "I remember last year reading about how he went out and threw a 200-pitch bullpen or something. I'm sure it was quite different for him to come out here and them wanting him on a pitch count and to kind of ease him into things. He's so used to going out there and going full bore right away. I'm sure it was an extreme shock for him."

For a while, each time Francona would take Matsuzaka out of a game while he had a gem in progress, it was a bit of a shock to the system of all those reporters who had chronicled him in Japan for so long and were now doing so in the United States. "Since he has so many complete games when he threw 160 pitches every outing, we all imagine Matsuzaka as a nine inning pitcher," said Hiroki Tohda of the Sports Nippon Newspapers, who made multiple trips to the United States in 2007 to cover Matsuzaka. "It's kind of weird to see him go off the mound after seven innings."

How many pitches can Matsuzaka throw in a game? "I think I can probably throw 140 to 150 pitches," Matsuzaka said. That comment was relayed to Varitek, who seemed a bit amused. "I don't know, only he really knows that. He's pretty special," offered the catcher. Make no mistake about it. The adjustment to pitch counts and bullpen usage in the Major Leagues was something Matsuzaka still wasn't comfortable with, even by the end of October. "It's a major [adjustment] and I have to say that it's probably still ongoing," Farrell said in early November 2007. "One other aspect of his personality that I've come to know is that he doesn't like restriction. He doesn't like a structure. Now, I want to be careful on how this comes across. He's very much a team player. But he doesn't like such a structured routine because he feels it's confining. That's when he feels it's confining to him. It doesn't give him that ability to freelance. He feels the limitation that can be frustrating to him. He understands it but he doesn't necessarily totally agree with it."

Another custom that was hard for Matsuzaka to deal with was when Farrell would come out to the mound for a chat in the middle of a sticky inning. That wasn't how it was done at Seibu, and Matsuzaka didn't much like seeing it happen in Boston, particularly when you consider the language barrier. "When I would talk to him in English, it would take some energy from him to translate that in his own mind and then decipher the meaning," said Farrell. "It got to the point, and again, this is the difference in baseball cultures and norms, that in Japan when a coach comes to the mound, it's to take that pitcher out of a game. He would rather there not be trips to the mound. My response was, 'Don't make me come out here.' It's almost like a time-out in basketball. You're trying to slow the momentum down and he understood that. But he felt like a trip to the mound was a little bit more of a distraction for him that negated the underlying purpose."

Despite some of the adjustments he continued to go through, Matsuzaka was on a complete roll, his best of the season to date. He had put three highly effective starts together, going 3-0 with a 1.87 ERA. The latter of those two outings propelled him to earn American League Player of the Week honors. It was debatable at that point who was hotter: Matsuzaka or the Red Sox themselves, who had opened up a double-digit lead in the American League East through just 40 games, making them just the second team in baseball history to build that big a lead in such swift fashion.

After a minor stumble in the Bronx—the Red Sox lost two of three to their rivals—it was off to Texas. Matsuzaka would lead that series off and there was no reason to think he wouldn't pitch another gem. But after a rain delay of nearly two hours, Matsuzaka stumbled around and was hammered for five runs in the fourth inning. Those who were privy to what was taking place in the clubhouse understood the mighty struggles of Matsuzaka. Those confined to the stands, the press box and television sets had no clue. How could they? "In the middle of the game," said Tom Werner, "I e-mailed Theo [Epstein] and asked him what was the matter. He told me that at the moment Daisuke was suffering through a stomach flu and was actually nauseous at the moment he was pitching. But Matsuzaka continued to pitch that night, actually even earning the win." What the Red Sox were watching was a man literally spilling his guts to win a baseball game.

Between innings, Matsuzaka would go into the clubhouse and receive fluids intravenously. There was in-game vomiting by the righty, who might have gone back out for the sixth had Francona not seen him doubled over in the dugout tunnel. After the five-inning, five-run performance in which Matsuzaka earned a 10-6 victory that ran his record to 7-2, he left behind a statement through a team publicist: "I tried my best to take the team as deep into the game as possible to fulfill my responsibility as the starter. I regret that I ended up being a burden on my teammates today. I'll do my best to prepare for my next start." What could have said more about the character of Matsuzaka than that statement? A burden? Huh? "He was dry-heaving in the concourse," Varitek said. "He battled. He got us as far as he could, and that was tremendous." A day later, Francona found himself marveling at what Matsuzaka did to help his team win. "He had no business being out there, pitching in that game," Francona said. "We've all had the flu, and you don't want to be pitching. You just want to get under the covers and be miserable." And you can't just chalk it up to a cultural responsibility. "That's probably part of what makes him so special," Francona said. "He could have said, 'Get somebody else out there' in the second inning and we all would have understood. That's not the [Japanese] culture, that's the person. He seems to get it, on a lot of levels."

Nobody besides Matsuzaka will ever know what kind of toll pitching through the sickness took on him. For when he was batted around by the Indians at Fenway five days later, he refused to make any excuses. "I think I was able to prepare for this start as I usually do," Matsuzaka said. One thing was clear: Everyone was willing to give him a mulligan after what he had been through in Texas. The Indians hit Matsuzaka around for twelve hits and six runs over 5^2/$_3$ innings, putting him in the loss column for the first time since April 17. At that point, Matsuzaka's ERA stood at 4.83. It was still fair to wonder exactly who he was.

His next trip to the mound was in Oakland on June 5, and Matsuzaka looked strong again, despite battling with the strike zone at times. He just couldn't get any runs. Matsuzaka threw 130 pitches over seven innings against the ever-patient A's and gave up two runs. He struck out eight. The Red Sox couldn't solve their former teammate Lenny DiNardo and lost the game by a count of 2-0. Matsuzaka continued to be diplomatic when asked about pitch counts in the Major Leagues. At the same time, he made it blatantly clear that his expectation is to pitch nine innings every game, and pitch counts weren't part of his vocabulary. "I haven't felt a difference but certainly in a situation like today, I probably would have been expected to pitch the entire game in Japan. Physically, I felt I could keep throwing, but as usual, pitch count is not something that I spend a lot of time worrying about." But the Red Sox, after making such a whopping investment in this man, weren't going to burn him out, even if it meant Matsuzaka would get a little frustrated from time to time. The more Matsuzaka pitched, the more it became apparent what a tough self-critic he was. Two runs over seven innings? Most starting pitchers would take that every day. Not Matsuzaka. "They are a team with great batters' eyes and are very patient," Matsuzaka said of the Oakland lineup. "But before I concern myself with the other team's lineup, I should assess my own pitching performance, which I wasn't very happy with today."

With the All-Star Game on the calendar just five weeks later across the bay in San Francisco, you knew somebody would ask Matsuzaka if he felt he'd make a return trip to Northern California at that time. He didn't exactly stump for himself. "I would certainly love to be chosen for the All-Star team. I think it would be a great honor to play in that game. But at the present moment, looking at my own performance, I don't think I'm worthy of being on that team." At that time, Matsuzaka was 7-4 and his ERA was 4.63. Not exactly All-Star numbers. If anything, his performances were a little on the uneven side. But there were enough flashes of brilliance to suggest he would figure things out to the point that opposing hitters would be very sorry once he did.

11

Marquee Matchups
(June 10–July 3, 2007)

DURING THE EARLY PART of the season, it seemed as if much of Matsuzaka's battle was internal. He was adapting to a new culture, a new pitcher's mound, a different sized baseball, a different strike zone, different ballparks and on and on. It was how quickly he could shrink those learning curves that would determine his success in his rookie season. But beginning with a trip to the desert of Phoenix, Arizona the second weekend in June, Matsuzaka was about to measure himself against some of the best who ever played the game. And it was against such immortals as Randy Johnson, Barry Bonds, and Greg Maddux that Matsuzaka would begin proving that he could hang with anyone on any level.

Randy Johnson is a lot of things Matsuzaka isn't. He is super-sized at 6-foot-10. He is left-handed. And he has a snarl and a coldness to him. Matsuzaka, on the other hand, is of average stature for a Major League pitcher. He stands at six feet and weighs 185. Unlike the Big Unit, Matsuzaka seems to have a smile for every occasion. In fact, it is one that lights up a room. When Matsuzaka is on the mound, the smile turns into cold concentration, but nothing that looks as intimidating as when Johnson puts that big body on the hill and looks 7-foot-10. Of course, Matsuzaka, being that he is right-handed, didn't figure to study Johnson as much over the years as marvel at him. Nonetheless, the June 10 matchup at

Chase Field marked the first time Matsuzaka ever pitched against a no-questions-asked, first-ballot future Hall of Famer. Johnson had won five Cy Young Awards and shared the World Series MVP with Curt Schilling—then a Diamondback—in 2001.

And Matsuzaka wouldn't just pitch against Johnson. He would literally face the man, as this Interleague matchup marked the first time Dice-K got to swing his lumber on American soil. Unlike some pitchers, who look and feel awkward with a bat in hand, Matsuzaka loves being a baseball player. During his time as a high school legend, Matsuzaka always handled the bat well. Though he didn't get to swing it much in Nippon Professional Baseball (he played in the Pacific League, which has the DH), the ability to put bat on ball was something he maintained. In fact, it was almost exactly one year before his start against Johnson—June 9, 2006—that Matsuzaka launched a home run for the Seibu Lions against the Hanshin Tigers. The highlight is readily available on YouTube, with Matsuzaka unloading on a near shoulder-high fastball by Darwin Cubillan and pummeling it over the fence in center for a two-run homer that gave Seibu an eventual 7-1 win. Cubillan, who hails from Venezuela, pitched 56 games in the Major Leagues, proving that yes, Matsuzaka could handle the bat against even a serviceable pitcher. "He loves to bat, he was a batter in high school and probably one of the disappointments in his [Japanese] pro career is that he played in the DH league here all those years," said Wayne Graczyk, a baseball columnist for the *Japan Times*. "Of course, he liked pitching, but he probably would have liked it a little better if he were in a league that did not have the DH so that he could hit because he liked to show off his hitting. He actually joined the home run contest one year before one of the All-Star Games. He hit a couple out. I think it was 2005."

Matsuzaka's bat, believe it or not, had already played a role earlier in the weekend. J. D. Drew, who was in the throes of a horrid slump at the time, grabbed a piece of Matsuzaka's wood and promptly drilled two homers and drove in seven runs in the Friday night game against the Diamondbacks. It was Rob

Bradford, a reporter from the *Boston Herald* who seems to leave no detail unchronicled, that uncovered the nugget. Bradford reported that it was an S318 Louisville Slugger maple bat that Matsuzaka had lent to Drew.

As happy as Matsuzaka was with bat in hand, he had no bold proclamations against the Big Unit. When Francona spotted Matsuzaka a day or so prior to that Sunday afternoon start, he joked, "Do you want to hit cleanup?" Matsuzaka's response? "Against Randy Johnson, no, no." The chance Matsuzaka had been waiting for came in the second inning as he dug in against one of the greatest pitchers who has ever stepped on a mound. Despite Johnson's advanced age, this was one of those days where it seemed the 43-year-old had been taking several gulps from the fountain of youth. The first pitch was a slider for a called strike. Then came an 85-mph slider that Matsuzaka cut on and missed. At this point, Matsuzaka broke into a small smile in the batter's box. After the game, he explained the root of his humor. "My first [at-bat in the Majors] just happened to be against Randy Johnson and when I stepped into the box for the first time and I saw his slider, for those of us who don't hit on a regular basis, I just thought to myself, this is an impossible pitch to hit." Still, Matsuzaka somehow fouled off a filthy slider. "Not a bad swing. He looks kind of hitter-ish," said a solid former Major Leaguer named Mark Grace, who was serving on this day as color commentator for the Diamondbacks. But Johnson then cut to the chase, firing 95-mph heat right by Matsuzaka, who struck out in his first Major League at-bat.

You can be sure, however, that none of the 46,622 fans who filed into Chase Field did so to see Matsuzaka or Johnson hit. They came to see the men pitch, and the duel was as tense as expected. The Red Sox scored first in the fourth, then the Diamondbacks tied it at 1 in the bottom of the inning. But Matsuzaka gave up an RBI double to Carlos Quentin in the bottom of the sixth and that proved to be the difference. Johnson, in six innings, gave up four hits and a run and struck out nine. Matsuzaka also went six, gave up the same four hits and had the same nine strikeouts. But

Matsuzaka gave up two runs and the Red Sox lost 5-1, thanks to a bullpen meltdown in the eighth. In the grand scheme of things, Matsuzaka offered this tease to the reporters who attended his post-game address: "Although the team lost, I saw some personal improvement." What exactly did he mean by that? "I think to put it very simply, I feel like the quality of the pitches I'm throwing is improving," said Matsuzaka. One thing that became clear to those who covered Matsuzaka is that he feared giving away any competitive advantages by what he said. Matsuzaka, when it came to the technical aspect of pitching, gave bare-bones information unlike, say, Schilling, who blogged about his at-bat to at-bat approach over the course of a start.

Johnson knew enough about Matsuzaka to know it meant something to beat him. "I had to throw my best game or at least match zeros with him, and I thought he threw pretty well," Johnson said. "It's definitely a morale booster for this young team to go up against someone of that stature who's getting a lot of publicity that they know that they can battle against that type of pitcher that comes in here." Believe it or not, it was Johnson's last win of 2007. Recurring back woes ended his season on June 28. But Matsuzaka—who clearly desired to have the sustained success of a Big Unit—was just about to hit his stride.

When the Red Sox ventured back to Fenway following their stay in the desert, Matsuzaka's record stood at 7-5. His ERA was at 4.52. In other words, a little good, a little bad and still an enigma in his rookie year. Going back to Boston felt even more like home than usual for Matsuzaka this time, for there were two familiar faces around. His first manager in pro ball, Osamu Higashio, was embarking on a week-long visit in Boston as both a member of the Japanese media and somewhat of a security blanket for his former protégé. When Matsuzaka broke in with the Seibu Lions at the age of 18, his manager had a reputation as being one of the best pitchers Japan had ever seen, as evidenced by 251 career wins.

With the Red Sox set to play the Rockies, second baseman Kazuo Matsui—Matsuzaka's teammate at Seibu for five years—

was also in Boston. With an off-day on Monday, the three men went out to dinner and reflected on old times. The next day, as Matsuzaka fired an early side session at Fenway, Higashio-san sat there on the bullpen bench with Farrell-san, i.e., Red Sox pitching coach John Farrell. "Mr. Higashio knows," Matsuzaka told members of the Japanese media. "Sometimes, I'd have to explain a lot to somebody. But he knows what's going on, what I'm trying to do." Michael Silverman, the excellent reporter for the *Boston Herald,* got more of a sense of that meeting, citing some technical adjustments that Higashio suggested to Matsuzaka. "Higashio knows about everything that concerns me and gave me pitching mechanics tips," Matsuzaka told Japanese reporters, one of whom, in turn, translated those quotes to Silverman. "Higashio has a keen eye about me. He already realized how I've changed my pitching in the U.S. and he asked me, 'Why did you change that?' So I answered the reason why I had changed my pitching in the U.S."

Perhaps Matsuzaka didn't need to make the changes. He was, after all, an international legend. Matsui, who had a very rough initiation to the Major Leagues with the New York Mets before finding a comfortable home in Colorado, seemed to take pride in the progress his friend was making. Naturally, over bites of cuisine, the men talked about how the adjustment was going. "He seems like he's getting more into this environment and American culture," Matsui said. "That's what he was talking about. At this point, I don't worry about anything about him. I'm happy that he's having a good time and is not injured. I experienced a few injuries. Not having injury and seeing how he's pitching, that makes me happy."

But it takes a pitcher to know a pitcher, and Higashio could tell that Matsuzaka, despite the flashes of brilliance, was not there yet. Sitting in the back work room of the press box that was built for the overflow of Japanese media, Higashio spoke for several minutes in a one-on-one interview the day before Matsuzaka's start against Bonds and the Giants. He spoke both broadly and specifically. "In the big leagues, being a good pitcher, you have to be really good at fielding and also pickoff attempts and control, command and also velocity," Higashio said. "Everything must be well-balanced to be a great pitcher. But soon, Daisuke will be a pitcher that a manager can definitely count on and a pitcher who can definitely formulate a game and construct a game on his own, with the trust in him from the manager. I saw Beckett pitch [earlier in the week], I like the pitching form of Beckett." Higashio had one final word before ending the interview. "I hope Daisuke picks up something out of Beckett also." For at that point in the season, Beckett had established himself as the true ace of the Red Sox. Nobody knew it at the time, but Matsuzaka was about to raise his own game to that level, at least for a short time.

If Matsuzaka truly wanted to be the best, he needed to conquer the best. Barry Bonds, who carries with him rumors of steroid use much like luggage, is one of the best hitters to ever play the game. Later in 2007, he would become the all-time home run champion, surpassing Hank Aaron's record of 755. Even before his body became over-sized, Bonds had been a megastar, someone capable of doing just about anything on a baseball field. Now he was so big he almost looked like a cartoon character. He came to Boston just eight home runs shy of Aaron's all-time record. If there was something that was easily noticeable about Matsuzaka, it was how much he enjoyed going up against the fiercest competitors. "In the rare opportunities I get to face such hitters, I would like to display a powerful style of pitching. It would be nice to find a little more velocity though," said Matsuzaka, with a grin on his face. In the Friday night opener of the series, which marked the first night Bonds ever set foot in Fenway, the left-handed slugger mashed a towering blast so far above the right field foul pole that it was almost impossible to tell if it was fair or foul. The umpire ruled foul. Bonds was otherwise tamed that night in a Boston win. He'd get his crack at Matsuzaka the following afternoon with a national television audience taking it in on FOX, not to mention all the people who were watching it in Japan.

The first at-bat came in the top of the first inning. With a runner on second and two outs, Matsuzaka was ordered to issue an intentional walk to Bonds. Matsuzaka had never issued an intentional walk in the first inning of a game back in Japan. "On a very personal level, the intentional walk as a strategy is not something I'm either used to or want to have to rely on a lot as a pitcher," Matsuzaka told the *Boston Globe*. By now, Bonds had become used to such cautious treatment. In the fourth, Matsuzaka's first pitch to Bonds was a high, inside fastball and it was ferociously ripped well foul down the right field line. The next pitch, also a heater, was crushed. But Bonds got under it just enough that it landed on the warning track in center for an out. Next time up, Matsuzaka threw all breaking pitches to Bonds, and it ended with a grounder to second. That was it for their one-on-one matchup, as by the time Bonds came up in the eighth, he dug in against another Japanese pitcher in Okajima, who froze him for a critical strikeout that paved the way for Matsuzaka's 1-0 victory which included eight strikeouts, three hits and no runs over seven innings. Matsuzaka was asked after the game if facing Bonds was a "special experience." "I've faced many great batters on the way, but he certainly emitted a great aura about him. That's rare to see even among those great hitters."

Bonds though, was not impressed with the way Matsuzaka came after him, especially after reading his pre-start quote about wanting to demonstrate his power. "If you say you're going to challenge me, then challenge me," Bonds said to Andrew Baggerly of the *San Jose Mercury News*. Noting that he had gotten good rips against the two heaters he saw from Matsuzaka, Bonds was displeased not to see another one. "He saw what happened the first time," Bonds said. "If you say you'll do it, do it then." But despite the somewhat innocuous quote that Bonds somehow viewed as bravado from Matsuzaka, the truth of the matter is that this wasn't some flamethrower of a pitcher. Sure, when Matsuzaka started with Seibu all those years back, his reputation was as a guy who would try to blow the ball by the batter and only go to Plan B when need be. Now he was very much a pitcher with a kitchen cabinet full of weapons. Why go fastball-heavy when you can get an out on something else?

Pitching in such a tight game didn't rattle Matsuzaka. Actually it was the opposite. "I love it," he said. For Matsuzaka, the true reason to cherish the day was that Higashio-san took in the whole outing from the second row behind home plate. "Ultimately I was able to show him what I think was my best performance, so I feel that he'll be able to return to Japan happy," Matsuzaka said following the game.

The next morning, which was Father's Day, Matsuzaka was not happy. The *Boston Herald* ran a Reuters photo from the game of Matsuzaka's wife, Tomoyo, holding their young daughter in the stands. Tomoyo had been photographed countless times before. That wasn't an issue. In fact, she was a well-known television broadcaster in Japan before marrying Daisuke. But Matsuzaka was so private about his child that many members of the Japanese media weren't even aware if he had a son or a daughter. The Red Sox PR staff had tried to make it clear to sports editors of major media outlets before the season that Matsuzaka had strong wishes to keep his child anonymous to the public. But a wire got crossed at the *Boston Herald,* and that memo was not clear by the time the paper was printed for that Sunday. Matsuzaka was nothing short of livid. According to a close associate of Matsuzaka's who is also Japanese and talked to Matsuzaka just about every day during the 2007 season, his outrage was all about being protective of his child. Maybe his daughter could be kidnapped if somebody knew what she looked like. The same associate said that if in Japan, a celebrity couple like Brad Pitt and Angelina Jolie had their baby photographed by the paparazzi, the eyes of the child would be blotted out of the picture. At any rate, Matsuzaka made it clear through the Red Sox that he didn't plan on talking to the *Boston Herald* for a long time, if ever.

A few weeks later, Gordon Edes of the *Boston Globe,* who was the first Red Sox beat reporter to be granted an in-depth sitdown with Matsuzaka, shed some insight into how much Matsuzaka's privacy, or lack thereof, weighed on him at times. "I think the biggest challenge so far has been my goal to protect my privacy and my family's privacy," Matsuzaka told Edes through a translator. "It's an important objective, but also one that is very challenging." Sure, Matsuzaka's privacy had been invaded in Japan as well, but that was his turf and he knew protocol. He was disturbed, for example, that a fan followed him as he drove out of Fenway one night.

According to Graczyk, who had long been in charge of printing a Japanese baseball media guide in English, the players had become a lot more protective in recent years about family information being made public. It was in large contrast to decades earlier, when Japanese players actually allowed their home addresses to be printed in the media guides. Leave it to Daniel Okimoto, the Stanford professor and long-time Lucchino confidant who served as a consultant during the negotiations to bring Matsuzaka to Boston, to best put the situation in perspective.

"You know that the press in Japan is intrusive, massively intrusive. They are like paparazzi," said Okimoto. "The written journalists, as well as the visual, they just follow players around and take any chance to accost them and ask questions, and they take liberties at sort of nuancing the answers. They are a very difficult press to deal with if you are a megastar baseball player like Matsuzaka. However, and this is a big however, the press tends to leave the private side of a notable private. The prime minister's children, for example, nobody ever sees a picture of his children. His wife goes with him on official trips. But they never invade the home. And there are not articles about his children. There are famous movie stars that have affairs and paparazzi are around snapping pictures of them with their boyfriends or girlfriends. That's all fair game. But when it comes to the private preserve of the family, the press backs off and respects the privacy of these prominent people. It's understandable that Matsuzaka would have been irate about that."

Again, Matsuzaka was from a completely different culture. And just because David Ortiz's little boy was seen on television every now and then running around in his mini-Red Sox uniform, that didn't mean Matsuzaka wanted his daughter to be seen in similar fashion. Perhaps it was good that the Red Sox got out of Boston after that game. There's something more relaxing for the team about being on the road, where a much smaller media contingent is with the team and the passionate fandom eases up to just the most faithful cult that actually follows the team on the road. Matsuzaka, though still mad at the *Herald,* was smiling again a day later in the clubhouse as his team began a three-game series in Atlanta against the Braves. It was in that first game of the nine-game road trip that Schilling's fastball had somehow dipped to the mid 80s and, unsurprisingly, the right-handed ace was shut down with a shoulder injury the next day. This would only increase the importance for Matsuzaka to turn into a co-ace along with Beckett. For Schilling was 40 years old, and there was no telling when he would come back, or how strong he would be when he did. Earlier in the year, that burden might have been too much for Matsuzaka. Not now. Clearly, he was in stride.

A twist of fate turned Matsuzaka's next start into yet another matchup with a living legend. Padres right-hander Chris Young had been involved in a brawl and was in the process of appealing his five-game suspension. In order to be prepared for when the punishment came, the Padres juggled their rotation so that Young would pitch the Saturday night game against the Red Sox instead of Friday. That Friday nod went to none other than Greg Maddux, meaning Matsuzaka would be pitching and hitting against one of his true idols. "When I found out that I would be pitching against Maddux, I felt very lucky," Matsuzaka said. "I thought there would be little chance our rotation would actually match up that way so I felt very lucky." For even a casual observer of Matsuzaka, it isn't hard to figure out why he would take to Maddux, who was well over 300 career wins. Both men were the most cerebral of pitchers. Though Matsuzaka threw much harder than

Maddux, both pitchers enjoyed being able to outthink the hitters by pinpoint location. And given that he was fifteen years Maddux's junior, of course Daisuke would look up to him.

Matsuzaka did something un-Maddux-like to start his outing. He walked the first three batters, mixing in a wild pitch along the way. He wiggled out of the inning giving up only one run. In fact, it would be the only run Matsuzaka would allow all night. Before jumping to the conclusion that Matsuzaka was getting used to yet another new mound, remember that PETCO Park was an old friend. It was there that Matsuzaka had put himself into the conscience of the baseball-watching public of America by winning the Most Valuable Player Award in the inaugural World Baseball Classic in March of 2006. Epstein, standing in the Boston clubhouse a couple of hours prior to Matsuzaka's return start in San Diego quipped: "We were hoping he'd get shelled so it would save us money on the posting fee. So much for that."

"When I stepped on the field, it was just as I remembered it, a very beautiful ballpark," Matsuzaka said. "As for actually pitching inside the park, just like last time, I allowed a few baserunners in the first inning, so it felt very similar to last time." As he had shown the ability to do so many times already in a Boston uniform, Matsuzaka was able to wash away that one bad inning against the Padres in which he was all over the place and look like a completely different pitcher the rest of the night. Though his pitch count—126—forced him to leave after six, Matsuzaka was in complete command. He struck out nine and allowed five hits and barely beat Maddux (six innings, seven hits, two runs) by a score of 2-1.

Matsuzaka knew what his pitch count was. He also knew he wanted to keep pitching. Francona had the unenviable task of being the voice of reason. "He said he still had more [in the tank] and I believed him. We'd like him to have more in August and September. He didn't look like he was tired to me." His final pitch of the night—a 94-mph fastball that whistled by Marcus Giles for strike three—proved that point. But it was the way Major League games get managed over the course of 162 games and Matsuzaka was trying to reach at least some degree of peace with that.

To those watching in Japan, it had to look downright eerie watching Matsuzaka pitch on a night the Red Sox were wearing 1982 throwback uniforms. Those grey road jerseys were very simple. Grey tops with black lettering "Boston" across the top of the jersey. There were no names on the back of the tops. Anyone who had seen Matsuzaka dominate for Yokohama in that 1998 Koshien tournament would see the resemblance between his high school uniform and the one he wore in San Diego the night of June 22. And to the fans of Japan, the image of Matsuzaka dealing for Yokohama on pure guts was indelible. Matsuzaka didn't learn until shortly before game-time he'd be wearing a Yokohama clone of a uniform. "I tried it on in the locker room and it certainly felt like I was going back to high school. It didn't feel strange though." Beating Maddux wasn't strange either. That was simply rewarding.

"Knowing how great a pitcher that he is, I knew I would have to do my best to hold their lineup to as few runs as possible," Matsuzaka said. "Facing him in the batters box, he threw a lot of two seam fastballs to me and I was able to see first-hand what a great pitcher he actually is. He's one of the pitchers I look up to so I felt very happy to actually be able to see his pitches live, first-hand." And the next day, there was more interaction between Maddux and Matsuzaka. This time, Maddux agreed to take part in the filming of a Japanese television special with Matsuzaka. The two men gathered in a room outside the Padres clubhouse and, with an interpreter between them, discussed the art of pitching. "It was a nice little chat," Maddux told Corey Brock of MLB.com. "I wish the cameras weren't around, but I enjoyed talking to him." Maddux gave Matsuzaka a signed baseball, which would undoubtedly become a cherished keepsake.

In a dizzying span of thirteen days, Matsuzaka had gone against three giants of Major League Baseball and showed that he belonged all three times. Only against Randy Johnson did he come out on the losing end. The Red Sox were starting to see a return on their $103.1 million investment. "We're very happy with him. He's pitching well," said Epstein. "He's done a good job of making adjustments to a new country, a new culture, a new team, new ballparks, a new mound, new baseball, new rotation every five days, that's a lot to ask of any one person. He's handled it really well. I still think the best is yet to come. His stuff can be better than what it is right now and I think it will be."

Matsuzaka closed out what wound up a brilliant month of June with yet one more tussle with Ichiro. This time, it was Safeco Field, Ichiro's house. For the third straight time, Matsuzaka was unable to get a win over the Mariners. This time, however, Matsuzaka had little to do with the losing outcome. In fact, he took a no decision. It was one of those rare spells during the season in which the team had hit a lull. They weren't hitting and the Red Sox lost 2-1 in 11 innings. But Matsuzaka was as sharp as he had been all year, limiting the Mariners to three hits and a run while striking out eight. The duels against Ichiro didn't have the same zest as the flashbulb fest at Fenway in April. Matsuzaka struck him out twice but also surrendered his only run of the game on Ichiro's defensive swing, which produced an RBI single up the middle. "Given Ichiro's great batting skill, I have no regrets about the pitch I made," Matsuzaka said. "I think it was really a testament to his skill that he hit that ball."

It was Matsuzaka's last start before All-Star selections, and perhaps a 10th victory would have earned him the nod. As it was, Matsuzaka stood at 9-5 and took pride in his June turnaround (1.59 ERA over five outings) that brought his ERA down to 3.80. "As I've said before, when it comes to my personal condition, I always feel that there's room for improvement but I will say that things seem to be getting a little bit better. My ERA was a concern and I wanted to make an effort to bring it back into the 3's," Matsuzaka said. When the All-Star teams were released on July 2, Matsuzaka's name was not on the list. Five other Red Sox were on the squad in Beckett, David Ortiz, Mike Lowell, Manny Ramirez, and Jonathan Papelbon. By virtue of the final vote conducted by

MLB.com, Hideki Okajima was the Japanese player from the Red Sox going to San Francisco. Matsuzaka, who has standards for himself that aim for the moon, didn't think he was deserving. He was thrilled for Okajima, and also his other All-Star teammates.

As the season got toward the midway point, there was no reason for Matsuzaka to stress about anything. He was starting to feel again like the ace he had been for so many years. With a dazzling performance at home against the Devil Rays on July 3 (four hits, no runs, nine strikeouts), Matsuzaka was 10-5 and his ERA was 3.53, the lowest it had been since April 22. A humorous moment developed during that game when Carlos Pena of the Devil Rays frustratingly asked for time-out and Varitek sheepishly apologized to the batter. "Sorry, he's got like forty pitches." The six or seven that Matsuzaka in fact did throw weren't getting hit by anyone.

Matsuzaka had turned in six commanding outings in a row, allowing two runs or less in each outing. The key during that stretch, which would be Matsuzaka's best all season? "Fastball command," said Farrell. The Red Sox themselves were on a bit of a fast track. No Schilling? No problem. Matsuzaka and Beckett, with help from Okajima and Papelbon in the bullpen, were anchoring a Boston team that led the American League East for the final eighty-four days of the first half. In fact, Boston's lead was double digits for a large margin of those days. Whatever struggles Matsuzaka had in April or May had become all but invisible from the memory banks.

"I think we have quite a pitcher," Francona said. "I think he's had to go through some adjusting because of cultural difference and all the things we talk about time and time again. But he's been a polished pitcher since the day we got him. He went through a lot of firsts. I think what he is now is a very, very valuable member of our staff and he's pitching like a veteran pitcher and that's exciting."

In actuality, what was most exciting was wondering what Matsuzaka might have in store the rest of the way. Legend had it that the bigger the games got, the larger Matsuzaka pitched. Red Sox Nation—primed for a return trip to the postseason after missing out in 2006—couldn't wait to see that.

12

Summer Wear
(July 8–29, 2007)

WITH JUST ONE START left in his first half-season as a Major League pitcher—which came in Detroit on the final day before the All-Star break—the Dice was rolling, there was no disputing that. For six successive starts, Matsuzaka looked like the international icon who prompted the outrageous posting fee of $51.1 million, posting an ERA of 1.29. He was giving the Red Sox durability and dominance in one filthy swoop. Conveniently, at the same time Schilling went to the disabled list, Matsuzaka pitched like an ace for the first-place Red Sox.

So what could there possibly be to worry about? Fatigue. Quietly, the Red Sox had become concerned that Matsuzaka's workload would start taking a toll in his first season of pitching in a five-man rotation, so they began doing some tinkering. For the first time all season, Matsuzaka was instructed not to throw a side session leading up to his start against the Tigers. And during that Sunday in Detroit, the concerns of Francona, Farrell, and undoubtedly the front office became justified. On a day his fastball was noticeably flat, Matsuzaka was hit hard. The Tigers, the same team Matsuzaka had fired that grand complete game against two months earlier, pounded him on their turf in Detroit. Over five disappointing innings, Matsuzaka gave up ten hits, six runs and three homers. Instead of overly scrutinizing the outing, Matsuzaka by this time realized that even established Major Leaguers have bad days. "When a game ends up like the way it did today, I tell myself that there are going to be days like this," summed up Matsuzaka, all but drawing up the "Mama always said there would be days like this" expression.

It was one of those days Matsuzaka's fastball didn't have zip and it wasn't well located. But to both the casual observer and the many on hand who knew him well, the prevailing thought was that Matsuzaka was tired. In the six brilliant starts leading into the bad performance in Detroit, Matsuzaka had averaged 118 pitches per outing. Then again, the amount of time he was spending on the mound was also an indicator of how well he was pitching. "Guys go through stretches, good pitchers, where they're out there because they're pitching well," said Francona. It was a bit of a double-edged sword. Still, the Red Sox were look- ing for a little more economy. "He's been known and he's made his livelihood over there in being able to throw a lot of pitches," said Varitek. "Hopefully we can get those down earlier in the game so we can get him extended innings later."

Hideo Nomo had proved more than a decade earlier that a Japanese pitcher could be dominant under the rigors of a Major League pitching schedule. In fact, the Japanese baseball-watching community considered him the ultimate samurai, not to men- tion a trailblazer who changed the perception of the way Major League teams viewed the talent level of Japanese players. How- ever, Nomo only prevailed in short doses—two to three years at a time—not long ones. Nomo had arm problems both in the middle and end portions of his eleven-year Major League career, in which he went 123-109 with a 4.21 ERA. By 2007, Nomo was still working out in hopes of making a comeback. But he hadn't pitched in the Major Leagues since 2005, and in his final two seasons he posted ugly ERAs of 8.25 and 7.24. It was a far cry from his brilliance years earlier, when he threw a no-hitter for the Dodgers in 1996 and another one for the Red Sox in 2001. Mike Piazza, a dominant right-handed bat in his heyday, was Nomo's first catcher with the Dodgers. "He threw a lot of pitches too, per at-bat. He always had a high pitch count," Piazza said. "He had no problem pitching past the century mark. Probably his arm got tired. This game is tough. You look back at some of the better pitchers in the game that threw a lot of complete games and had longevity and traditionally, aside from Nolan Ryan, not too many of them were power guys."

Roger Clemens and Randy Johnson, both of whom were certain to go to the Hall of Fame on the first ballot, were obvious exceptions. Schilling, who always relied on power, had significant arm injuries in the middle of his career, but emerged into a durable workhorse later. He was still pitching at 40, though he added a changeup and began relying more on his curve to make up for some of his loss in velocity. Tom Seaver, a first-ballot Hall of Famer, also had longevity but he transformed into more of a finesse guy during the latter stages of his career. Pedro Martinez was an example of an elite power pitcher who started to break down in his mid 30s, though in his case, it was many years after some baseball executives had predicted, given his slight frame and explosive delivery.

But before Matsuzaka could be put in the same context of those giants of the game, there would be a lot of baseball in front of him. He was just halfway through his rookie year. Sure there were some rough outings in Matsuzaka's first half of baseball in the Major Leagues, but he headed into the break with good numbers (10-6, 3.84 ERA). His 123 strikeouts were fifth in the Major Leagues. In the moments after that game was complete, six Red Sox players packed their bags and boarded owner John W. Henry's Learjet in order to be transported to the All-Star Game in San Francisco. It was the very same plane that Matsuzaka had boarded roughly seven months earlier upon deciding he was going to sign with the Red Sox. But Matsuzaka was not an All-Star, so there was no reminiscing on Henry's jet. Though Matsuzaka had numbers that could have warranted consideration for the All-Star squad, he told those who asked that Beckett, Papelbon, and

Okajima were the three pitchers on the Sox who had pitched like true All-Stars in the first half.

While six of his teammates went to soak in the All-Star hype, Matsuzaka took a three-day break with his family, some of which was spent in Pittsfield, a western Massachusetts town located in the scenic Berkshires, a popular summer getaway for New Englanders. Before Matsuzaka left for his R&R—and in essence it was his first chance to take a breather since signing with the Red Sox—he fielded a question about his first half. "I don't have any specific thoughts looking back on the first half, but maybe I can take the time to look back once the whole season is over," Matsuzaka said. "Looking at some of the games when I do get hit up and when I do lose, it seems to be a very similar pattern, so I think my objective in the second half is to avoid that pattern and do my best to help this team win."

Even without Matsuzaka, the All-Star festivities were another event Japan could take pride in. Okajima was there representing the Red Sox. The great Ichiro—who was about to become the first player in history to hit an inside-the-park home run at an All-Star Game—was also on hand. And so, too, was Dodgers closer Takashi Saito, the 37-year-old who was in the midst of his second dominant season since coming over from Japan. Saito had pitched for Matsuzaka's hometown team in Japan, the Yokohama BayStars. Because they are in the Central League, Saito rarely interacted with Matsuzaka and the Seibu Lions of the Pacific League. But like anyone from Japan, Saito was well aware of Matsuzaka and all he had come to represent. Therefore, his opinion on Matsuzaka's early assimilation to the Major Leagues was worth hearing.

"Ever since he's been over here, I feel like he hasn't reached his actual total potential," Saito said. "He has a lot more to give, a lot more to offer. For example, I think he's still trying to tinker with his form, still trying to work out various mechanics. I know that once he gets some time to completely adjust, I know he'll do a lot better. I think his stats actually speak for themselves right now, but in the future I think you'll probably see him up here [sitting in an All-Star press conference] every year."

With another half-season to go, Matsuzaka would continue the search for the stardom he had made his sizable following accustomed to. And he would find out if his body could withstand the rigors of a 162-game schedule on United States soil. While everyone fixated on the specific baseball differences, it seemed that something was overlooked. Here was a man pitching in a foreign land, continents away from home. Few—if any—American baseball coaches could relate to the differences in culture more than Jim Colborn, who was the pitching coach for the Pittsburgh Pirates in 2007. He was not only a pitching coach for the Orix Blue Wave in Japan for a four-year stretch, but later a Pacific Rim scout for the Mariners. As a Major League pitching coach, he had Japanese pitchers such as Nomo and Kazuhisa Ishii.

"I think people might underestimate the cultural differences more than the actual training differences," Colborn said. "The different pace of the baseball, the language and the food. The strangeness of it all." Colborn noted that what competitors seek in the heat of battle is comfort. And in the case of a player in a foreign land, it took energy to find comfort. "You're constantly on a negative balance in terms of feeling good," said Colborn. "You just lose a little every day and you gain it back with sleep, you gain it back with a good meal. But the next day you're still a little bit below your level than the day before. I guess I can relate to it more having gone over to Japan."

Once the break was over, Matsuzaka's fatigue didn't just go away. His first start of the second half came on July 14 in Boston's third game of a four-game series with the Blue Jays at Fenway. And it seemed to be a repeat of Detroit. Again, Matsuzaka didn't have his best fastball. He also lacked command. And in a clear sign he was battling to find his mechanics, Matsuzaka pitched two innings completely out of the stretch, even when there were no baserunners. For Matsuzaka, going to the stretch is something he does only when he's trying to fix a flaw. He mentioned that it was something he frequently did in Japan in order to improve balance. In fact, the practice was not altogether uncommon for pitchers in Japan. There were times during Spring Training when Matsuzaka would do his entire bullpen session out of the stretch. But nothing helped on this night. He gave up two homers and four runs, three of which came in his final inning, the sixth. But the Red Sox battered the Blue Jays anyway, helping Matsuzaka pick up win No. 11. Not that the "W" was much reason for consolation. "I think I was disappointed from beginning to end," Matsuzaka said of the outing.

And his workload again became a story, thanks to agent Scott Boras revealing to the *Boston Globe* the details of a conversation he had with Matsuzaka in San Diego back in June, when the Red Sox were playing the Padres. "I'd rather see him throw closer to 100 pitches than 120 pitches," Boras said to the *Globe's* Nick Cafardo, repeating what he had told Matsuzaka directly some three weeks earlier. Though Boras had not made any direct requests to the Red Sox about Matsuzaka's pitch load, Francona still had a good time with it. "I have a lot of respect for Scott, I really do," Francona said. "He can run the pitching when he lets me run the contracts, how's that? Is that a fair tradeoff?"

Quips aside, Matsuzaka's entire pitching schedule, from the day he took the mound to the four or five in between, is something that Francona and Farrell spent a lot of time discussing. The Red Sox, as detailed an organization as there is in the game, ran charts on everything regarding their pitchers. How many pitches did they throw on the side? How many throws of catch were there between starts? "I think the big thing for us right now is to not only try to understand but learn the in-between days," Francona said. "We feel like the game, we've had under control. It's been pretty consistent all year. We really watch workload. By workload, that doesn't mean pitch count, that means workload." The Red Sox would leave no detail unexplored in their quest to get things just right with Matsuzaka. Francona revealed that he had a 45-minute conversation in Detroit with Takanori Maeda, Matsuzaka's personal masseur that he had brought over from the Seibu Lions, to get an understanding of exactly what made the pitcher tick. "We just talked about the different cultures, different ideas," Francona said. "It's helpful. The more we learn, the better we are. I think everybody understands that we're really in this together. We're just trying to learn as much as we can."

Matsuzaka, at least publicly, downplayed any fatigue he might have been feeling at that time. "Of course, I feel a little bit of fatigue, but I wouldn't call it extreme," Matsuzaka said. "I think how I feel right now is par for the course in what I have experienced in previous seasons." It's just that in previous seasons, Matsuzaka wasn't under nearly the same microscope he would be under during his first season in the majors. The Red Sox had made a lavish investment in the man, and there was curiosity to see whether he would reach not only everyone else's expectations, but his own.

The main thing the Red Sox were conscious of was managing Matsuzaka's workload. Deep into July, Matsuzaka was in the top ten in the Major Leagues in total pitches thrown. And the maintenance of Matsuzaka continued when Farrell again instructed the pitcher to skip his side session leading up to his July 19 start at Fenway against the White Sox. This was the second time in three starts Matsuzaka didn't have the comfort of refining things leading up to his outing. Aside from what country Matsuzaka was in, this notion of cutting back on work was extremely foreign to him. For anyone who has spent any time absorbing the culture of Japanese baseball, it is readily apparent that the theme is to work yourself into the ground. Though the Japanese writers, one after the other, seemed convinced that the modifications to Matsuzaka's throwing program had to be ticking him off, the pitcher himself would make no such statements to the media. "I am not allowing myself to get too anxious about my preparation between starts," said Matsuzaka.

In truth, Matsuzaka eased into the American throwing program far better than some of his Japanese predecessors. Take the
case of Ishii, who was a rookie under Colborn with the Dodgers in 2002. The lefty had no interest in pitching in exhibition
games during his first Spring Training. Instead, he wanted to
keep throwing in the bullpen. At last, Colborn and manager
Jim Tracy talked Ishii into a start late in Spring Training and
he went two solid innings. That left the Dodgers with precious
little time to get him stretched out. But the next two exhibition
starts, Ishii lasted less than two innings. "We were left with a
fifth starter that hadn't gone longer than two innings all spring,"
remembered Colborn some five years later. But Ishii dominated
in his Major League debut on April 6 of 2002 against the Rockies, pitching 5 2/3 innings and striking out 10. The Dodgers did
everything they could to ease his adjustment, even putting a net
under the dugout tunnel near the team's batting cage that he
could throw at between innings. "Ultimately all you care about
is his performance," Colborn said. "You don't really care how he
does it. If it takes him throwing a ball against the wall between
innings then go ahead." Ishii had a decent first season (14-10,
4.27) but wound up hitting a rookie wall. His ERA in the first
half was 3.58, compared to 5.57 in the second half. Ishii was out
of Major League Baseball following the 2005 season, when he
was just 32 years old.

There was no reason to suspect Matsuzaka would flame out
like that. He was putting too much time and thought into making the adjustment, and so were the Red Sox. "He's been great,"
credited Francona. "When you get players of that caliber that
are good, we do want to listen to them. We want to know what
makes them tick and what makes them good. I don't think we
were ever striving to change for change. This guy is pretty good.
It's been interesting. It's been enlightening. We're trying to learn
too." Besides, Matsuzaka was on a different level than Ishii,
given his status as an international icon. Matsuzaka had produced excellence at every level, from high school on up, and

that was on display many times during his first year with the Red Sox. But Matsuzaka struggled for the third start in a row, this time against the White Sox after the skipped side session. The problem this time was control. In just five-plus innings—Matsuzaka was removed after walking the bases loaded and giving up an RBI single to start the sixth—he issued six walks, his career high to that point. It was hard to know if Matsuzaka was rusty from skipping his customary bullpen session, or if he was still tired. Whatever the case, White Sox second baseman Tadahito Iguchi—who had faced Matsuzaka over ninety times in Nippon Professional Baseball—knew that this wasn't quite the same pitcher he remembered hitting against so many times earlier. "I faced him many times," Iguchi said a day after the showdown at Fenway. "It was same as usual except I don't think he was in his best condition and I'm really looking forward to facing him again in Chicago." As it turns out, Iguchi would be traded to the Phillies one week later and would have to wait until Spring Training 2008—at the earliest—to get another look at Dice-K.

But amid the concern about Matsuzaka's latest so-so effort, Farrell cited a reason for optimism, noting that he actually believed Matsuzaka had more life on his fastball than in the previous two starts. What was separating Matsuzaka from his six-start streak just a few weeks earlier when he was so tough to beat? "The difference to those compared to tonight was just repeating a consistent release point," Farrell said. "One of the positives that he and we all need to take from this is we see some velocity creep back up there and there was definitely life in his body, life in his arm and he had some power to all his stuff."

Farrell's silver lining came to fruition five days later. Matsuzaka, again thrust into duty against one of the star pitchers in the game—this time Cleveland's C. C. Sabathia—made a strong statement that his second wind had arrived when he took the ball at Jacobs Field. As usual, Matsuzaka's day would start hours before he pitched. In sort of a surreal sight, Matsuzaka, dressed in a workout shirt and his uniform pants, stepped on the game mound four hours before the game's scheduled first pitch and mimicked his delivery. He went to that full windup, paused his hands in front of his head like he always does, and then unleashed his right arm for delivery. It's just that there was no baseball in his hand. This was shadow pitching, something that other Red Sox pitchers such as Jonathan Papelbon did a lot of. But it was none-theless unusual to see a starting pitcher out there on game day in public view so long before the game would start. But Matsuzaka was a perfectionist and if he was going to be pitching at Jacobs Field that night, he wanted to get a sense of exactly what it felt like to pitch at Jacobs Field.

As much as the Red Sox took every precaution to make sure Matsuzaka didn't tire himself out, the one thing they never minded was his undying commitment to get his blood flowing in the hours leading up to his start. "That's something I wish would rub off on our culture," Francona said. "I know there's ways you're trying to meet in the middle. I never could understand, and again, pitchers are a different breed. You don't understand them to begin with. You see some guys, you look up at 6:30 and they're sleeping on the table and then 20 minutes later, they've got the biggest day of their week. Bronson [Arroyo] was like that. And I love Bronson. But that was his routine and he was good." Every pitcher indeed had his own quirks. Schilling paced around the clubhouse in full uniform for hours on days he was pitching as a clear intensity burned from within. Beckett did a lot more talking to teammates than the other starters on days he was pitching to the point where it was hard to know he was starting that night. It worked for him.

Clearly, what worked for Matsuzaka was work itself. It was the culture he came from, and he was very much a conformist in that way. Three hours before the start against the Indians, Matsuzaka walked back into the clubhouse drenched in sweat. "Now not all pitchers are comfortable doing that," Francona said. "I don't have any problem with a guy being out there. I think that's more on the positive side than worrying about a guy wearing out."

And for the first time in a while, Matsuzaka looked anything but worn out during his start against the Indians. He outdueled eventual Cy Young Award winner Sabathia, 1-0, picking up all five of his strikeouts at big junctures of the game. The punchout had been a weapon of choice for Matsuzaka in Japan, as four times he produced more than 200 strikeouts in a season. And that was pitching in a six-man rotation when he'd make fewer than 30 starts in all but one of those 200-K seasons. Matsuzaka was among the American League leaders in strikeouts for much of his first season but in late July, he still didn't feel the superiority he had for all those years in Japan. "Going forward, I'd like to become the type of pitcher that can get strikeouts at will," Matsuzaka said. "But until I'm at that point, there's still a long, long way to go."

As for the Red Sox, October continued to seem like a near lock. Their lead was consistently between seven to nine games as the end of July neared. After the team started its two-city road trip with five wins in the first six games, Matsuzaka pitched the finale at Tropicana Field, a domed stadium that houses the Tampa Bay Devil Rays. Just as in most years, the Devil Rays were one of the worst teams in Major League Baseball. But Matsuzaka had the misfortune of facing their best pitcher, left-hander Scott Kazmir. And the Red Sox were also weary, not only from the road trip, but from a twelve-inning game the night before Matsuzaka's Sunday afternoon start. Matsuzaka pitched well, but so did Kazmir. A scoreless duel entering the bottom of the seventh inning, Matsuzaka hung an 0-2 splitter to a nondescript hitter named Dioner Navarro for a solo home run. After a single, Matsuzaka was removed and the Devil Rays broke the game open against Manny Delcarmen. It could have been a different game if only Matsuzaka could have put away Navarro. But the pitch obviously didn't do what he wanted to do, which prompted a Japanese reporter to pose an excellent question after the game.

The reporter asked Matsuzaka what his feel for the slicker and slightly heavier baseball was at that point in the season, compared to his final two years with Seibu. "If my feel for the ball while I was pitching for Seibu was about a ten, I'd give myself about a six right now," he said. But as he usually did with his answers, Matsuzaka wanted to make sure people knew he was just responding honestly to a question and not making an excuse. "Still, I think the important thing is to pitch well in challenging spots."

With two months left in Matsuzaka's first Major League season, his arm appeared to be holding up, despite the natural phase of "tired arm" that every pitcher seems to go through over the course of a 162-game season. But one interesting trend had emerged. Through Matsuzaka's first twenty-two starts, exactly eleven were after the standard rest time of four days and eleven were with the five-plus days of rest Matsuzaka was so used to during his years in Japan. In the eleven starts with the extra rest, Matsuzaka was 7-3 with a 3.30 ERA. In the eleven on standard rest, he was 5-5 with a 4.19 ERA. "That was another transition that Ishii wasn't quite able to make," noted Colborn. "The second half of the season, when there just aren't as many days off, each second half he kind of ran into a wall. It's a little different pace." Would Matsuzaka be able to run over the wall instead of into it? In August and September, the answer to that question was all but certain to become apparent. At times, neither Matsuzaka nor the Red Sox would like the answer.

13

Rookie Wall
(August 4–September 14, 2007)

IF THERE WAS A point at which Matsuzaka started riding a wave of momentum toward the Rookie of the Year Award, it was August 4, when he met up with Ichiro and the Mariners for the fourth time of 2007. Farrell checked out Matsuzaka's pre-start bullpen session and the word that probably came to his mind first was, "Wow." The pitching coach relayed to Francona that Matsuzaka had everything in his arsenal working. Mind you, pitchers don't always carry a great "bullpen" into the game, but on this occasion Matsuzaka did. In a performance that was as workmanlike as it was dominant, Matsuzaka held the Mariners to six hits and two runs while striking out ten batters for the first time since April 17. Maybe the July fatigue was turning into an August rejuvenation, for this was Matsuzaka's third terrific outing in a row and it ran his record to 13-8. At this rate, he would easily get the 15 wins everyone seemed to predict back in the spring, and maybe even 20, which is the benchmark for an elite pitcher. Though there was sentiment from a small faction of writers that players with a rich history in Japanese Professional Baseball didn't deserve much consideration for an award given to rookies, 20 wins would make Matsuzaka a very difficult name to avoid checking off if he could keep going strong.

Even a couple of weeks after the season had ended, Farrell didn't flinch when asked the one outing of Matsuzaka's that sort of stuck out in his mind above the others. "Seattle in August," said Farrell. "He was dominant in that game, I thought." Farrell was so excited about the performance that he used it to drive home what he thought might be some motivational points to Matsuzaka a few days later. The Red Sox were in Anaheim at that point, and Matsuzaka came to the park in the morning for an early workout because he was going to fly to Baltimore ahead of the team, where he'd be opening a series that weekend. "When I saw that type of performance in Seattle, I think all these things loop back into how he's received and viewed in Japan," said Farrell. "You look at the games he pitched in Seattle, those didn't happen just by chance. He's three hours closer to Japan. Those games are televised back there. He's competing against Ichiro. There are so many other components to those games against Seattle that really drive him. I told him, 'You're looking at possibly the best hitter in the American League in Ichiro, the batting title winner. There's no reason you couldn't be the best pitcher in the American League. You two are on a par.' Maybe he could use that as a bit of a motivator." The slicing up of the Mariners in Seattle would be followed by a fourth consecutive sharp showing at Camden Yards in Baltimore the night of August 10, as the weary Red Sox were starting their third leg of a lengthy road trip that started in two West Coast cities—Seattle and Anaheim—and concluded in the land of the crab cakes. Matsuzaka was in prime position for win number 14 after limiting the Orioles to one run over seven innings and striking out seven in the process on a night he was matched with one of the best pitchers in the league in Erik Bedard. Eric Gagne, who had been acquired a few days earlier to give the Red Sox another dominant closer—albeit to be used in a setup role in front of Jonathan Papelbon—was given the responsibility of preserving Matsuzaka's 5-1 lead in the eighth inning. Just a few minutes later, Gagne had given it all back. The Orioles won it in the bottom of the ninth on a sac fly against Hideki Okajima and what looked like a sure win for Dice-K was transformed into a no decision, not to mention a bad loss for the team. Still though, Matsuzaka was looking good. His ERA in the heavy-hitting American League was, at this point, 3.59. The Red Sox pretty much felt good whenever he took the ball figuring, at the very least, he would put them in position to win. Nobody knew it at the time, but the lost opportunity in Baltimore wound up being highly symbolic of the way things would go for Matsuzaka for the next several weeks.

In fact, Matsuzaka's 2007 season was never the same after that point. Bad luck did not get Matsuzaka five days later in a rare Wednesday afternoon game at Fenway against the Devil Rays. This time, it was just bad pitching. For the first time since that flat Sunday before the All-Star break in Detroit, Matsuzaka had very little working and the Devil Rays let him know about it, pounding eight hits and six runs over six innings. One trend that did continue for Matsuzaka was that all of his worst outings seemed to come on the standard four days of rest that Major League pitchers typically perform under, rather than the extra day that Matsuzaka had become so accustomed to in Japan, and that the Red Sox always tried to give him whenever possible. There was no need for the Red Sox to be stubborn in this matter and they weren't. Matsuzaka had very little familiarity pitching every fifth day and it wasn't something the club would force, especially when days off could be used to the pitcher's benefit. In fact, with a pair of 40-year-olds in the rotation in Schilling and Wakefield, the extra time off would help just about everyone out. In the case of Matsuzaka, it was easy to see why the rest helped him so much. With his strikingly close attention to detail and his intense preparation between starts, all the time he could have was for the best. "I'm very disappointed," was how Matsuzaka would sum it up after the game. In truth, the disappointment was just about to start after what had mainly been a solid first season to that point.

What prompted the start of Matsuzaka's free-fall? "I don't know if maybe it was the combination of the game in Baltimore where he pitched well and didn't get the win, and then he got knocked around against Tampa Bay, and the expectation of that elusive 15th win, trying to get to 15 and staying up with Beckett the way he was accumulating wins, and Wakefield was also, I think he began to do a little too much to try to keep that pace and lost some of that feeling and trust in his secondary stuff that makes him so good," said Farrell.

Next up for Matsuzaka was another matchup with the Devil Rays, and this one at Tropicana Field with two extra days of rest. What Francona did was slot Julian Tavarez into the rotation for one start so that each pitcher could get an extra breather. In particular, the move seemed designed for Dice-K, who would wind up making six of his last seven regular season starts on more than four days of rest. Clearly, the Red Sox were playing for October and they felt they needed to have Matsuzaka at close to peak form. Beckett was a true horse, but with the age on both Schilling and Wakefield, they couldn't be counted on quite as much as in years past. Matsuzaka was going to need to be there when it counted, and the Red Sox were doing everything they could to make sure he made it through the marathon. "Numbers-wise, I don't think there's any getting around it," Francona said. "He's been more successful with the extra day. It doesn't always work out that way where you can do it. It's nice when you can. I don't think he feels any urgency to have the extra day, but the numbers do bear it out." And, again, with that extra day, Matsuzaka looked good at Tropicana Field. In a performance eerily similar to his game there a month earlier, he was done in by one bad pitch which was deposited over the wall by B. J. Upton for a two-run homer in the bottom of the sixth, which gave Dice-K and Boston a 2-1 loss. It was the same score Matsuzaka lost by in his previous visit to St. Petersburg, and at that time of the season the continuation of a troubling trend in which the Red Sox didn't score for Matsuzaka. In Matsuzaka's first ten losses, the Red Sox scored a total of nineteen runs while he was in the game. If there was a constant to Matsuzaka's rookie year, it was that he never looked for any type of excuse. Always, he put a loss on himself. "I don't think I'm particularly

stressed out about the fact that these games haven't turned out in
our favor," Matsuzaka said following that game. "Anything I do
feel frustrated about is really about my own pitching."

Maybe Matsuzaka put too much on himself at times. "He
takes a tremendous amount of responsibility towards his position
and what it means for the team," said Farrell. "When he wasn't
receiving the win in some cases, I think there was a tendency for
him to maybe try to do more. That's where we saw the pitch dis-
tribution start to become more fastball-oriented. He was trying
to do too much to get a win. Inevitably, that can work against a
guy." The wall—real or imagined—that many rookies face was
about to serve as an annoying barricade for a while. And it came
at a most inconvenient time, as the Yankees, who had surged during the second half to get to at least a level in the standings where
the Red Sox couldn't help but take notice, were next up. Part of
the thinking in the way Francona lined up his rotation for crunch
time was that Matsuzaka, Beckett and Schilling—in that order—
would pitch in each of the three-game series against the Yankees,
the second of which would come at Fenway on September 14. But
before that, there was the three-game Bronx showdown which
the Red Sox rode into with some momentum after obliterating
the White Sox in a four-game sweep at Chicago by an aggregate
score of 46-7. Contrast that with the Yankees, who had lost an
extra-inning game in Detroit at 3:30 a.m that same weekend, and
lost three out of four to a Tigers team that had been playing bad
baseball at the time. While Matsuzaka and the Red Sox were rest-
ing up for the big series in the Big Apple during Monday's welcomed off-day, the Yankees were still in Detroit, where they'd cap
that disastrous Detroit weekend with a 16-0 loss in which veteran
Mike Mussina was so bad he was bounced from the rotation. The
Red Sox led their rivals by eight games entering the series, and it
seemed that all that was necessary to avoid any kind of drama in
the division race was for Boston to win one game.

There was no better time for it to happen than the opener,
with Matsuzaka on the hill in a showdown with Andy Pettitte.

But one thing quickly jumped out about Matsuzaka in this one. His fastball was mainly around 90 and 91 instead of the 92–94 he frequented when he was at his sharpest. It wasn't as if lack of rest could be pinpointed this time around. Matsuzaka came in with the extra day to recuperate. But the Yankees, the offensive juggernaut that they were, quickly struck for two in the first and another one in the fifth. The Red Sox did enough against Pettitte and the game was tied at 3-3 entering the bottom of the seventh. But an old friend—and now very much a nemesis—named Johnny Damon spoiled the night for Matsuzaka by hooking a two-run homer down the line in right field. Matsuzaka had been uneconomical, throwing 110 pitches over 6$\frac{1}{3}$ innings. He produced just two strikeouts. It was Matsuzaka's third loss in as many starts, marking the second time all year he'd lose that many in a row. Even with all that said, Matsuzaka had still hung pretty tough against an opponent that could flat-out pound on opposing pitchers. "I look at the game in New York and Johnny Damon jams himself and hits a ball 315 feet for a home run," said Farrell. "But otherwise, he pitched his ass off in that game."

Kazuhiro Takeda, who served as the pitching coach for Team Japan during Matsuzaka's legendary run during the World Baseball Classic in March of 2006, was at Yankee Stadium for the game, serving as a broadcaster. He couldn't believe this was the same Matsuzaka he had witnessed during his magical international run 17 months earlier. "I saw him pitch but that's not even half of what he can do," noted Takeda. "The season is long over here and he's getting quite tired but I think he's trying to save himself for later also." Takeda met with Matsuzaka the day after his velocity-deprived outing against the Yankees. There were clearly adjustments Matsuzaka was adapting to throughout his first season, the texture of the baseball most prominent among them. "Here, it's more slippery," Takeda said. "I feel I've watched him pitch a lot and I feel he still has to get used to the ball and it's going to take a bit more time." The tight leash and attention to pitch count would weigh on Matsuzaka throughout his rookie year. Though he was mum about it publicly, the people who knew Matsuzaka the best could sense it gnawing at him. "He definitely wants to stay in and pitch more, run up the count a little more," Takeda said. "I talked to him and he said he wants to pitch at least 120 pitches every outing." In actuality, Matsuzaka averaged 109 pitches over his 32 starts. What was most interesting about Matsuzaka's postgame address after the loss in New York was that he claimed to be "minimizing the strikeout" in order to go deeper into the game. However, that logic, when relayed to Francona and Varitek, was met with strange looks. "When you're a strikeout, fly ball pitcher, it's hard to force too much contact but still be aggressive," said Varitek, the catcher and captain.

If Matsuzaka's Rookie of the Year chances were beginning to slip away, he didn't much care. In fact, he seemed to share the belief of Bill Ballou, the veteran Red Sox beatwriter for the *Worcester Telegram,* who thought veteran Japanese players had no place in the discussion for the Rookie of the Year Award. Ballou, in fact, along with one other voter, didn't even put Hideki Matsui on the ballot in 2003, which helped cost the Yankees' outfielder the award in a narrow defeat to Angel Berroa of the Royals. Four years later, Ballou's stance, if anything, had only gotten stronger. But in a way, Matsuzaka was shooting a hole in Ballou's theory by having some lumps that seemed very rookie-like. Ballou and Francona would often have spirited debates about such matters either on the field during batting practice or in the manager's office. Francona, who clearly had a comfortable relationship with Matsuzaka despite the language barrier, decided to ask his pitcher for his thoughts on the Rookie of the Year at a time when not only was fellow Japanese teammate Hideki Okajima a candidate, but so was Sox second baseman Dustin Pedroia. "He had an interesting answer," said Francona. "He said, 'I've already been Rookie of the Year.' And he pointed at Pedroia and said, 'That's your rookie of the year.' I remember thinking, it was just in passing, but I remember thinking, that's a pretty mature attitude. I don't want to hurt someone's chances of receiving awards, ever, but I loved his attitude." Matsuzaka, in fact, had been the Rookie of the Year for the Seibu Lions after going 16-5 with a 2.60 ERA in 1999. But there would be no controversy this time around. Though nobody wanted to quite say it at the time, Matsuzaka was pitching himself out of the discussion for Rookie of the Year. By November, it was indeed Pedroia who had won the award, while Matsuzaka finished a distant fourth.

Especially in late August, there were far more relevant matters at hand. The Red Sox were swept in those three games in New York, dropping their once whopping lead down to five games. At the same time the Red Sox were trying to open their lead back up, they were focused on helping Matsuzaka finish his first season in strong fashion, considering that he would be needed during the month of October. Though every Matsuzaka start seemed to have a twist to it that made it unlike all the others, his next turn after Yankee Stadium was truly bizarre. The venue was Fenway Park, the opponent was the Toronto Blue Jays, and the occasion was Labor Day. It's just that the night began as anything but labor for Matsuzaka. He blew a fastball by Vernon Wells on the first pitch of the game and seemed to stay in that general area of dominance through his first five innings. Unlike in New York, when the zip was gone, Matsuzaka appeared refreshed. The fastball was humming, the offspeed stuff was dancing and the Blue Jays generally seemed perplexed.

The Red Sox, for one of the few times in a while, had no problem smacking the ball all over the park in support of Dice-K. They had built a 10-1 lead by the time Matsuzaka took the ball for the sixth. And then? Complete disaster. Practically everything Matsuzaka had built up until that point of the night seemed to be shredded by what was almost a complete collapse. There was a walk, a hard single, a bloop single, a strange chopper that Matsuzaka deflected to turn into a hit to bring one run home. And then there was a laser of an opposite field, three-run homer to right by Troy Glaus. A game that had once been 10-0 was now 10-5. Matsuzaka gave up two more baserunners after the homer and was removed from the game. By the time the inning finally ended, the Red Sox were ahead by a precarious one run, and only because rookie Jacoby Ellsbury made a sliding catch to prevent the tying run from scoring. Matsuzaka wound up getting the win—despite the ten hits and seven runs allowed—but it didn't seem to matter. Again, all eyes were on Matsuzaka. How could he lose it so quickly? Why was he in a slump? Was he really worth all the money?

For the American media that tried to make sense of Matsuzaka's highs and lows, some of the more frustrating moments would come during the post-game press conferences. Masa Hoshino, a Harvard graduate and an easygoing man, was always cordial and concise in translating Matsuzaka's answers to the press. Perhaps he made Matsuzaka sound more like an Ivy Leaguer at times than a baseball player, but other than that, Japanese reporters who were fluent in both languages thought that the theme of Matsuzaka's answers were translated properly. But it just seemed like Matsuzaka—be it the language barrier or protecting a competitive advantage—would give precious few details into his successes or his failures. Matsuzaka was asked following the strange Blue Jays meltdown why his last inning was so different than his first five. "Certainly there were a few bad breaks in a row. I felt that I could pitch well enough to cover those bad breaks, but since I wasn't able to, that led to that big inning in the sixth." Because that answer didn't really say anything, there would be follow-up upon follow-up. "As I mentioned before, I think it was just the bad breaks and my inability to cover those moments. I think that was the main difference." And, as in every single time that Matsuzaka would struggle, he was asked if fatigue was a factor. "I personally don't think it's a problem," he said.

Five days later, there were problems all over the place as Matsuzaka aimed for win number 15 in Baltimore. If you take a quick glance at Matsuzaka's first season, it seems apparent that his high moment was the complete game gem against the Tigers on May 14. It can be said with even more certainty that the true low point of 2007 for Matsuzaka was the night of September 8 at Baltimore

against a terrible Orioles team. The Red Sox had staked Matsuzaka to a 4-1 lead after two innings and it seemed as if everyone
would just be able to put it in cruise control for the rest of this Saturday evening. But then came the kind of disastrous inning that
had found Matsuzaka a few times over the course of 2007, but
none as bad as this complete implosion. The third inning started
in the following fashion: single, double, walk, walk, single, walk.
Two of the walks forced in runs. The score was now tied at 4
and the bases were loaded with nobody out. Maybe Matsuzaka
could minimize the damage and hold it right there, it seemed,
after he struck out Aubrey Huff and got Jay Payton on a popup.
Up stepped a man in Scott Moore whom only the most die-hard
of Orioles fans had even heard of before. Matsuzaka threw the
23-year-old prospect a tasty, 2-2 fastball and Moore ate it up,
sending a grand slam over the wall in right-center. Just like that,
the worst start of Matsuzaka's career to date was over. He had
been slammed for six hits and eight runs over 2²/₃ innings. His
ERA now stood at 4.44. His record was 14-12. Over a five-start
span, Matsuzaka had been anything but the sometimes dominant
innings-eater the Red Sox so often counted on during the first half
of the season. Instead, he went 1-4 with a 9.57 ERA in that skid,
and the 2-1 loss to the Rays marked the only time in those five
starts Matsuzaka didn't give up five runs or more.

While the nature of Matsuzaka's struggles were sometimes a
mystery, that was not the case in Baltimore. For all the talk about
Matsuzaka's deep arsenal of pitches, he had an amazing depen-
dence on his fastball that night against the Orioles, and really,
over the last few weeks. Where a changeup or a curve could have
thrown the Orioles off their rhythm, Matsuzaka kept trying to
pound in the hard stuff. It was reminiscent of some of his early
years in Japan, where he would do the same thing at times, especially when he was starting to get hit. His manager during his
first few years with the Seibu Lions remembers some of the growing pains. "Back then, he felt he had to prove something so he
was going at full force and full velocity," said Osamu Higashio.

"Because of that, he didn't have the command of his pitches." Another difference back then was that Matsuzaka's fastball in his late teens and lower 20s was consistently in the mid to upper 90s. Now, he was mainly around 93–95. That was not going to stop a Major League hitter who was zoned in on heat. Farrell expressed concerns about Matsuzaka's over-reliance on the hard stuff, both directly to the pitcher and in the media. "He's recently had a tendency to just rely on his fastball solely and trying to generate as much power as possible," Farrell said after the Baltimore bashing. "As a result, I think he's sacrificing location. He's somewhat gone away from his offspeed pitches and hitters have had a chance to go in and look hard and not really have to guard too much against anything soft in a pitch mix."

One thing Francona spoke of quite often when it came to players, particularly ones without a lot of Major League experience, was the need to slow the game down. Matsuzaka was not doing this. Not with his pitches and not with his heart rate. It seemed obvious by the fact that there were so many isolated bad innings throughout the year that when things went bad, he didn't yet have the capacity to turn the tide. "In a nutshell and trying to keep it simple, I think when the ballpark is getting loud and the game is getting fast, he's getting hard [with his pitches]," Francona said. "Sometimes hard, harder, hardest isn't necessarily the best. If you're able to throttle back and throw all your pitches, again, that's pitching. And it's certainly easier said than done. But we've got to try to get back to that in those situations."

There was an eerie comparison to be made within the confines of the Red Sox's clubhouse. Go back one year earlier and Josh Beckett was the new guy in town. He was the one who came over with a legendary reputation in big games—albeit for the 2003 Florida Marlins and not in Japan. Beckett spent his first season in Boston trying to announce his presence by gunning one 97-mph heater after another. The curve and the changeup that had served him well in the past were put on the back burner. By overthrowing his heat, Beckett often left it over the middle. The end result? An uneven 16-win season in which the 36 homers allowed and a 5.01 ERA were better indicators of the way he pitched. Beckett couldn't quite slow his problems down in the middle of the season but he seemed to come to grips with it all during the winter at his ranch in Texas. He went on a mission during the offseason in terms of lifting weights and increasing his workout routine, and he came to camp looking like a new man. Beckett in 2007 was not just the ace of the Red Sox, but perhaps the premier ace in baseball. His curve was back, so was his changeup. And more importantly than that, he had the confidence that all elite pitchers need. Schilling wasn't so sure the Beckett comparison applied. He just thought the year was one big adjustment for Matsuzaka that nobody could truly relate to. "Josh was, I think, still trying to get used to a lot of things from a stuff standpoint and he still is," Schilling said. "I think, Daisuke from a stuff standpoint, is still very aware of his stuff. There's a whole lot more on him than I think you can expect from somebody. He's got Red Sox Nation, the nation of Japan, but he's not going to make excuses. He's going to make adjustments." And Schilling also had a more clinical look at Matsuzaka's over-reliance on heat. "That's not exclusive to those two guys. That's what happens when a power pitcher struggles," said Schilling. "A lot of times you go away from pitching and you try to get out of trouble by throwing. That's a lot of people."

But Matsuzaka clearly wasn't a lot of people. He was a legend in Japan—an international icon. Not only was his status slipping back home, but his new fans were getting a little unimpressed by what they were watching every fifth or sixth day. Don't think for a second that Matsuzaka didn't feel this burden. If anything, his expectations were enormous. "I think he feels a tremendous responsibility to carry his share," said Francona. "Sometimes you go through rough times. We need to make sure we help him. Coaching or managing in Boston is different than somewhere else. It's not just all about x's and o's. We can help with all that stuff and we do. But there's other things on the periphery. Part of our responsibility is to help make it easier for him to succeed. I think we understand that also."

Things were at such a bad point that the pitcher was asked after the Baltimore game if he was worried about not being part of the postseason rotation. "I haven't thought out that far yet," Matsuzaka said. "I think right now, what I need to do is really take care of my job that's been laid out right in front of me and into the future. I feel that there's really no benefit or positive value of worrying about something that's so far ahead." He did acknowledge, however, that his funk was nothing less than serious. "I would agree that right now is sort of a testing time period for me where I need to be patient but at the same time I feel like I'm the one guy dragging on this team a little bit," he said. "For that, I feel very apologetic." For the only time all season, Matsuzaka didn't speak to the Japanese media after the game, instead using his brief session with the American writers as his only words of the night. His reasoning was that in Japan, the losing pitcher seldom speaks to the media, so he figured the Japanese writers would understand his reluctance to talk.

As for the way Matsuzaka was pitching, Boras claimed not to be surprised, instead all but suggesting in an interview with the *Boston Herald*'s Rob Bradford that he viewed Matsuzaka's first season more on the context of what he did the first 4½ months than the whole body of work. "If you go back and look back at what I said was going to be the only issue with Daisuke and it has come to be true, and that is, pitching in the Major Leagues, it's stressful physically and mentally," Boras said during that interview. "This was a new experience for Dice-K. This year, I think he's done tremendously well. When you look at particularly his first four, four and a half months, that's how I'm gauging Dice-K. I knew that the last month and a half was going to be very difficult because of what would be a new world physically and mentally for a Japanese pitcher. I think Boston recognizes that and is doing a very good job of managing and bringing Daisuke to where he can perform at his best in his first season."

The Red Sox had put so much time and energy into getting Matsuzaka and doing whatever they could to make him comfortable once they got him that they weren't about to lose faith in him. A big, three-game series with the Yankees loomed at Fenway Park and Matsuzaka would keep his turn in the rotation for the Friday night opener on September 14. But first, there would be an impromptu birthday gathering. With Matsuzaka's actual birthday on September 13—an off-day for the team—the Japanese media serenaded him with a cake the day before just outside the Boston clubhouse. It was quite a bizarre scene for the American media, as they could never imagine doing such a thing for say, Curt Schilling, or anyone for that matter. But the two media contingents just had different ways of doing things. "I hope I will have a better happy birthday next year," Matsuzaka said to the reporters upon blowing out the candles, which was a candid admission that the season wasn't going quite as he'd hoped. But he would be 27 the next time he pitched, and there would be no better time for Matsuzaka to truly come of age. With that off-day preceding the Yankees series, all the idle time was left to again focus on Matsuzaka and whether he'd have a second wind in him down the stretch. On the morning of the Yankees' opener, the *Boston Globe* ran a graphic demonstrating Matsuzaka's total number of pitches in each professional season. Already in 2007, Matsuzaka had thrown 3,125, the most he had thrown in any season since 2001, when he fired 4,072 pitches. But he came out against the Yankees and demonstrated some sheer will against the most relentless lineup in the game. As was often the case, he threw a lot of pitches, including 27 in the first inning alone. But he continually wiggled his way out of trouble. The Yankees mustered four hits, two runs and five walks off him over 5²/₃ innings and 120 pitches. But Dice-K did strike out seven and he had a 7-2 lead when he walked off the mound. Win number 15 was a given. Or it least it seemed so. But the trusted 1-2 bullpen combo of Hideki Okajima and Jonathan Papelbon suffered a nightmare collapse, getting tagged for six runs in the eighth.

As crushing a loss as it was—the Yankees closed within 4½ games in the American League East—there was some hope that Matsuzaka was on the verge of a resurgence. "I thought he pitched with a lot of heart," Francona said. "When he left the game, we were in good shape." By the end of the weekend, Matsuzaka was in a good enough mood that he had no problem whatsoever participating in the initiation prank the Red Sox played on the rookies. Even after a tough Sunday night loss to the Yankees in which Roger Clemens out-pitched Schilling in one of those epic duels between veterans, the Red Sox dressed all the rookies up for a late-night flight to Toronto. Okajima and Jacoby Ellsbury returned to the lockers in the clubhouse at Fenway Park, only to see the female pirate outfits that had been left for them. Clay Buchholz, fresh off a no-hitter a few weeks earlier, was now Minnie Mouse. Brandon Moss was Dorothy from the *Wizard of Oz*. Dice-K? He was dressed as Dipsy, a bright green Teletubbie from the hit cartoon show which features rotund space creatures. The sheepish grin on Matsuzaka's face as he trudged through the clubhouse was fairly priceless. Matsuzaka had been a star all his life, but he had no problem being "one of the guys." It was one of the things that endeared him most to his manager and his teammates. Sure, Matsuzaka's rookie year wasn't as easy as he had hoped. But he didn't sulk or act like less of a teammate because of it, which was impressive when you consider the language barrier. The loss to the Yankees was undoubtedly one of the toughest of the year, but Matsuzaka helped create some levity. Francona spoke about it the next day, before the Red Sox got ready to take on the Blue Jays. "I didn't think that there was much that could make me laugh last night. There was," Francona said. "Watching Dice-K go through the security, it was hard not to laugh. Just sitting back there in the back and the players always go first and I'm looking at Dice-K and I'm thinking, somebody wrote a check for [$103.1] million and he's going through the line as a rodent or whatever. Remember when I said in Spring Training he gets it? I think he gets it. The look on his face, it was hilarious."

At this point of the season, the Red Sox needed all the levity they could get. Their lead over the Yankees, which had been 14½ games on May 29, was down to 1½ by the time the Red Sox got swept right out of Toronto on September 19. Still, there wasn't a doubt the Red Sox would make the playoffs. If nothing else, they could win the Wild Card, thanks to a late-season collapse by the Tigers. But the Red Sox were worried about their own team. For the first time all year, there was a tenseness about the team. Injuries had played a role in the demise, without question. Gifted slugger Manny Ramirez didn't play from August 29 to September 24 because of a strained left oblique. Kevin Youkilis, the gritty first baseman, missed a week in mid-September after being belted on the right wrist by a Chien-Ming Wang fastball. Gagne had been brought in to bolster the bullpen in late July, but had been an unmitigated disaster, and a sometimes ailing one at that. And Okajima, the less-heralded Japanese pitcher on the Red Sox, hit a wall himself late in the season and was far less effective than he was earlier in the year. But of all the questions the Red Sox had, perhaps the biggest was whether they could get Matsuzaka right before October. After Matsuzaka's Yankees' outing, Francona and Farrell outlined a period of seven days rest for him before he'd next pitch. Part of it was to get Matsuzaka some time to work out some kinks on the side. Another part was to line things up before the postseason. "At some point, there was going to be a three-day extra rest period," Francona said. "We elected to do it now as opposed to before a playoff game. It just didn't seem to make a ton of sense. Rest is great, but if there's any rust, let's have it now and get guys on a schedule and turn them loose." As confident as the Red Sox remained in Matsuzaka, nobody truly knew what he would offer at the most critical point of the season. It was impossible to know, given that he was still in the midst of his first journey through the marathon that is a Major League Baseball season. There weren't many starts left for Matsuzaka in 2007. All you had to do was look at a calendar to know that. But the ones that were left were all big.

14

A Bubbly Finish
(September 22–30, 2007)

THERE WERE TWO STARTS left for Matsuzaka in his topsy-turvy 2007 regular season. And both, believe it or not, would lead to champagne. By the time the Red Sox arrived at Tropicana Field—yes, Matsuzaka was pitching in the dank, domed stadium in St. Petersburg for the third time in two months—they were ready to solidify the postseason berth that had seemed inevitable since May. This, even though the Yankees had come back with such fury in the American League East that they were nipping on the heels of the Red Sox. The Wild Card race was a completely different story. The Tigers—American League champions the season before—had bottomed out over the season's final few weeks, making it clear that both the Red Sox and Yankees would be postseason participants. By the time Matsuzaka took the ball that Saturday night (September 22) in St. Petersburg, a Boston win combined with a Detroit loss was all it would take to clinch a playoff spot. The Tigers took care of their end of the bargain, taking a 7-4 defeat against the Royals that ended while the Boston-Tampa Bay game was still in progress. So Dice-K, refreshed after his longest break of the season, could be the man to seal the deal for the team that had invested so much time and money in acquiring his services.

Matsuzaka came out of the gate with three shutout innings and by the time the sixth inning rolled around, he had himself a 5-2 lead. Once again, win number 15 seemed in the cards. But the Devil Rays got one back in the sixth. Then came the seventh. It never failed, it seemed, that there could be one inning that would ruin an otherwise solid night at the office for Dice-K. This one truly snuck up on everyone. He had retired the first two batters of the inning on popups and was a mere out away from his finest seven-inning outing in weeks. In fact, it would have been the first time he had pitched as many as seven innings in a game since August 10 at Camden Yards. But the final out never came. Matsuzaka walked two batters in succession. And because of the way he can fall apart in an inning, not to mention that one of the most productive hitters in the league for the season was coming to the plate in Carlos Pena, out came Francona with the hook. "Carlos Pena is standing up there looking like he's about 6-foot-8," Francona would say later. In came lefty specialist Javy Lopez and out went the baseball. Pena nailed a three-run homer that turned a Matsuzaka win into a Matsuzaka no decision. After the game, Farrell had an interesting point about the back-to-back walks. Matsuzaka was so accustomed to being on the mound without a leash in Japan—basically every game was his to win or lose until he dropped—perhaps he tightened up when he knew he was closing in on the pitch count the Red Sox had penciled in for him. "He probably sensed that the seventh inning was going to be his last inning," Farrell said. "He probably tried to overthrow some pitches that led to the walks. He looked like he was trying a little bit too hard to get the final out in the seventh."

Trailing in the game 6-5, the Red Sox were in danger of putting their postseason clincher on ice. But they would rally, with Jason Varitek belting a game-tying homer to lead off the ninth and Julio Lugo crashing through with a two-run blast later in the inning. Before the game, Francona indicated that the Red Sox wouldn't have any type of celebration because their eyes were on the bigger prizes. But because of the way they won, and a little bit because of how stressful things had been lately, they did allow themselves to enjoy the moment for a bit. When the players came off the field, they gathered in the clubhouse over a modest display of champagne and beer and had a toast, with Francona congratulating them on the accomplishment and giving an encouraging reminder of what was ahead. By the time the media was allowed in a few minutes later, all the remnants of the party were basically gone.

Matsuzaka had pitched well enough to enjoy the moment, even if he didn't have a win next to his name. Ever since those nights in 1999 when he attended those Yankees-Braves World Series games, Matsuzaka had envisioned himself as a participant in October, Major League style. Now, his chance was just a short time away. That was just another reason he was determined to get his pitching back in sync by the time the season reached its urgent stage. Matsuzaka stood outside the clubhouse and spoke to the media in a dark hallway. "There would have been nothing greater than getting the win and being the winning pitcher on the night that we clinched," Matsuzaka said. "Now that I'm at this point and looking at the situation, I'm pretty happy that we were able to make the playoffs and I'm excited to move forward."

The one thing the Red Sox always did during Matsuzaka's struggles was to keep a confident public façade. In fact, their positive reinforcement with Matsuzaka himself probably played a role in the bend but don't break mentality he would show various times throughout the season. Matsuzaka would be given some constructive criticism during the year. But it was never done in negative fashion. As an example of the power of positive thinking, consider Farrell's response when a Japanese reporter correctly pointed out to him that Matsuzaka had won exactly two games over the last two months. "A pitcher getting a win is reliant on a number of things, his offense, his defense, the bullpen that comes in behind him," Farrell said. "I think we're

all well aware that in the first half Daisuke had 10 wins and
he sits here today with 14. He has pitched well enough to win
many other games, much more than the 4 he's had in the second
half. Things have to fall right. Unfortunately tonight, Daisuke
was in line for a win, as he's been many other times, but it just
didn't work out for him tonight." But it also wasn't like Farrell
to just blow smoke. He found some tangible evidence behind
his silver lining. Unlike that dreadful night in Baltimore two
weeks earlier, the fastball was at least now taking an occasional
backseat to the supplementary pitches, which were so good in
Spring Training.

   "I think over the past couple of starts, he's used his curve
ball and really his changeup with much more frequency and
much more effect. I think what it's allowed," said Farrell, "is
some relaxation to filter into executing his fastball." Relaxation
was an interesting choice of words. In fact, nobody—be it the
organization, the fans or definitely the highly-interested Japanese media—seemed to be at ease with how things were going
for Dice-K. He remained unpredictable deep into his rookie year,
which isn't to say it was a failure. It's just that the money—
$103.1 million was ingrained on the brain—and legendary repu-
tation back home preceded him. The Red Sox needed Matsuzaka
in the playoffs. They couldn't have Beckett as the lone stalwart,
and even if Schilling was a big-game pitcher beyond reproach,
he was now a six or seven-inning guy at best and one who now
pitched with less of a margin for error than he ever had before.
Tim Wakefield, with 17 wins in 2007, was second only to Beckett on the staff. But his health was declining so badly as the season wore on that his October status was anything but certain.
Fifth starter Jon Lester, the talented 23-year-old lefty, had been
cancer-free for less than a year and he was still working his way
back to top form late in the year. This made it more imperative
than ever that Matsuzaka step up and make his combination
of power and finesse something the Red Sox could use to their
advantage in October.

Because he's a pitcher and not a prophet, Matsuzaka didn't know at the time that this would hardly be his last time to pitch in a clinching situation. Opportunity Number 2—and that wouldn't be the last one either—would come in his next start. It was September 28, a gorgeous summer-type night at Fenway Park with a full moon hovering over the right field light tower. And it was Dice-K's last regular-season turn of 2007 and the radar was on him that night against the Twins. The Red Sox needed a win and a Yankees' loss at Baltimore to at last clinch the American League East that they had led since April 18. The Red Sox had clinched a spot in the postseason. But winning the division— something the Red Sox hadn't done since 1995—would allow the team to open the playoffs with homefield advantage. The Red Sox were also battling the Indians for the best record in the American League, which would give them homefield advantage for the entire postseason. The possible clinch party was a mere sideshow to what really mattered. The Red Sox still hadn't set their postseason rotation and Matsuzaka was going to help determine it.

Dialed in right from the bullpen, as Francona would put it later, Matsuzaka came out blazing, striking out the first two batters on the night. There was nothing laborious about the performance. The ball was popping out of his hand, much like it did on some of his best outings of the year. Free and easy was Matsuzaka, recalling memories from that May night when he went the distance against the Tigers. And the radar gun readings served as proof of the way he was changing speeds and staying away from the unpredictable pattern that had betrayed him at times in the second half. From the 90s to the 80s to the 70s on the radar gun, Matsuzaka was clicking. He did give up a pair of runs in the seventh, cutting his lead to 4-2. As a sign of his lack of fatigue, Matsuzaka threw a 95-mph fastball for a strikeout to start the eighth. Still, there was a fleeting moment in the eighth when it seemed his rebound night could go up in flames. With one on and one out, the dangerous All-Star Torii

Hunter represented the tying run. But this time, Matsuzaka dipped down to 83-mph for a changeup and got a 5-4-3 double play to end not just the inning, but his night. In finally winning his 15th game—the number so many prognosticators picked back in March—the key number of the night was eight. Matsuzaka had not gone eight innings in 15 starts. This was the first time he did it since July 3. He did it while throwing 119 pitches, 77 of them for strikes. There were just two walks.

But after Jonathan Papelbon closed down the Twins like he usually does—with a dominant ninth—the Red Sox still hadn't clinched anything. It seemed the party was going to have to wait another night. The Yankees would build a 9-6 lead entering the late innings against a real bad Baltimore team and had their all-world closer Mariano Rivera lined up to pitch the ninth.

So Matsuzaka and Francona both held press conferences after the Boston game had ended thinking full well that the division race had at least one more day left in it. Francona was always looking big-picture and he was noticeably relieved by what he had seen from Dice-K. "He kind of rose to the occasion," the manager said. "He understands the magnitude of these games. He was ready to go. That was good to see." Good to see, because of the time of year it was. Next time Matsuzaka pitched, it would be October, and any hiccups could derail an entire season not just for an individual, but for a team. So yes, Francona wasn't going to understate how important Matsuzaka's final tune-up was. "Yeah, I can spin it any way I want, and I will. But that was great to see." For Matsuzaka, it was much needed. And the way he looked at it, his will played a role as much as his stuff. "It was an important game so I really wanted to win today and as I was pitching I just kept telling myself that we were going to win today," said Matsuzaka. For all the trials and tribulations of his first Major League season, the one thing that could never be taken away from Matsuzaka is that he always wanted the ball. "I think the thing that's most reassuring is his competitiveness and his heart," Francona said. "He's not going to back down from anybody."

Heart cannot be measured. But statistics can. And now that his regular season was over, there was a full slate of numbers to view. The overall body of work didn't look so bad, particularly when you consider some of the late-season lumps. Not only did Matsuzaka pitch 204²/₃ innings to lead the staff, but he had 201 strikeouts, sixth in the American League. If the 4.40 ERA was a little blah, Matsuzaka's .246 opponents batting average was a clear sign that he was anything but a comfortable at-bat. Though he wasn't a true rookie by the assessment of many, there was nonetheless an interesting rookie stat to highlight his season. Matsuzaka became just the eighth first-year Major Leaguer to record 15 wins, 200 strikeouts and 30 starts. He would throw 3,479 pitches on the season, the twelfth highest of any pitcher in the Majors. Matsuzaka's 108.7 pitches per game was the top mark in all of baseball. If nothing else, Matsuzaka proved he was durable by undertaking such a load and never coming down with any sort of injury. Nobody could dispute that the rigors of the longer season had taken a toll. Matsuzaka's ERA before the All-Star break was 3.80 and after it swelled to 5.19. But the one stat that jumped out at the eyes was the marked difference when Matsuzaka had more rest between starts. Under the standard four days of rest that Major League pitchers are accustomed to, Dice-K was 5-7 with a 5.29 ERA in 13 starts. In the 16 starts in which he had five days rest, Matsuzaka was 9-4 with a 3.83 ERA. In the three starts he had more than five days rest, Matsuzaka was 1-1 with a 3.66 ERA. On Boston's staff, it was actually seamless to give Matsuzaka that extra day whenever there was an off-day, because that also enabled Francona to get his two 40-something pitchers— Schilling and Wakefield—an extra breather. "I think as he gets more accustomed to the five-day rotation, I think some of those numbers will find more of a common ground," said Farrell. "I think what we'll always do, because we feel good about the depth of our rotation, is we'll always look to give off-days when they appear in the schedule."

If you wanted an assessment of Matsuzaka's first season in the bigs, you'd best ask someone other than the pitcher himself. "I think I'll talk about that when the season is actually over," he said. The season, indeed, was not over. Not even a little bit. The Red Sox hoped it was just getting started. They appreciated that Matsuzaka was not just another player on the team and that he was in the midst of overcoming major cultural changes, both in baseball and in life. "Just to accomplish going through a year here with all of the things that have been thrown at him, you have to be very, very tough," Francona said. "Any time you're not having the success you're accustomed to or you want to have, I think, as professional athletes, everyone has a certain amount of confidence, but at times, it can't be at its very peak when you're giving up runs or you're not getting hits, that's human nature."

Before Matsuzaka ever became part of Francona's staff, the front office had dissected every element of the man and determined that he would make it in America against the best hitters in the world. Were they still confident a season in the books later? "I think he's had a very successful first season," Epstein said. "He's certainly laid a baseline of performance out there that he can improve upon going forward as now a 27-year-old next season. He's made a lot of adjustments this season, probably more than any of us could appreciate. He's handled it well while having a season where he's made every start, throwing 200 innings where he's striking out a lot of guys and doing some things that really bode well for the future. Certainly the second half there were probably more bumps in the road then he's used to or he anticipated. But as a whole, this was a successful first season."

Oh, about that Yankees-Orioles game. After Matsuzaka had beaten the Twins, some players—including captain Jason Varitek—showered and headed home. Others, such as veterans like Mike Timlin, Lowell, and Alex Cora, sat on the clubhouse couch and watched their rivals play out the rest of their night in Baltimore. Reporters were milling around, stalling a little. Meanwhile, the most optimistic Fenway fans kept their Friday night going by watching the Yanks and O's on the center field Jumbotron. If ever the Yankees could melt this one away, it sure would be one strange celebration at Fenway. Lo and behold, the Orioles kept coming and Rivera kept giving up hits. Baltimore tied it at 9 in the ninth at which point Sox PR maven John Blake hollered, "Clubhouse is closed [to the media]." Reporters scurried upstairs to the press box and began crafting their stories, still not knowing if the AL East race was over.

But an inning later, with players still on the couch and Francona, Epstein, and Henry taking in the game from the manager's office, the Orioles won it on a walkoff bunt single by Melvin Mora. Fenway Park erupted as the thousands of fans who remained in the stands celebrated the Sox division title. The Red Sox also erupted in their clubhouse, pouring beer and champagne all over each other. The handful of players who had left all seemed to make it back in time for the joyous celebration. Matsuzaka, his eyes covered by goggles, joined in the fun, that smile of his once again gleaming the way it had on Henry's jet all those months ago. It was Matsuzaka who clinched the win that made the Red Sox division champions for the first time since 1995, and for a night, his late-season stress all seemed to float away amid the sprays of champagne and the stench of cigars. The Red Sox took the party to the field, cheered on by their always-supportive fans. Papelbon, decked out in boxer shorts and a tee-shirt, started doing the Riverdance from the pitcher's mound. Matsuzaka looked on and simply laughed at the goofball closer. What else was there to do? The entire season had been a crash-course for Matsuzaka on surviving and thriving in the Major Leagues, and now there was a moment when everyone could just relax and enjoy the ride. Most of the players—including Matsuzaka—went to a bar that is connected to Fenway Park and celebrated more with the fans. Matsuzaka stood there, beer in hand, his translator by his side, and again, soaked in the moment. It was as if he was thinking, "I'm not in Japan anymore." And he was right. This was Boston. Crazed Red Sox Nation. It was October, and the region was ready to become even more gripped than usual by the exploits of the local nine. It was that time of year, and yet another first for Matsuzaka was on deck: pitching in the playoffs for the Boston Red Sox.

15

Early Playoff Pitfalls
(October 1–15, 2007)

BY THE TIME OCTOBER rolled around, it hardly seemed to matter that the Red Sox had struggled for much of September. They were a confident bunch that took over first place on April 18 and never let it go, despite that hard late charge by the Yankees. And their Division Series draw was a good one. The Los Angeles Angels of Anaheim were beat up by injuries and frankly, they just weren't on the same level as the Red Sox. Meanwhile, Francona had spent much of the month prioritizing the health of his players to make sure they were all fresh and as ready as humanly possible for a time of year in which all facets of a team need to be clicking. Manny Ramirez and Kevin Youkilis were back from their ailments, and ready to roll. J. D. Drew, who had been a bust for much of his first season, was finally starting to take the type of swings the Red Sox envisioned when they invested $70 million in him. Okajima had been given a rest in September and was ready to conquer October much like he had for most of the regular season. Then there was Matsuzaka. How could anyone know quite what to make of Matsuzaka when the postseason started? He had produced only one truly top-notch outing in September, but fortunately it was in his last start.

One of the big questions in the days leading up to the Division Series against the Angels was who Francona would go to as

his Game 2 starter. The whole world knew that Beckett was going
to start Game 1. Those who like to speculate were steered in the
wrong direction for Game 2 when Curt Schilling was scratched
for non-health reasons in the final regular season game. It seemed
that Schilling, who had pitched far better than Matsuzaka down
the stretch and had an impeccable history of postseason success,
was going to get the ball in Game 2 and his late scratch was only
further proof. But about an hour before Francona formalized his
rotation to the media, a story broke that Matsuzaka would follow Beckett. Was it a leap of faith in Dice-K? Perhaps a little.
But, in truth, there were other factors at work. Tim Wakefield,
a 17-game winner during the regular season, was unavailable to
pitch in the Division Series because of ongoing arm-back issues.
And the Red Sox felt that Schilling, who was rebuilding his arm
throughout the course of the year following his midseason injury,
needed as much rest as he could get before opening what the Red
Sox hoped would be a full month of intense starts. The way the
off-days were set up in a postseason schedule that was newly
installed for 2008, the Red Sox would be able to pitch their
Game 1 and 2 starters twice in the best-of-five series if it went the
distance. "Within a five-game series, the two guys who physically
we felt could bounce back the best were Beckett and Dice-K,"
said Farrell.

It had been a methodical process for everyone involved to get
Matsuzaka back in full working order by October, and the Red
Sox were hopeful they had done just that. "I think [his last regular season start] was a huge step, particularly for his confidence
knowing he came away with a win," said Farrell. "He takes such
pride in pitching deep in the game, and having completed eight
innings is another added component, added belief that he is ready
for the postseason." The bright lights would be shining on him,
and Matsuzaka always seemed to enjoy that. "I think this stage
will be a good place for him to show what he can do," Francona
said. In a year of firsts for Matsuzaka, he was ready to have his
next big one. The first start on the stage that is Major League

Baseball's postseason. "Almost everything was new to me this year, so every experience I had I felt, you know, I decided early on that it was going to be a learning year for me," Matsuzaka said two days before Game 2. "Now that I'm at the very end, I just feel that I want to go into this game in the best shape that I possibly can."

A couple of hours after Matsuzaka was done speaking with the media, all Beckett did was pitch one of the best playoff games in Boston Red Sox history. He was ridiculously overpowering and yet efficient, firing a four-hit shutout at the Angels. Of his 108 pitches, 83 were strikes. Beckett struck out eight and walked none. It was this type of textbook power pitching that led Matsuzaka's former Seibu Lions manager Osamu Higashio to say four months earlier that he wanted his former pupil to pitch more like Josh Beckett. Who wouldn't want to pitch like that? But Beckett was in his prime of primes and Matsuzaka—though he had dominated like a Josh Beckett in Japan—was still learning about life in the Major Leagues. In other words, Beckett would be one tough act for Matsuzaka to follow in Game 2 and he didn't even come close to doing it. Relieved to see that all of Matsuzaka's pitches didn't come screaming in at the corners like Beckett's had forty-eight hours earlier, the Angels worked Dice-K hard. They didn't score in the first inning, but managed to make Matsuzaka throw 31 pitches. The Red Sox did Dice-K a favor by scoring him two in the bottom of the first. But instead of keeping momentum on his side, he pitched tentatively and gave it right back. In that second inning, Matsuzaka was again throwing a lot of pitches and not commanding particularly well.

Former Major League pitcher Steve Stone, serving as a color analyst for the nationally televised audience on Turner Broadcasting Systems, told his viewers that "MLB scouts tell me Matsuzaka is a power nibbler." The Angels weren't biting. They crowded the basepaths in that second to score three runs and take a 3-2 lead. It was yet another 28 pitches in the inning, giving Matsuzaka a whopping 59 through two. As much as the Red Sox

hoped that the worst parts of Matsuzaka's first year would go
away for October, the most recurring one of all was back in full
view. "If there was one thing that became a little bit of a trademark or a label for him, it was the one [shaky] inning within a
game," Farrell said. "Come to find out, that was the same way
in Japan. It wasn't like he was experiencing something new. All
of a sudden, because of a ball that was hard hit or squared up or
whatever, there would be a tendency from him to begin to nitpick
and nibble a little bit too much."

Matsuzaka settled down briefly in the third and fourth,
throwing 10 pitches in each of those innings. But after getting
the first two batters in the fifth, Matsuzaka again started experiencing one of those sudden implosions that had marked his first
year. There was a liner just off the glove of first baseman Youkilis that probably could have ended the inning. But Matsuzaka,
in a clear mental mistake, forgot to cover first. Then, there was
a stolen base and a ball four pitch so far out of the zone that it
skipped away from Varitek for a wild pitch. Things were getting
messy and Francona came out to get Matsuzaka. The pitcher
tilted his head and then took what looked like a stressful deep
breath. That was it. His first Major League postseason entry
(4²/₃ innings, seven hits, three runs, three walks, three strikeouts)
was not about to join Koshien and the World Baseball Classic in
the annals of Dice-K lore.

But the Red Sox did Matsuzaka a favor. They produced
a stirring win to make his personal performance as close to a
non-story as it could be. In the bottom of the ninth inning of
a tie game, Ramirez unloaded for what is known in Japan as a
sayonara home run. On American soil, it is simply referred to
as a walkoff. It came against Francisco Rodriguez, one of the
league's dominant relievers. At any rate, it was a majestic shot
that soared like a rocket over the giant Coke bottles that rest on
top of Fenway Park's Green Monster. With one swing, the Red
Sox had taken a 2-0 lead in the best-of-five series and Matsuzaka would only have to pitch again in the Division Series if it

stretched to a winner-take-all Game 5. That didn't seem likely the way the Red Sox were playing. On the heels of such an exciting ending, Matsuzaka was reduced to sidebar status instead of front-page news, at least in the United States. In fact, Francona was asked only one question about the righty in his post-game press conference. "It was a lot of pitches. A lot of deep counts. I thought even when he worked and started ahead, he found a way to get himself back into hitter's counts," the manager said. "But the one thing I will say, he didn't cave, he didn't give in." Matsuzaka's briefing with the press was short and sweet, and American writers, pressed for deadline at that point, were more interested in recording all the nuances of Ramirez's monster blast. Standing in the middle of the clubhouse instead of the interview room reserved for the winning pitcher, Matsuzaka said, "There wasn't anything I could be really happy about tonight. I wished I could have gone deeper into the game and built a better game overall. I think I approached the game in the same way that I approached the regular season games. That being said, the results were somewhat disappointing for me. Personally tonight was a disappointment but I'm very happy the team was able to win."

It was a crash course on playoff baseball for Matsuzaka. Hitters intently look over every pitch in the postseason with an eye on tiring out the opposing starter. And the one thing Matsuzaka was truly struggling with at this late juncture of the year was fastball command. That is a crucial thing to be lacking in postseason baseball and not many pitchers can thrive without it. Unless you are precise in your execution, you will often suffer a similar fate as Matsuzaka and be gone by the fifth inning. At least for one round, Matsuzaka's lack of command was inconsequential. The Red Sox went all the way to Anaheim to play one baseball game, as Schilling stepped up in big fashion and stifled the Angels to give the Red Sox a three-game sweep. This would create a mini-vacation for the team, as the American League Championship Series against the Cleveland Indians did not kick off until

October 12, some five days after the Division Series ended. For Matsuzaka, the break would be even longer. When it came time for Francona to announce his next pitching rotation, Matsuzaka was no longer second out of the gate. Beckett, naturally, was up first again. But this time Schilling vaulted past Matsuzaka, as the 2-3 spots were flip-flopped. Though some pitchers would have to be coddled upon receiving news they were moving down in the rotation, Francona appreciated Matsuzaka's selflessness on issues like this. "That wasn't hard," Francona said. "He would take the ball whenever you gave it to him. I don't think there was much ego there. He just wanted to know when so he could prepare. There was never a worry about him taking the ball or him being upset. He's such a good kid. He just wanted to know so he could prepare."

With Game 3 not slated until October 15, a full ten days after Matsuzaka had last pitched, the right-hander pitched a simulated game at Fenway on the day before the ALCS started. In fact, Matsuzaka tried to make his simulation as real as possible. He even went out there in his full game uniform, which is highly unusual for a pitcher throwing against teammates. The sky was cloudy and Matsuzaka's mood also seemed to have a little gloom. He wasn't sharp in the simulated game and a couple of teammates who wished to remain nameless noted that the pitcher's fastball command was, well, lacking. Then again, the rust served as further evidence of why the simulation was necessary. "He left some pitches over the plate, which I'd rather him do than hit [Doug] Mirabelli in the back," Francona said. "I think it was pretty well worth the while." At the most critical time of year, Matsuzaka remained most unpredictable. But his upside still made him better than the alternatives. Because the Red Sox boasted such a strong bullpen, they weren't asking the world of Matsuzaka in the postseason. They were hoping for five or six strong innings, at which point Francona could turn to Okajima, Papelbon and the others. As it turns out, though, Matsuzaka's first start of the ALCS would wind up being more pressurized than his first turn of October. After the locked-in Beckett fired off another gem to win Game 1, Schilling and the bullpen let the Red Sox down in an extra-inning defeat in Game 2. The series shifted to Jacobs Field in Cleveland for Game 3, and an electric Monday night crowd, antsy to see the Indians win their first World Series since 1948, waved white towels in unison to try to get the home team revved up.

Matsuzaka gave the packed house an even bigger shot of adrenaline in the bottom of the second inning, when he hung a meaty fastball on the inner third of the plate to Kenny Lofton and the fan favorite knew what to do with it, putting it just over the wall in right for a two-run homer that broke the scoreless tie. Ryan Garko was on board for Lofton, and he, too, reached on a pitch that didn't go where Matsuzaka wanted it. "To me, he gave up two runs on two mistakes," said Farrell. "It was a 2-0 cutter to Garko that he lined up the middle for a base hit and then he misfired on the fastball to Lofton that he just hits out." Entering the fifth inning, Matsuzaka had settled down nicely, and Lofton had done the only real damage. On the same mound where Matsuzaka shut the Indians out, 1-0, on July 24, he seemed to be turning in another strong performance. But then came the fifth. There was a one-out single, then a wild pitch and a walk. An RBI single up the middle by Asdrubal Cabrera made it 3-0. With runners at the corners, Sox second baseman Dustin Pedroia tried to end the inning by ranging up the middle, then stepping on second and firing to first for what could have been a huge double play. But Travis Hafner just beat it out, pushing another run across and putting the Sox in a 4-0 hole. Matsuzaka's night ended when Victor Martinez literally stuck his bat out and check-swinged a single into left field. Out came Francona. FOX play-by-play man Joe Buck didn't couch his words as Matsuzaka exited the stage. "Matsuzaka, the big investment brought over from Japan, two postseason starts in his first year with the Red Sox, he has not been able to give Boston five innings."

Francona thought that type of statement was an over-generalization. "You're talking about the best teams in baseball [in the playoffs]," Francona said. "There were some games he could have gone longer but because they were playoff games and our bullpen was so good, we'd take him out. We did that with Schill too. Schill didn't go deep but he pitched pretty well too. That sometimes was as much because of our bullpen as opposed to how a guy is pitching and what's in our best interest in winning a big game." You couldn't help but wonder if Matsuzaka's 2007 season had ended right there on the mound of Jacobs Field with that hook from Francona.

The Red Sox, all of a sudden, had lost their swagger. They weren't hitting and Matsuzaka (4²/₃ innings, six hits, four runs, two walks, six strikeouts) again left something to be desired. The game ended with a 4-2 loss that pinned Boston in a 2-1 series deficit with two more games looming in Cleveland against a red-hot Indians team that had already knocked the Yankees out of the postseason. Could the Red Sox be their next high-budget prey? The money the Red Sox had spent to bring Matsuzaka over was just another symbol of their financial clout. But in October, it was all about momentum, not dollar signs. And the Indians were looking like the money team. By the time the game ended, Matsuzaka was still decompressing in public view. As reporters entered the clubhouse, the pitcher was still in uniform, still sitting in front of his locker and still looking like a man in disbelief. He sat there for an hour and never did speak to the assembled press. Finally, he issued a statement through his translator: "As you saw, I allowed them to score first and I wasn't able to hang on after giving up the lead. I wanted to do everything I could today to win and hand it over to Wakefield in a good way."

But instead, the ball was handed to Wakefield in the least desirable fashion imaginable. Not only had Wakefield been idled for sixteen days, but he was less than 100 percent and basically gutting it out so he could be there for his team. Wakefield hung tough for four shutout innings but faltered in the fifth, at which point the Indians broke the game open with seven runs. The Red Sox didn't start scoring until they were already way down, belting three straight solo homers to make for a more respectable final score of 7-3. Just like that, the Red Sox were on the brink of elimination, trailing the best-of-seven series 3-1. Another loss and they'd be home. Another loss and Matsuzaka would have months to stew over his Game 3 defeat.

The Red Sox did have one thing going for them, however. And it was one big thing. They had the hottest, most confident pitcher in baseball going in Game 5 in Beckett. In case Matsuzaka was worried about not having the chance to pitch a Game 7 at Fenway, Beckett told his teammate not to worry. "You're going to get a chance to pitch again," Beckett promised Matsuzaka. Other teammates did all they could to keep Matsuzaka's spirits above water. "We'll just have to pick him up," said veteran reliever Mike Timlin. Could that be done even with the obvious language barrier? "We'll find a way to cross that [barrier]," said Timlin. "We've got two interpreters here, we're all right." There was an obsession from the media in the way Matsuzaka had stewed at his locker for so long following Game 3. "He lost. How would you take it?" Timlin said. "He took it pretty hard. It's the playoffs. You want to win, you want to do well for your teammates. You take it hard. I would have been the same way. It's a thin line. You go out there and you do well, you're OK. You do bad, how do you handle it?" Timlin, who takes pride in being a spiritual leader for his teammates, wasn't going to let cultural barriers prevent him from doing it again in this case. "I know you guys [in the media] are worried about Dice-K," said the 41-year-old reliever, who would soon be the proud owner of four World Series rings. "We're not worried about him. We'll handle what we need to handle. This is a 30-man family. If one guy falls down, the rest of us pick him up. That's just how it's been all year long. It will be the same way now."

If Matsuzaka was going to get a pick-me-up, Beckett was going to have to be the one to put it in motion. It was Beckett who was entrusted with getting the series back to Boston, where the Fenway crowd could undoubtedly sway the momentum back on the side of the Red Sox. And it was Beckett—who struggled so much in his first season in Boston—who Matsuzaka was so often compared to. The line of thinking with several members of the Red Sox organization, Francona prominent among them, was that if someone with Beckett's caliber of stuff could struggle so much in Year One in the American League East and prove it to be an aberration, then why not Matsuzaka? And the problems the two pitchers encountered—taking the cultural aspect away for a minute—were eerily similar. Beckett so often left his fastball in hittable locations in 2006 and wasn't able to utilize his offspeed stuff effectively. It was the same thing that was haunting Matsuzaka. A couple of days before he was entrusted with winning Game 5 and getting Matsuzaka another chance to pitch, Beckett was asked if it was valid to compare his 2006 to what his teammate was going through a year later. "Yeah, I mean, I see some of the same stuff. You know, you have to make a lot more adjustments here, whether you're coming from the National League to the American League . . . I've obviously never played in Japan, but I would assume that you still have to make some adjustments," said Beckett. "Pitching in the American League East and pitching to some of these teams out of our division, you have to learn how to make adjustments, because great hitters, that's what they do, they make adjustments while they're at bat, from pitch to pitch, and you have to defense what they're trying to do."

But in the middle of the season, when everything is going at full speed, it's not as if the human mind can always just slow everything down enough to make those adjustments on the spot. It took Beckett a full year. And judging by most of the stats, Matsuzaka actually had a better first year in Boston than Beckett did. From the ace on down, the Red Sox still believed Matsuzaka could get it done. Considering all the money the Red

Sox had poured into the Dice-K fund, there never seemed to be any kind of resentment from within the clubhouse. "We back Daisuke," said Beckett. "We still believe every time he goes out there that we're going to win. It doesn't have anything to do with the money that they're paying him or anything like that, it's just that we believe in him because we know he's trying. He's really giving it his all."

Francona was puzzled and maybe even a little annoyed that the media was making such a big deal about Matsuzaka's stare-down with his locker after Game 3. It isn't part of the manager's protocol to go into the middle of a clubhouse to see how his pitchers are acting in the immediate aftermath of a loss. Francona was a player himself, so he knows those moments are built on emotion and that the athlete's engine is still burning. In large part because of the big deal that was being made of Matsuzaka's reaction, Francona checked in with the pitcher a day or so later to double-check that everything was OK. "He just wanted to get it out of his system," Francona said. "He said, 'I didn't want to go back to the hotel sitting on this one.' He just needed to process it. He was frustrated, he was disappointed and he just wanted to get out it out of his system so he could kind of start fresh, which is what he needed to do." By the time Matsuzaka got around to talking again a few days later, he was equally perplexed at how much was made of his actions in the clubhouse immediately following a tough defeat. "I might have appeared very upset, but I wasn't as upset as everybody thought."

Nobody could make Matsuzaka's frustration go away quicker than Beckett, who was on the type of October roll most pitchers can only fantasize about. And it was Beckett who got Matsuzaka one step closer to redemption. He simply refused to let the Indians clinch on their own field. The Red Sox were going back to Boston and Beckett made sure there would be more baseball to play. The flame-throwing righty who owns a ranch in South Texas was a true cowboy in this one, striking out eleven Indians over eight innings of one-run baseball. The Red

Sox were headed back to Fenway and Matsuzaka was gaining more confidence that his season was not over just yet. In fact, Matsuzaka had been told by so many people that he still had another game to pitch that he began looking at it more as fact than positive reinforcement. "In our communication, we always kept talking about, 'You're going to get another opportunity in this series.' We always kept gearing things up for Game 7 in his mind," said Farrell.

16

Seventh Heaven
(October 21, 2007)

By the time Curt Schilling (seven dazzling innings) and J. D. Drew (first inning grand slam) had officially punched the ticket for Game 7 of this riveting and momentum-swaying ALCS, Matsuzaka was left somewhere between glowing and grinning. In the immediate aftermath of Boston's 12-2 romp in Game 6, Matsuzaka couldn't seem to get the smile off his face. Really, Matsuzaka had been in a good mood for the past few days. Part of the thinking behind his hour-long stew session after Game 3 was so that every negative vibe could get out of his system. He had a unique way of rejuvenating in quick order. When Matsuzaka was smiling, it could become a little infectious, no matter what language you spoke. "I think he was very, very eager to pitch Game 7," Francona said. "I think that's what maybe gets lost in the shuffle. If you saw his emotions after a [bad] game, he'd be real down. But he'd show up the next day raring to go. He'd be the first guy there in the dugout, big smile. He was always real good about that."

Teammates feed off each other, especially championship teams like the Red Sox that pride themselves on having good chemistry. And this is why, even after Matsuzaka's back-to-back shaky October outings, there was a confidence behind the man taking the ball in the winner-take-all game. "He was kind of grinning in here when we won," said Sox closer Jonathan Papelbon. "That grin to me kind of meant, 'It's up to me to keep the ball going, keep the momentum in our dugout,' and I think he's up to the challenge. I think he likes the challenge." It seemed like Matsuzaka just couldn't wait to pitch. Schilling— who shared Matsuzaka's thirst to be on center stage in the big moments—had mentored him in a chat leading up to the Game 7 start, emphasizing some keys to better fastball command, which would undoubtedly be key to a successful start in Game 7. And more than anything, Matsuzaka was eternally grateful that the promise made by multiple members of the Red Sox—that Game 3 was not his final act of 2007—was anything but hollow. "After the last few games, I believed I was going to have a chance to throw again," Matsuzaka said. "My teammates kept insisting I would have another chance. Everybody on my team told me to be ready for the next chance that I would have, so I was waiting for my turn to come." And now that his turn had indeed arrived and he was finished talking to the media about the biggest start of his career to date, Matsuzaka left Fenway Park wearing a casual black sports coat and jeans. By the time he came back a day later, Game 7 was on the docket and Matsuzaka had the privilege—or was it the pressure?—of trying to pitch the Boston Red Sox into the World Series.

Given Matsuzaka's recent lack of success, how could he remain so enthused about such a pressurized game? Because these were the type of moments he craved and in a way, felt he was born to pitch for. Go back to Koshien or the World Baseball Classic or some of the bigger games he pitched for Seibu, or even his Major League debut in 2007 or his dream matchup with Greg Maddux later that season. There was a common denominator in games like that. Matsuzaka would typically find his way in the winner's circle. Maybe Matsuzaka couldn't quite overcome all his adjustments on a start-by-start basis in 2007, but he seemed to have a way of coming through in the bigger games. There's a certain type of athlete that thrives the most when the pressure is at its peak. "When you look at any kind of championship personality, they relish that opportunity," said Farrell. "I think he saw that as another opportunity, to not only contribute to what our common goal was but also it was a chance at redemption."

It was a prime-time Sunday night evening at Fenway with a certifiable buzz of intensity that only comes with a winner-take-all contest. Matsuzaka, wearing red sleeves under his jersey and carrying his usual red glove in his hand, walked to the bullpen for his pre-game warm-ups, with the cheers swelling as he worked his way toward the outfield. The season had been a climb for Matsuzaka, sometimes a decidedly uphill one at that. But he was now in the biggest game imaginable, the type of high-stakes Major League drama he could only dream of pitching in when he was in Japan.

By the time Matsuzaka began pitching, he displayed why there seemed to be so much confidence in him when maybe his recent track record didn't give anyone justification to be hopeful. Matsuzaka came out for Game 7 carving the strike zone. It was like he stopped thinking so much and just went back to the innate type of pitching ability he had displayed so often in the first half of the season. His fastball comfortably in the mid 90s in the first inning, Matsuzaka began his evening by shattering Grady Sizemore's bat on a popup to second base. It was a succinct, 13-pitch, 1-2-3 inning that ended with Matsuzaka blowing a 96-mph heater by Travis Hafner. The next inning, there was more of the same, as this time Dice-K retired three straight on just eight pitches. In all, Matsuzaka sent down ten of the first eleven batters he faced. From his perch next to Francona in the dugout, Farrell was buoyed by how free and easy Dice-K looked. "He showed in his delivery—not only was the body language upbeat and it had purpose—but there was an energy about himself where it was not too much where it was taking him out of his game or out of his delivery but I think there was this confidence that he was showing on the mound and the relaxation in his delivery allowed him to command his fastball."

Matsuzaka held a 3-1 lead entering the fifth and looked primed to perhaps even go a few more innings. But even on a night when it seemed to all be going so well, the one sticky inning got him and shortened the performance. He got some fortune at the start, as Lofton clubbed one off the Green Monster in left, only to have Ramirez fire a strike to second to cut Lofton down. An exuberant Matsuzaka clapped into his glove. But there were two singles that immediately followed by Franklin Gutierrez and Casey Blake, setting up runners at the corners with nobody out and the ever-dangerous star Sizemore looming in the batter's box. A couple of weeks after Game 7, Farrell pointed out how a new-and-improved approach—one he hopes will be a staple of Matsuzaka's in 2008 and beyond—could have prevented that rally from getting started. "I think that's where it gets back to being able to attack right-handers on the inside half of the plate. What we've seen is that he'll have a tendency to attack right-handers on the outside part of the plate." As harrowing a sight as Sizemore had to be at that point in time, Matsuzaka did minimize the damage, getting a sacrifice fly to center. And with Hideki Okajima poised to come out of the bullpen and face on-deck hitter Travis Hafner, Matsuzaka was determined not to let that happen. As a nine-pitch at-bat with Asdrubal Cabrera intensified, Okajima paused and basically waited in the bullpen. He was hot, and ready to come in. Matsuzaka rubbed the sweat on his forehead, pulled his cap down slightly and then scrunched his nose before unleashing the 2-2 changeup that Cabrera swung right through. Matsuzaka offered a slight fist pump following one of his best changeups in weeks. He hopped off the mound following pitch number 88, the lead still intact at 3-2. This time, Matsuzaka finally reached the five-inning plateau. As he walked in, Francona extended his hand out and Matsuzaka shook it. Matsuzaka then disappeared into the tunnel, probably hoping his night had more pitches in it. But that was it. Francona's bullpen had several arms on this night, even Beckett's if the situation called for it.

To Matsuzaka, this was still a strange thing, coming out with games hanging in the balance and his arm still strong enough to throw another 30 or 40 pitches. In Japan, he always went out to the mound with a long rope. There was never any thought about pitch counts or lining up the bullpen. If there was one adjustment that never did sit quite right in Matsuzaka's competitive stomach during Year One, it was the in-game hook. To the core, he still viewed himself as a nine-inning pitcher. "He wanted to finish things he started," Francona said. "But we have an obligation not only to Daisuke, but also to the organization, to keep guys healthy. We tried to explain that. Sometimes I think he understood it, sometimes I don't think he did. We still have a ways to go. I think there was a frustration on his part that he wanted to pitch longer."

But Matsuzaka never mixed frustration with sulking. As much as he loved to keep the ball in his hand for as long as he could, he let it go after coming out of the game. For example, Matsuzaka was every bit as riveted over the final four innings of Game 7 as his teammates. He witnessed his friend and countryman Okajima stand up marvelously to the pressure he faced. The lefty mowed through the Indians in the sixth and navigated his way out of a first and third, one-out jam in the seventh. Much like Matsuzaka, the other Japanese pitcher on the Red Sox seemed to have a nerveless quality about him when the occasion called for it. The Red Sox padded the lead to three runs in the bottom of the seventh when Pedroia belted a crowd-pleasing, two-run homer to left-center. When Okajima got into trouble by allowing two baserunners to start the eighth, Francona went to Papelbon, his fireballing closer. Papelbon got through the inning unscathed, then watched the Red Sox explode for a virtual series-clinching six runs in the bottom of the eighth. All that pressure of being down 3-1 suddenly came crashing down into a state of euphoria for the Red Sox. Papelbon ended Cleveland's near dream season in the ninth, with center fielder Coco Crisp crashing into the wall in right-center to end the magnificent ALCS with a highlight-reel catch. The Red

Sox then mobbed each other in celebrating their second trip to the World Series in four years. On Page 1 of the next morning's *Boston Globe,* there was a terrific photo of the players piling on top of each other. Matsuzaka, wearing a red pullover, stood on the periphery and just had an enormous smile as he surveyed the scene. In 2004, the Red Sox had come back from a 3-0 deficit to beat the Yankees in the ALCS. This time, it was 3-1. And this time, there were new faces on the scene, including Matsuzaka, who was now going to pitch in the World Series—the event he attended as an awe-struck fan eight years earlier.

He took a measure of pride in being able to take the ball in a game of such magnitude. "Same as it was in the WBC last year, I felt very lucky that this start came along and belonged to me, but I also felt that with the momentum we had going into the game, there was no way we were going to lose," Matsuzaka said. Matsuzaka liked the end result of Game 7, but he knew that he had hardly produced a vintage performance. "I'm not 100 percent satisfied with my own pitching," said Matsuzaka. "I want to address some of those things in my next outing, not to make a big deal out of it, but the world's biggest stage is still waiting for us, and I'd like to see what I can do."

What Matsuzaka rediscovered in Game 7 was his control, as evidenced by the zero walks. "If he does that, he's going to be much better," said Epstein. "You don't get beat in the American League by the solo home run. It happens to everybody. You get beat by big rallies, by walking guys." The nibbling version of Matsuzaka didn't show up for the final game of the ALCS. Instead, in a refreshing throwback to his best moments of the season, he went after hitters. And he didn't go after them with sheer tenacity, but also by taking something off of it when he had to. There was something particularly heartening about Matsuzaka finishing his Game 7 performance with that gorgeous changeup that Cabrera didn't come close to. "That's a pitch he's going to need moving forward," Epstein said. "It was a great pitch for him in Japan the last couple years, and somewhere that got lost along the way this season. If he can bring that back to go with his breaking ball and fastball command, that's taking it to the next level." Where did the changeup go? There didn't seem to be a clear answer. But with a start still to go for Dice-K in the World Series, the return of the pitch could, if you pardon the pun, become an important change in momentum for Matsuzaka. "He's got an 80 changeup on a 20-80 scale in Japan. Let's be honest: it was hardly here this year," Epstein said. "You know, we got away from that. It's something that makes his fastball, so we've got to get back to that."

It all sounded so simple, keeping the changeup and other supplementary pitches as part of the equation. But when a pitcher loses a feel for certain pitches, he no longer has the conviction to throw them. And that left Varitek—for that one ill-fated stretch late in the season—calling for an awful lot of fastballs and cutters. "And as a result, becoming more velocity-oriented, the feel for the secondary stuff started to diminish until making a counter adjustment within the last six to seven weeks of the season," said Farrell. The important thing for the Red Sox was that Matsuzaka had his changeup back when he needed it most, and he used it to get perhaps his most important out of the entire season.

Though Matsuzaka didn't have all that many chances to just unwind and savor the moment in 2007, the clinch party after Game 7 offered one of those opportunities. The party flowed from the clubhouse to the Fenway Park field, where thousands of fans stayed well after the game to cheer on the American League champions. But the pennant flag wasn't the only one on Matsuzaka's mind that night. There were some fans in the stands who were hoisting a Japanese national flag. Japanese media relations coordinator Sachiyo Sekiguchi and Okajima's translator Jeff Yamaguchi arranged for the flag to be brought to the playing field. Once it got there, Matsuzaka and Okajima held it proudly for one photo opportunity after another. They also had the American League trophy and were just as proud to show off that new toy.

"I know his face was full of smile," said Sekiguchi. "You know his smile. It's like a million dollar smile. He looked so happy holding the trophy with Okajima. For me, it's priceless. I had to make it happen. Those two really contributed big time to the team winning." Yes, without the contributions of their two Japanese players, the Red Sox well could have been on the golf course during the final month of October instead of at the World Series. Okajima had come out of nowhere to become a bullpen force all year. Matsuzaka? Even with the ups and downs, he was the only pitcher on the team to make all of his starts and he did win Game 7 of the American League Championship Series. For a man who liked to perform in the spotlight, the biggest one of all was on deck. In his first Major League season, Daisuke Matsuzaka was going to get the opportunity to start a World Series game. In other words, there was a giant reward coming for all the struggles he fought through in the course of Year One.

17

A World Series Hit
(October 27–28, 2007)

HIDEO NOMO WAS THE unquestioned trailblazer for Japanese
pitchers, proving with emphasis back in 1995—and even later
by throwing two no-hitters—that scouts had another country to
find quality Major League arms in. But Nomo never got to start
a World Series game, not for the Red Sox or any of the other
teams he pitched for. Neither did Hideki Irabu, Tomo Ohka, Kaz
Ishii, Masumi Kuwata, Masato Yoshii or Mac Suzuki. It seemed
that an overriding theme to Matsuzaka's inaugural Major League
season was all the firsts, and here was perhaps the most compelling one yet. Matsuzaka was getting the ball in Game 3 of the
World Series in Denver against the Rockies, at which point he
would become the very first Japanese pitcher to start a World
Series game. There would be some 250 members of the Japanese
media on hand to chronicle the moment. In fact, after Beckett
(4-0, 1.20 ERA in 2007 postseason) turned in his latest October
clinic to down the Rockies in Game 1, Okajima was the player
who got to make history in Game 2. The lefty who had helped
to ease Matsuzaka's adjustment all year and vice versa, spotted
winning pitcher Schilling in the sixth inning to become the first
Japanese-born pitcher to so much as appear in a World Series
game. Not only did the lefty pitch, but he was nothing short of
phenomenal. Okajima was perhaps the catalyst of Boston's 2-1

victory in Game 2, firing 2¹/₃ perfect innings and striking out four. Just a week after being on the brink of elimination against the Cleveland Indians, the Boston Red Sox were now feeling downright invincible. They were two precious wins away from a world championship.

Matsuzaka was on deck for the first game in Denver. The man who had pitched on all those different mounds in Japan—not to mention Sydney and Athens for Olympic Games—and all the various ones throughout his first year in the Major Leagues was set to deal with the high altitude and thin air of the Rocky Mountains for the first time. It was a park that could make offspeed pitches flatter than a pancake. All this against a lineup that had wrecking-ball potential. How could anyone really know what Matsuzaka was going to do in this opportunity? The unpredictability factor was high, as it had been for him the previous several weeks. But he was going to get to meet up with an old friend. Kaz Matsui was the Rockies' leadoff man and Dice-K's teammate in Seibu for five years. They had visited back in June, when the Rockies were at Fenway. They had also dined in California last winter, when Matsuzaka had just learned he was coming to the Boston Red Sox. "When we had dinner prior to the season, we just told each other that we should both do our best this year," Matsuzaka recalled. Here they were, months later, in the World Series, which was a long way from the Seibu Lions for both men. Whatever disappointment Matsuzaka had from his first season was currently on the back burner as he eyed championship glory. "I just want to play my small part and help the team win," Matsuzaka said the day before taking the ball. "Just because you have a long career doesn't necessarily mean that you get to be in this position, so today I feel very happy. In thinking about this, I've been thinking about this throughout the Series, but tomorrow I just want to use this last bit of strength to do my best to help the team win."

All year long, Matsuzaka was aware of the calendar. He knew the Red Sox had aspirations of being in the World Series and he knew he'd want to have something left in the tank if they got there. Both the Red Sox and Matsuzaka carefully monitored his workload all year long to try to avoid first-year burnout. In the end, the diligence seemed to pay off, as Matsuzaka would indeed have enough for that final act of 2007. Farrell observed Matsuzaka in the bullpen the night of Game 3 and felt much the same confidence that Team Japan pitching coach Kazuhiro Takeda did the night of the final game of the World Baseball Classic Final. "It was evident when he was warming up," said Farrell. "So much can be said the way an individual pitcher is warming up in the bullpen. The expressions on his face, the confidence he shows, the action on his pitches. It doesn't always guarantee a good performance, but it was clear he felt very good about himself warming up in the bullpen that night."

The first real pitch Matsuzaka threw all night was to his old pal Matsui, who promptly rifled it into right field for a base hit that J. D. Drew misplayed, allowing the leadoff man to reach second. But Matsuzaka was unfazed, bouncing right back with a strikeout and then making a tremendous backhand stab on a grounder by Matt Holliday and catching Matsui in a rundown between second and third. The Rockies were held off the board in the first inning of their first home game of the series.

One of the true benefits for Matsuzaka in pitching on the road in the World Series was being able to bring his bats. This wasn't a pitcher at heart. This was a baseball player at heart. Just as Matsuzaka showed with that first inning fielding play on Holliday's crisp grounder, he liked to be involved in all aspects of the game. He just loved to hit and hadn't been able to get enough tastes of it since high school. The DH was in effect for Seibu also. So for the last nine years, Matsuzaka would only get to hit on special occasions. And unlike Spring Training, when Francona gave the pitcher specific instructions not to swing the bat, Matsuzaka was sure to be hacking in this setting. Months later, Francona still got a kick out of Matsuzaka's eagerness to bat, and the disappointment at not being able to do so in Spring Training. Francona had witnessed Matsuzaka's 2006 home run for Seibu on youtube.com. "I showed him his home run," Francona said. "I said, 'I'm aware that you can hit a little bit but you're not swinging it.'" Still, Matsuzaka eagerly went up to the plate in those Spring Training games played in National League parks with batting gloves on both hands. And with great pain, he stood there like a statue.

During the regular season, Matsuzaka was only able to get four at-bats, and they all came against future Hall of Famers Randy Johnson and Greg Maddux. Unsurprisingly, Matsuzaka went 0-for-4. But that didn't do anything to diminish his confidence as a hitter. "When we were getting ready for the postseason and obviously the World Series, because pitchers were going to hit, he was chomping at the bit to get in the cage and swing," said Farrell. "We had to almost hold him back a little bit not to get too aggressive for fear of straining something because those guys hadn't swung the bat all year." The rust did show in Matsuzaka's first at-bat in Game 3. Batting in the top of the second inning against Rockies starter Josh Fogg, Matsuzaka took sort of a half swing on strike three, foul tipping the curveball into the catcher's mitt. "After the first couple of swings he took in his first at-bat, maybe he was just setting them up," World Series MVP Mike Lowell would say later.

What Matsuzaka was setting the Rockies up for was a feeling of agony as big as any they'd feel in the entire series. Fogg got himself into all kinds of trouble in the top of the third, giving up three runs on a night his team was essentially playing for survival. After Manny Ramirez was thrown out at the plate on a base hit by Jason Varitek, Fogg had a golden opportunity to keep the game at 3-0. This, even after he walked Julio Lugo with the bases loaded. There were two outs and all that was standing between Fogg and the end of the inning was Matsuzaka's rust-filled bat. Nonetheless, Matsuzaka stood up there, waved the bat back and forth a couple of times, and then unloaded on Fogg's first pitch. Again, it was a curveball. This time, Matsuzaka timed it just right, hammering it hard on the ground and past the glove of Rockies third baseman Garrett Atkins. Lowell and Varitek came racing home and Matsuzaka had just flattened the Rockies. It was now 5-0 and everyone in the Red Sox dugout was erupting with glee. "I was pumped up," said Lowell. "Any time you score two runs, but especially coming from a pitcher . . . For an American league guy to come up with a big hit like that, I think it was unexpected."

Utility infielder Royce Clayton was not on the active roster for the World Series, but he was wired up by FOX. "Everybody's safe," hollered Clayton, who then turned to Coco Crisp and said, "He's Ichiro!" In this case, Ichiro couldn't have done it much better himself. And who would have thought that Matsuzaka would get a World Series hit before Ichiro? Ichiro still hasn't been lucky enough to play on the grandest stage baseball has to offer. Making Matsuzaka's hit sting just a little more was the fact that Jacoby Ellsbury followed with an RBI double to make it 6-0. And then, the Rockies had to go to their bullpen, even with the pitcher's spot due up in the bottom of the next inning. "It was a huge lift for us," Farrell said of Matsuzaka's batting magic.

The pitching change allowed Matsuzaka—who by this point had reached third on Ellsbury's double—to briefly retreat to the dugout and sip on some water. By this time, the Boston dugout was becoming a rowdy place. They were on a mission to win a World Series and after Matsuzaka's back-breaking hit had Game 3 turning into a potential romp, it was as if everyone could start sniffing the finish line. "Any two-out hit is welcome. When it came from Dice-K, you could see his eyes light up and then he's running the bases," Francona said. "Then they're making a pitching change and he comes in the dugout and everybody is all over him. You see the smiles break out. That was great."

When the Red Sox spent all that money to bring Matsuzaka to Boston, they certainly didn't have any grand visions of clutch hits in a World Series game. "I was actually stunned when he hit that single," said Werner, who was watching from the stands. "Of course he had batted only four times this year, and I was unsure how often he had batted in Japan. At any rate, I realized after he had hit the ball through the middle that you should never underestimate an exceptional athlete."

Once Matsuzaka got back on the mound in the bottom of the third inning, he went back to the business of keeping the Rockies from getting the type of clutch hit he had produced. Matsuzaka had gotten all of his confidence back, pitching even better than he did in Game 7 against the Indians. FOX analyst Tim McCarver, who had also called the ALCS, noted the difference in Matsuzaka to his nationwide audience. "There's a rhythm, a flow and a cadence to Matsuzaka that we have not seen, certainly in the two league championship games against Cleveland," McCarver said. Matsuzaka was just dealing, which is the last thing the Rockies needed to see with a six-run hole in their face. The thin air that was supposed to unnerve pitchers didn't seem to play any kind of factor for Matsuzaka. "While acknowledging it, we tried to put it aside too and not let it affect him," said Farrell. "We felt like his changeup would become a much more important pitch than maybe his curveball. That being said, he spent some time knowing that would be a pitch he'd need." And even still, Matsuzaka snapped off some nice curveballs. His fastball was also pinpoint, such as when he struck out Matsui in the third on 95-mph filth on the lower, inside corner.

The at-bat that best demonstrated what type of zone Matsuzaka was in for Game 3 of the World Series came in the bottom of the fourth against Todd Helton, who has been one of the best pure hitters in baseball for the last decade. Helton stepped up with one out and nobody on and grinded out Matsuzaka in a way that nobody had all evening. As the 12-pitch at-bat neared its conclusion, Helton hammered a fifth consecutive foul ball, and the sixth of the at-bat. Matsuzaka pounded his right leg with his hand in pure annoyance. Then he looked in at Varitek and shook off the captain not once, but twice. Finally, Matsuzaka got the finger he was looking for and dropped an 82-mph breaking ball right past a frozen Helton. This, after eight straight fastballs.

This was the precise type of hard-soft adjustment Matsuzaka had failed to make so many times during September, but he was now getting it done at the most crucial point of all. Matsuzaka took a three-hit shutout into the fifth.

When Matsuzaka took the ball for the sixth, he felt like he could pitch all night. He started with a quick groundout but Helton again worked him hard, this time for an eight-pitch walk. Then Matsuzaka walked Atkins on four pitches. He retrieved the baseball from Varitek and got ready to face Hawpe. But then, you could see Matsuzaka's mouth twitch open a little. Francona was up off the steps and on his way to the mound. The manager never made visits just to talk to a pitcher. That duty always went to Farrell. Knowing that his night—and probably his first season in Boston—was over, Matsuzaka took a few steps behind the mound. If Matsuzaka could have run away from Francona, he probably would have. "I did feel that I wasted some pitches there in the sixth, but with our lead I didn't think that I'd be asked to come out there," Matsuzaka said. This coming out of games thing—so foreign to Matsuzaka during his years in Japan—was the one adjustment he didn't even come close to making by the end of 2007. "I think he hated it," Francona said when asked how Matsuzaka felt about coming out of games. When Matsuzaka at last did walk off that mound after pitch No. 101, the Rockies still hadn't scored against him. But that changed when lefty specialist Javy Lopez didn't do his job, giving up two straight hits. In fact, the Rockies would eventually close the gap to 6-5 before the Red Sox regained control with three in the eighth and another in the ninth.

Matsuzaka was a World Series winner in the first World Series start by a Japanese pitcher. And on this night, he was also a hitter, one who supplied a big knock to aid the cause. "I can't say that I'm a confident hitter, but I love hitting," Matsuzaka said. As for the pitching—which consisted of three hits, two runs and five strikeouts over 5$\frac{1}{3}$ innings—Matsuzaka had done his job. "I think that I felt more pressure going into Game 7 of the

LCS, so today was easier mentally," he said. "But the team won, and I didn't wind up being the one to stop our momentum. So in that sense I feel very relieved." By this time, the Red Sox were your virtual buzz-saw. There wasn't going to be any stop to their momentum until they hoisted that trophy. When Matsuzaka got to his locker following Game 3, he noticed that somebody had put a game-ball in there for him. Matsuzaka had the ball delivered to his mother, who had traveled from Japan to witness her son—the one she named after another baseball player—pitch in the World Series. Back in Japan, everyone had their eyes on Dice-K and the Red Sox. The World Series games were on the big-screen television sets at the electronics stores in Tokyo. "I felt like I was in Best Buy on Route 1 [in Massachusetts]," said Ian Macaulay, a Red Sox fan who spent the World Series in Japan on business.

It was interesting that Matsuzaka floundered in his first two postseason starts but then came up big amid the pressure of Game 7 of the ALCS and Game 3 of the World Series. Then again, Farrell, who had viewed Matsuzaka so closely all year, didn't think it was that big of a surprise. He thought there was something to the mystique Matsuzaka had built as a big-game performer. "I think if you go back and look at the common traits of those elite performers, the higher the visibility, the more the importance or consequence to a given game, the more they're able to remain calm and focused," Farrell said. "Manny has it, Beckett has it, Dice-K's got it, Curt's got it. You see guys do these type of things, and it isn't a mistake. It's a major part of their individual fabric that allows them to remain calm in those key moments."

There was also another way to look at it. Matsuzaka's postseason run was somewhat a microcosm of his season. Some ups and some downs in a tight rope to ultimate success. "Early on, in the postseason, things didn't go his way, but he made adjustments," said Epstein, "just as he's made adjustments all year long. He was able to get himself in a good place and let his ability take over. Shoot, he won Game 7 of the ALCS, he won Game 3 of the

World Series, and did it by pitching some pretty good baseball. We're proud of him, he did a good job."

After Matsuzaka put the Red Sox at the doorstep of the World Series championship, all that remained was the coronation. Not that the Red Sox were going to look ahead. "We don't want to eat the cake first, before your birthday," the goofy Ramirez said after Game 3. "We've got to wait and see what's going to happen [in Game 4]." By the end of Game 4, there was the baseball-celebrating equivalent of cake and ice cream—champagne and cigars. There was enough to go around for everyone. The Red Sox, just as they did in the 2004 World Series, recorded a sweep and celebrated on their opponent's field. The final nail in Colorado's coffin came in Game 4, with the Red Sox sending Jon Lester to the mound for the finale. The left-hander overcame cancer a year earlier and was making his first career postseason start. Lester was tremendous and the Boston bats did just enough for a 4-3 victory that was complete when Jonathan Papelbon struck out Seth Smith to end it. A euphoric Papelbon threw his glove about twenty feet into the air. The Red Sox from the United States, the Dominican Republic, Puerto Rico, and, yes, Japan, mobbed each other in a pile of pure joy. Matsuzaka was among the first ten players to get out to the middle of the celebration. Standing behind Manny Delcarmen and next to Schilling, Matsuzaka was wearing both a hooded sweatshirt and, naturally, a smile.

As Werner entered the celebratory clubhouse a little while later and saw Matsuzaka drenched in champagne, his mind couldn't help but wander back to November. "I actually went up to Matsuzaka in the locker room and reminded him what we had said at the dinner at my house," said Werner. "That it would be our dream to have Dice-K pitch in a World Series game wearing a Boston Red Sox uniform. I certainly didn't expect that he would be doing so in 2007, although of course we were hopeful. Matsuzaka had a broad smile on his face when I reminded him of our dream." Back at that introductory dinner at Werner's house, a replica of the 2004 World Series trophy was brought into the room so Matsuzaka could check it out. Here they were, eleven months later, and Matsuzaka was hoisting the real thing, albeit the 2007 model. "Wow, this is heavy," Matsuzaka told a large group of Japanese reporters. "This is the second time for me to touch the trophy. It is heavier than my daughter." But perhaps not quite as heavy as the burden he had felt at times during the season.

For weeks, Matsuzaka said he would not reflect until the season had actually ended. Now that it had, he finally allowed himself to look back just a little. "There were many hard things for me," Matsuzaka said. "However in the end it all finished as the best result, which was good for me." And it was pointed out to him that he faced so much pressure from both sides of the Pacific Ocean. Again, Matsuzaka welcomed expectations because he had perhaps even greater expectations for himself than everybody else did. "I want to be a player who can be counted on and can fulfill fans' expectations the next year and so forth, too," he said. The one thing Matsuzaka didn't feel like doing was taking much credit for the team's overall success. "I thought my contribution was very tiny," he said. But Matsuzaka did take a measure of pride in what he did in Game 3. "As for the World Series, since I thought that I contributed something to the team, I am very glad," he said. "The road to here was rocky, but I am very glad that I reached here. It is finished."

The championship taste was so fine that Matsuzaka was already eyeing more where that came from. "Although I think to clinch the championship for consecutive years is very difficult, I want to experience this many times," Matsuzaka said. "Only one championship is not my goal. I want to have it several times. It is good to clinch the championship so soon, but I want to experience it many times."

There was more celebrating to do. Matsuzaka brought the World Series trophy out to the stands and showed it to his mother Yumiko, father Satoru and younger brother Kyohei. Later on, as the Japanese media huddled around him and took more photos,

Tomoyo Matsuzaka had a little secret that she no longer felt the urge to keep. "Should we tell them, should we tell them?" Tomoyo asked her husband. The pitcher gave her the approval, and it was then the Matsuzakas first publicly revealed that they had another baby on the way—in March. The season had finally ended, but the Matsuzakas had a new beginning to look forward to. And ironically, Daisuke Matsuzaka's second child is scheduled to be born just before the dawn of the 2008 season, at which point Matsuzaka also hopes to have a fresh start in a place that will be no longer foreign to him.

Epilogue

Two days after the Red Sox won the World Series, Matsuzaka took a joy-ride through the streets of Boston. This was the championship parade, and Matsuzaka rode on a "Duck Boat" with Jon Lester. The last two starting—and winning—pitchers for Boston in the 2007 World Series were united on a spirited ride during the sparkling early afternoon of October 30, when life was pure bliss for the baseball players and fans of Boston. As the procession started moving, the streets were filled with cheering fans backed by their thick Boston accents. "Dice-K" bellowed one euphoric spectator after another. Matsuzaka was left waving and smiling for hours on end. This was truly a magical way for him to end a year that had defined the word *battle*. He looked like he was floating through the streets. For the first time all year, Matsuzaka could exhale and not worry about cultural barriers or imposing hitters. As it turns out, the struggles were all worth it. He was a member of the World Series champion Boston Red Sox in a season he hadn't even pitched up to his full capability.

The fact that it ended so well provided optimism going forward. "It's human nature," said Farrell. "The last experiences you have are probably the ones you hold on to the most throughout the offseason. For it to be on an upswing in that stage in a World Series, obviously that's going to be a positive. I firmly

201

believe there's going to be an opportunity for him to reflect over the offseason and think about the challenges that he faced and I think he'll continue to learn even though games aren't going to be played."

By going 15-12 with a 4.40 ERA in the regular season and 2-1 with a 5.03 ERA in the postseason, Matsuzaka turned his entire body of work into a bit of a grey area. Was it a success or not? The question was not easy, considering the various factors that surrounded it. In truth, there probably wasn't a concrete answer. "He, himself, the person, is a very committed, extremely competitive individual," Farrell said. "From just a baseball standpoint, this is someone who is very strong physically, very strong mentally, and I think to encounter and embrace all those adjustments or challenges that he faced and still come out throwing 200-plus innings, to me, it's a very successful year."

To the people of Japan, who seemed to take Matsuzaka's success or lack thereof almost personally at times, the ending provided satisfaction that simply wasn't there for a great part of the year. "We got a little bit disappointed in his performance in mid-August and early September," said Hideki Okuda, the seasoned baseball journalist from Sports Nippon Newspapers. "He re-focused in mid-September and got better. He got out of the game in the middle of the fifth inning in the first two playoff games but he got better. We are happy about his strong finish."

While Okuda, a Japanese man who has lived in the United States since 1990, had his take, so, too did, Jim Allen, an American man who has lived in Japan since 1984. "His season was disappointing only because he had so many mediocre and poor games," said Allen, who covers baseball for the *Daily Yomiuri*. "Each one is a small blow and they were remembered this season. But now that he's a champ, people's memories will wash that away and he will be a hero when he comes back."

The Red Sox tried to stay as far away as they could from public perception of Matsuzaka in Year One. They stressed from the second they signed Matsuzaka that it was not about one year.

It was a six-year commitment, one the Red Sox hope will go even longer than that. Matsuzaka is 27 years old, and that's a prime age when pitchers start to peak. After a full season of crash-course learning, Matsuzaka will have a full winter of absorption under his belt before taking the ball for the first time in 2008. "Any player having to play in the Major Leagues has to go through a period of adjustment," said Werner. "This was exponentially harder for Matsuzaka because of the language barrier and the grueling demands of a season. The travel alone must have been quite wearing. What he accomplished was extraordinary and I would expect that his learning curve is such that next year he ought to be even better. I don't want to place any unfair burden on him but now that he has helped win a World Series, he should be even stronger." Expectations from the fans and media might be diminished after Matsuzaka's up-and-down results of 2007. But the Red Sox and Matsuzaka himself are looking for a higher level of performance.

"I feel like Daisuke's '07 season is analogous to Beckett's '06 season," said Epstein. "I think he's smart enough and gifted enough to take the lessons he's learned this year and make changes over the winter—and then take his game to an even higher level next year." Schilling, who is as observant and analytical a teammate as there is in the game, has unabashed optimism for what Matsuzaka will do going forward. Doing a radio interview on WEEI-850 AM in Boston as he drove into Fenway for the World Series parade, Schilling offered the following thought: "You're talking about a guy who literally is a few small corrections, fixes, changes, whatever you want to call them, away from winning 20, 25 games. No question. You don't get the reputation and do what he did in that league over there without being somebody who can make adjustments and get better."

Farrell reinforced those necessary adjustments to Matsuzaka during an exit interview of sorts at Fenway Park a couple of days after the World Series. "He knows that he's got to still use hard and soft and not become too one dimensional or predictable," said Farrell. But if there was one thing the pitching coach drilled into Dice-K on his way out of Fenway and into the wintertime, it was the importance of fastball command. As Beckett or Schilling can attest, fastball command pretty much sets up everything for a power pitcher. "It's going to allow him the ability to use his secondary stuff knowing he can get a strike when needed with a well-located fastball," said Farrell.

With Matsuzaka's rich arsenal of pitches, improved control of the fastball will open up the rest of the kitchen sink for him. And because hitters—particularly the stronger ones in the American League East—so love to extend their arms, Matsuzaka must do a better job of using the inner half of the plate. The lack of being able to do that in 2007 was probably the biggest reason Matsuzaka frequently had high pitch counts toward the middle part of the game, and also why he often couldn't put away hitters after getting ahead in the count.

"I think his ability to pitch inside, just from a pure baseball standpoint, will help him," said Farrell. "He needs to pitch inside to right-handers more and to use the hitters' defensiveness to his advantage. We all witnessed how many times he would get ahead of hitters. If you were to categorize him, he is a power pitcher but what he began to do was kind of nitpick a little bit, even with power stuff."

Also, Matsuzaka has expressed an interest in improving his English, which will lessen the need for interpreters and increase the type of one-on-one dialogue that can be so useful throughout a baseball season. "You get frustrated because you want to talk to him like you talk to the other players," said Francona. "Especially a guy that's not from here, you probably need to talk to more. The better the communication—and it's not fair, but unfortunately that probably falls on him—and if he can [communicate better], it would certainly help. And I think he has interest in doing that."

When you consider the language barrier, it was rather impressive how well Matsuzaka did blend in with his teammates in 2007. Sure, he had the natural kinship with Japanese teammate

Hideki Okajima and translator Masa Hoshino. But Matsuzaka did anything but isolate himself. He made friends quickly. Julian Tavarez, the jovial right-hander, always chatted and joked with Matsuzaka and played catch with him, even getting into the uncomfortable catcher's stance. Schilling, Beckett, and Wakefield always made the effort to talk to Matsuzaka, be it directly or through translators. And perhaps most importantly going forward, Matsuzaka and catcher Jason Varitek formed a bond that transcended cultural barriers.

The day after the World Series parade, Varitek stood in a near-empty clubhouse at Fenway Park and discussed all things Dice-K with a small group of reporters. "I love him," Varitek said. "He's got a tremendous smile, which everybody knows. I had a very joking relationship with him, which for me is kind of out of the box. He's just fun. He just looks like he really enjoys the game." Varitek, whose mind is in constant motion throughout the course of the 162-game season and into October, was able to slow down a little once it all ended and elaborate just on what it all must have been like for Matsuzaka. "People don't understand the elements that changed for him," Varitek said. "Everything had a huge effect on him. You had more change in his game than any other player."

What also came across to the captain was how badly his new teammate wanted to succeed. In other words, Matsuzaka might have been pushing the envelope too hard at times. "You always sensed he wants to be in a certain place and in trying to get there, he would try different things," said Varitek. "There was just a lot of changes for him—different hitters, different umpires, mounds, the baseball, media coverage from different countries, new teammates. I could go on and on. It's not excuses but there are those elements he had to deal with he did such a great job in handling. Next year will be a lot easier because he can just focus on playing." Matsuzaka's end goal is no secret to anyone who has spent much time with him. "He just wants to be great and he's learning from himself what it will take to be great," Varitek said.

The one thing Matsuzaka never spoke much about in 2007 was his personal life. He has always been a private person by nature. But it was relevant to wonder if he enjoyed living in Boston. Before becoming the Japanese media relations coordinator for the Red Sox in 2007, Sachiyo Sekiguchi had an existing friendship with Tomoyo Matsuzaka. So how did Tomoyo and Daisuke enjoy Boston in their first year? "They love it," Sekiguchi said. "They love living in Boston."

In the immediate aftermath of the World Series, there was one phrase Matsuzaka kept repeating in his dialogue with the Japanese media. "It is finished," said Matsuzaka. In reality, it is just getting started. And by the time it is over, Matsuzaka hopes to become the first Japanese pitcher to have sustained greatness in the Major Leagues.

His second Major League season will start not in Boston, but Tokyo of all places. On November 14, 2007, the Red Sox and Oakland Athletics were formally scheduled to begin the 2008 season with a two-game series at Tokyo Dome, to be played March 25–26. Unless there's a conflict with the birth of Matsuzaka's second child, he is all but certain to pitch one of those games. But this time, Matsuzaka will be in Japan as a visitor. Boston is his home, and it is one that figures to get more comfortable each year as cultural barriers continues to break.

Index

About the Author

Ian Browne is a beatwriter for the official Major League Baseball website, www.mlb.com. He has chronicled the inner workings of the Boston Red Sox on a daily basis since the start of the 2002 season and had a front row seat for Matsuzaka's initiation into a new culture and a new baseball world. He lives in Boston, Massachusetts.